The United States Flagbook

The United States Flagbook

Everything About Old Glory

ROBERT L. LOEFFELBEIN

McFarland & Company, Inc., Publishers
Jefferson, North Carolina, and London

Cover photograph by Teresa A. Turko, Garland, Texas.
Reprinted by permission from 1991 *Parade*/Kodak "Let
Freedom Ring" photography contest.

British Library Cataloguing-in-Publication data are available

Library of Congress Cataloguing-in-Publication Data

Loeffelbein, Robert L.
    The United States flagbook : everything about Old Glory /
Robert L. Loeffelbein.
        p.   cm.
    Includes bibliographical references (p.   ) and index.
    ISBN 0-7864-0156-7 (sewn softcover : 50# alk. paper) ∞
    1. Flags — United States — History.   I. Title.
CR113.L64   1996
929.9'2'0973 — dc20   96-20026
                                                            CIP

Manufactured in the United States of America

McFarland & Company, Inc., Publishers
  Box 611, Jefferson, North Carolina 28640

To those who have served our flag,
even unto death.

Table of Contents

"A thoughtful mind, when it sees a Nation's flag, sees not the flag only, but the Nation itself; and whatever may be its symbol, its insignia, he reads chiefly in the flag the Government, the principles, the truths, the history which belongs to the Nation that sets it forth."

— Henry Ward Beecher

Acknowledgments

One does not succeed in a research undertaking of this scope without a lot of help from a lot of kind people who take their time to answer a multitude of questions and furnish myriad bits of data, history, and nostalgia, and to help search out photographs, with everything going together to make a cohesive story. It is rather like putting a jigsaw puzzle together.

Those who have helped include caretakers of history, business persons, members of all sorts of organizations, writers, and other researchers. To one and all, I dedicate this reference tome by way of thanks. I couldn't have done it without you.

Thanks to:

All the flag companies I queried, including the National Banner Company of Dallas, TX; National Capital Flag Company of Alexandria, VA; Colonial Flag Company of Coshocton, OH; Valley Forge Flag Company of Great Neck, NY; Dettra Flag Company of Redwood City, CA; Ace Banner and Flag Company of New York, NY; American Flag and Banner Company of Westlake Village, CA; John Ewing and Company of Buffalo, NY; Eder Manufacturing Corp. of Oak Creek, WI; Adventure Creations of San Clemente, CA; Advertising Imports of Atlanta, GA; United States Flag Service of Frederick, MD; Flags International of Osceola, IN; Robert Wagner Flag Sales of Elverson, PA; and Annin and Company of Roseland, NJ.

All the special organizations and those representing them, including Dr. Whitney Smith, executive director of the Flag Research Center of Winchester, MA; the Reverend Robert H. Schuller, paralegal Victoria S. Millay, and Diana O'Connor of the Crystal Cathedral Ministries of Garden Grove, CA; the staff at Flags International, Inc., at Trenton, NJ; the North American Vexillological Association; directors D.S. Mohr and William Jayne, Public and Consumer Affairs Service, National Cemetery System, Department of Veterans Affairs; librarian Anthony Martin, former president George F. Cahill, and President

Daniel R. Fleck of the National Flag Foundation of Pittsburgh, PA; Mayor Jess Hughston of Pasadena, CA; Caryn E. Eaves, public relations manager, Pasadena (CA) Tournament of Roses; staff at the United Nations Bookstore in New York City; Patricia R. Olkiewicz, film/photo specialist with the U.S. Olympic Committee's Department of Information Resources in Colorado Springs, CO; Charles G. Cumpstone, Jr., assistant recorder for the Imperial Council of the Ancient Arabic Order Nobles of the Mystic Shrine in Chicago, IL; Dr. Conrad Swan, York herald of arms for the College of Arms in London, England; Ted R. Cormack, director of public relations with the Braille Institute of Los Angeles, CA; Karen L. Stiver, administrative assistant, Francis Scott Key Foundation, Washington, DC; and Sharon Banks, special projects coordinator, Virginia Beach (VA) Center for the Arts.

Various governmental agency correspondents, including Ann Higgins, Presidential Correspondence Unit; U.S. senator Slade Gorton; William F. Gavin, assistant director of the U.S. Information Agency; Patricia White, acting director, Public Liaison Staff for the General Services Administration in Washington, DC; Terrence L. Sparr, executive assistant to the secretary of administration for the governor's office in Harrisburg, PA; Patricia Rakowski, secretary to the mayor in Waukesha, WI; Robert K. Stevens, deputy chief of protocol for the mayor of Los Angeles, CA; Donald M. Fraser, mayor of Minneapolis, MN; Michael J. Styles, public information director of San Diego, CA; Harold A. Milley, manager of the George Washington Bridge for the Port Authority of New York and New Jersey in Fort Lee, NJ; Richard Sullivan, Myron Leslie Hurwitz and Ellen Hemminger, information officers for the Port of New York Authority in New York City; R. James Pope, supervisor of parks and recreation, Public Utility District #1, Chelan County, WA; Muriel Crook, secretary to Sheriff Michael P. Seniuk of Mineola, NY; James J. Farkas, Office of the Chief of Police in Muskegan Heights, MI; Birgitte Jeppesen and Annette Jacobsen of the Aalborg (Denmark) Tourist & Convention Bureau.

The many Chambers of Commerce contacted, including Ellen Kornfield for the Philadelphia (PA) Convention & Visitors Bureau; the Tourist Promotion Division for the Rhode Island Development Council in Providence, RI; Janet M. Leight of the Central Baltimore County Chamber of Commerce in Towson, MD; Helen MacDonald of the Lexington (MA) Chamber of Commerce; Martha M. Doss of the Lexington (VA) Visitors Bureau; Hazel G. Freeman of the Colton (CA) Chamber of Commerce; Margaret R. Fox and Jeanne P. Vasold of the Tourism Council of Frederick County in Frederick, MD; Diane McNatt of the Greater Pittsburgh Office of Promotion in Pittsburgh, PA; the Greater Richmond (VA) Chamber of Commerce; and Betsey Hoyt, public relations manager, Lake Havasu Area Chamber of Commerce at Lake Havasu City, AZ.

Many units of the military, including the Historical Reference Section of Headquarters Marine Corps in Washington, DC; Thomas B. Profitt, chief,

Heraldic Services and Support Division of the Army at Cameron Station, VA; Quinn L. Hawley, commander CHC for the Bureau of Naval Personnel in Washington, DC; J01 Rebecca Fox Celli, Public Affairs, Hawaiian Sea Frontier, Pearl Harbor, HI; Joseph A. Leonski, chief warrant, USMC, Public Affairs Office, Marine Barracks, Washington, DC; the Naval History Division of the Office of Naval Operations in Washington, DC; Michael J. Crawford, head of the Early History Branch at the Naval Historical Center in Washington, DC; J.J. Holloway, Jr., rear admiral, USN, superintendent of the U.S. Naval Academy at Annapolis, MD; William B. Dermady, assistant public affairs officer at the Naval Training Center at Great Lakes, IL; the Audio-Visual Branch of NASA in Washington, DC; Major Daniel R. Schmidt, USA, Community Relations Division, Office of the Secretary of the Army, Washington, DC; Colonel Charles R. Spittler, AGC Commanding, Institute of Heraldry, Cameron Station, Department of the Army, Alexandria, VA; Public Affairs Office, Ft. Lesley J. McNair, U.S. Army District of Washington, DC.

A multitude of contacts at various museums and libraries, including Edgar M. Howell, curator of the Division of Military History at the Smithsonian Institution in Washington, DC; Sher S-King, Department of Prints and Photographs, National Portrait Gallery, Smithsonian; Public Inquiry Mail Service at the Smithsonian; DeAnne Blanton of the Military Reference Branch at the National Archives and Records Administration in Washington, DC; William H. Davis of the Projects Branch at the National Archives; George P. Young, archives technician, National Archives–New England Region, Waltham, MA; Crystal Brooks–Cross of the Office of Presidential Libraries at the National Archives; Timothy Sullivan, library assistant, Cooper-Hewitt National Design Museum, Smithsonian Institution, New York, NY; the Prints and Photographs Division, Library of Congress, Washington, DC; John T. Curry, archivist-in-charge, Book Collection for the General Services Administration at the Harry S Truman Library in Independence, MO; Fred Pernell, assistant chief for references, Still Picture Branch, National Archives at College Park, MD; staffers at the University of Maryland rare books collection; John M. Adams, director of libraries for the Tampa-Hillsborough County Public Library System in Tampa, FL; the Tampa (FL) Municipal Museum at the University of Tampa; Joanna Norman, Photographic Collection, Florida State Archives, Tallahassee, FL; Linda Ziemer, Prints and Photographs Section of the Chicago (IL) Historical Society; Scott S. Sheads, park ranger, Ft. McHenry National Monument and Historical Shrine in Baltimore, MD; David T. Hedrick, special collections librarian for the Musselman Library at Gettysburg College, Gettysburg, PA; Kenneth Fieth, director of archives, Gary Layda, photographer, and Virginia R. Lyle, metro archivist, all for the Metropolitan Government Archives at the Public Library of Nashville and Davidson County, Nashville, TN; J.D. Young, historian for the Custer Battlefield National Monument at Crow Agency, MT; Lori Marie Thillman, assistant director of the Waterloo (NY) Memorial

Day Museum; Andrew Kraushaar, reference archivist for the Iconograph Collections of the State Historical Society of (Madison) Wisconsin; James Folts, associate archivist for the State Department of Education at the University of the State of New York in Albany, NY; James L. Hansen, genealogy/reference librarian for the State Historical Society of Wisconsin at Madison, WI; Allen R. Hoilman, cataloguer for the Curation Branch of the North Carolina Museum of History in Raleigh, NC; Catherine H. Grosfils, AV editorial librarian for Colonial Williamsburg, VA; Ruth Levin, registrar for the Bennington Museum, Bennington, VT; Mariam Touba, reference librarian for the New York Historical Society in New York City; Patricia A. Hobbs, curator of collections, Woodrow Wilson Birthplace and Museum, Staunton, VA; Barbara R. Luck, curator for the Abby Aldrich Rockefeller Folk Art Museum in Williamsburg, VA; Dr. Robert Bishop, director of the Museum of American Folk Art in New York City; Ann Bregent, documents librarian at the State Library of Olympia, WA; Naomi Allen, Reference Services, Commonwealth of Massachusetts State Library, Boston, MA; R. Eugene Zapp, reference librarian, Department of Rare Books and Manuscripts, and Henry F. Scannell, reference librarian, Microtext Department, Boston Public Library; director Rodney Armstrong and Patricia Figueroa, Reference Department, Library of the Boston (MA) Athenaeum; Jennie Rathbun, the Houghton Library, Harvard University, Cambridge, MA; Philip Bergen, librarian, the Bostonian Society, Old State House in Boston, MA; Ron Crozier, librarian, Santa Barbara (CA) Museum of Art; Chris Steele, curator of photographs, Massachusetts Historical Society, Boston.

A number of persons representing commercial businesses, including Penny Rutherford Sitler, advertising manager for Draper Shade and Screen Company in Spiceland, IN; Georgia L. Grove, consumer information coordinator for Coca-Cola USA in Atlanta, GA; Lawrie Pitcher Platt, director of external affairs, Tupperware World Headquarters in Orlando, FL; Joel Nichols, division vice president of advertising for Woodward and Lothrop in Washington, DC; A.M. Johnson, director of industrial relations for Eastern Products Corporation in Columbia, MD; Brenda Matthews of the public relations department of R.J. Reynolds Tobacco Company in Winston-Salem, NC; Barry D. Heasy, general manager, Deranleau's Appliance and TV, Lewiston, ID; the public relations office of Boeing Commercial Airplane Group in Seattle, WA; Jane Andrade, director of Public Relations for the Brown Palace in Denver, CO; Kevan Burke of NFL Properties in Los Angeles, CA; Bobbie Michael, administrative assistant for J.R. Simplot Company of Boise, ID; T.F. Schmit, vice president of AAA Automatic Flagpole Company of Maywood, IL; R.D. Musser III, president of the Grand Hotel, Mackinac Island, MI; Nancy Montgomery of John Wanamaker, Inc., of Philadelphia, PA; Susan L. Kelly, director of public affairs, Hudson's, Southfield, MI; Barbara C. Zibell, consumer affairs administrator for William Wrigley, Jr., of Chicago, IL; and Janice Madhu, Reproduction Department, George Eastman House, Rochester, NY.

Several syndicates and individual publications, as well as their representatives, including Judy Colbert of the Los Angeles Times Syndicate in Los Angeles, CA; Ben F. Phlegar, executive editor, and Susan J. LeClair of the U.S. News and World Report, Washington, DC; Marcia Terrones for *Playboy* of Chicago, IL; Bunny Hoest for William Hoest Enterprises of Lloyd Neck, NY; George Pipal, vice president for United Media of Santa Rosa, CA; Audrey Weinstein for *Star* Magazine of Tarrytown, NY; John Chan, Photo Department, Parade Publications of New York City; Allsport Photography of Santa Monica, CA; Katharine Burns, Editorial Rights and Permissions, *Reader's Digest*, Pleasantville, NY; and HG Publications, Inc., of Beverly Hills, CA.

A short list of individuals, including John J. Daly of Washington, DC, for use of his "A Toast to the Flag"; Neil B. Watson, superintendent of the Green-Wood Cemetery of Brooklyn, NY, for his information concerning the grave of Captain Reid, who made the first Stars and Stripes; Dana Walk, Lewiston, ID, for allowing the use of a photo of her flag-painted house; Robert Wells of Kennett Square, PA; Teresa Turko of Garland, TX, and Kathy Brownell of Jamestown, RI, both for furnishing their photographic winners in the *Parade*-Kodak "Let Freedom Ring" contest.

Preface

My research for this book was exhaustive, taking time over a 12-year period. My purpose was to compile the definitive reference source for the Star-Spangled Banner and all things pertinent to it.

In order to transmit a vast amount of previously scattered information in an orderly fashion, I used the federal Flag Code (Title 36, Ch. 10, secs. 170–178), which codifies the customs for display of and conduct toward the flag, singing of the national anthem, and reciting the Pledge of Allegiance as an outline. Relevant information is gathered under each section of the code.

It is my particular hope that this book will find its way into the hands of young people, who should grow up knowing the history and meaning of our national flag, and of all those people in government work of one sort or another, who also should be aware of what our flag stands for and how it should be treated. The book has been written in a popular vein and I hope it will prove interesting, not only as a reference and supplementary textbook, but as nonfiction browsing enjoyment for the average person.

Research included many supplementary sources besides the federal Flag Code itself and visits to the Flag House museum and Fort McHenry. It included a number of past presidential proclamations, a revised Flag Code bill sponsored by former senator Birch Bayh, and literally hundreds of newspaper and magazine articles. I also read every book about the flag I could locate, including a number now out of print and available only in rare book collections.

A unique feature of this book is its critique of the federal Flag Code, section by section, showing where it is outmoded and how it should be usefully updated. Historical notes show how some sections came about, why they are as they are, or why they have been or should be changed. For example, for the section discussing the code regulation for allowing the flag to fly 24 hours a day, I researched 33 sites where this has been done with official sanction during United States history. For the section listing flag-flying holidays, I researched the histories of these holidays. Where mention is made of the national anthem or the Pledge of Allegiance and how each is to be used in conjunction with flag display, I present appropriate history. I have even included a number of lyrics submitted over the years to replace those of the hard-to-sing national anthem.

For the section discussing cleaning and storing of the flag, I researched modern technologies and inventions and discussed how new flag materials and automated flagpoles have made code changes necessary. Where the church pennant, battle streamers, and the United Nations flag are discussed, I present the reasoning behind their usages.

In discussing the history of the flag, I show the various designs used, as well as various designs already on file in the eventuality of future state additions (such as Puerto Rico, Guam, or Micronesia).

This history replaces the Betsy Ross myth, telling the more likely story of how a Navy captain designed the Star-Spangled Banner. It discusses the fact that the United States flag has never been dipped to any person, and why. It tracks down the inspiration for the "Uncle Sam" appellation. It discusses the misuse of flying the flag upside-down as a distress signal and misuse by states in half-masting it, and even examples of misuse by the military and other government offices. It explains how flags are reconstructed by museums. And it discusses the problem of how outdated United States flags are to be treated, which also isn't covered by the Flag Code.

The federal Flag Code assigns no penalties for flag desecration, so this book also covers the prototypal penalties imposed by states, like Virginia, that took an early stand on putting teeth into the federal Flag Code.

Also covered are many interesting sidelights: the gardener who grew a living flag replica in flowers; the unique picture taken with thousands of sailors posed into a huge flag design; a lady who has crocheted flags; the largest flags ever flown; and much, much more.

My objectives — as an avowed flag waver and veteran of two wars — are: (1) to present an up-to-date, complete-in-one-book reference on our national flag, appropriate for both research and general reading; (2) to show, through research and anecdotal material, how our American Flag Code has been outdated and ignored, and how it can be updated to make it once more pertinent and positive; and (3) to make the entire project intriguing to the average American, especially young people. I'd like to see flag etiquette proudly and knowledgeably observed, all over the country, once more. We can use a dose of patriotism today.

BOB LOEFFELBEIN
August 1996

Introduction

Doesn't anyone know how to display the United States flag anymore?

Believe it or not, for the most part, United States government officials don't. The United States Park Service doesn't. Most military personnel don't. Most city, county, and state officials don't. Most of our Pan-American and Olympic Games officials don't. Most movie producers and television network officials don't. Most owners and managers of theme parks don't. Most owners and managers of sports arenas don't. Most parade managers and sponsors don't. And most business managers don't. Despite the fact that the rules of proper flag display are spelled out in the United States Code (Title 36, Ch. 10, secs. 173–178 — the "Flag Code"), these rules are ignored every day. The examples — only a few of the many documented — are here to prove it.

EXAMPLE: Almost daily throughout the year, scores of United States flags — an average of 250 per day — are raised briefly over the Capitol, then lowered. These flags are then passed on to people who have requested flags that have flown over the Capitol. This program has become so popular that it is now widely publicized. And it's been going on a long time. Chris Benza, the self-styled "Flag Lady," even went on television's old "To Tell the Truth" show (September 26, 1972), telling viewers how they could secure these flags.

Anyone can get a flag that has been flown over the Capitol for a few seconds — certified by a machine that forges the name of the Capitol architect — by contacting his or her congressional representative or senator. Cost varies depending upon fabric (cotton or nylon) and size. Does this program violate the Flag Code in any way?

ANSWER: Quite apart from the fact that all United States flags are equal — that is, flying over the Capitol does not make one any better or more valuable than another — there is a violation taking place. The regulation governing raising and lowering of the flag states that, once up, the flag doesn't come down until sunset (U.S. Code Title 36, Ch. 10, sec. 174[a]). The code also states (Sec.

1

174[b]) that the flag should be lowered "ceremoniously." It's hard to believe that those in charge of raising and lowering nearly 90,000 flags a year have much time for ceremony.

The program for handing out flags that had flown over the Capitol began so long ago that no one involved remembers when it started or who started it. Records, however, show that six flags were given out in 1937. Originally it was just a matter of passing along to some worthy group the tattered and presumably historic remains of the big 8×12 foot ensigns that flew night and day from east and west fronts of the Capitol building. These wear out at the rate of about 18 a year. That wasn't enough to meet the demand, so some bright senator or congressman procured a smaller flag on his own, had it flown briefly and certified, then sent it off to some cherished constituent, who probably bragged around until others started asking for the same favor.

By 1945 about a thousand flags a year were being so used. By 1993, more than 300 flags per day (excepting days at half-staff) were being run up and down on three poles. Some stayed up less than 30 seconds. The greatest number flown on a single day was on July 4, 1976, when 10,471 were raised and lowered to satisfy Bicentennial orders. The second most prolific day was July 4, 1960, when over 5,000 were raised to commemorate the new 50-star flag.

To add another wrinkle, sometimes banners other than the current 50-star flag are used. Special requests for 13-star flags have been filled. Then there was the first-grade class at the Carlton Palmore Elementary School of Lakeland, Florida, which sent Senator Lawton Chiles a class-made 13-star flag, unevenly but enthusiastically stitched, to be sent up the flagpole. Their request was granted, as was that of Marion Hendrickson, an 86-year-old resident of the Lutheran Retirement Home in Northwood, Iowa, who submitted (via Rep. Neal Smith) a 50-star crocheted model. That flag was later displayed by the Worth County Historical Society for the Bicentennial summer.

EXAMPLE: Flag Day (June 14) in 1980 was celebrated in the nation's capital by rolling out flat, on the Washington Monument grounds, the largest United States flag in the world, 86,310 square feet, covering an area of two football fields. It took 25 members of Iron Workers Local #5, two forklifts, and a crane to get its seven tons spread out. Then a news photographer from the Washington Star, not satisfied with the immensity, asked a group of 12 people to walk out onto the flag and pose on one of its stars. The picture was printed, so evidently none of the editors noted anything wrong. Were there no violations of the Flag Code here?

ANSWER: First of all, the Flag Code states (sec. 176[b]) that the flag should not touch the ground. As for allowing 12 people to stand on a star, the code states in sec. 178(e) that the flag should not be displayed in a manner that permits it to be easily soiled (for example, on the ground and underfoot); and sec. 176(g) states that nothing should be placed on any part of the flag — not a "mark, insignia, letter, word, figure, design, picture, or drawing of any nature." Nor, presumably, a person. What's more, another section of the U.S. Code — Title 4, Ch. 1, sec. 3 — establishes that the photographer was also guilty of a violation by exposing the spectacle of the "marked" flag to public view.

Why was the flag rolled out on the ground in the first place? It was the kickoff of a project in which the flag was to tour the country, with promoter Len Silverfine trying to raise enough in donations (about $55,000) for it to eventually be hung on New York's Verrazano Narrows Bridge, replacing a somewhat smaller one that had been torn apart by winds there during the Bicentennial year.

EXAMPLE: The United States Park Service has ringed the base of the Washington Monument with American flags, flying 24 hours a day. Is this display in keeping with the code?

ANSWER: At one time, the Flag Code implied (by referring to "the universal custom") that the United States flag should not be flown between sunset and sunrise. However, as the code states in sec. 178, "Any rule or custom pertaining to the display of the flag of the United States of America, set forth in sections 171 to 178 of this title, may be altered, modified or repealed, or additional rules with respect thereto may be prescribed, by the Commander in Chief of the Armed Forces of the United States, whenever he deems it to be appropriate or desirable, and any such alteration or additional rule shall be set forth in a proclamation." Accordingly, President Nixon, in Presidential Proclamation #4064 of July 6, 1971, stated:

> The Washington Monument stands day and night as America's tribute to our first President. The fifty American flags that encircle the base of the Monument represent our fifty states and, at the same time, symbolize our enduring Federal Union.
>
> As this Nation's 200th year approaches, I believe that it would do all Americans well to remember the years of our first President and to recall the enduring ideals of our Nation.... NOW, THEREFORE, I ... do hereby proclaim that, effective July 4, 1971 the fifty flags of the United States of America displayed at the Washington Monument in the District of Columbia be flown at all times during the day and night, except when the weather is inclement.

This proclamation allows the exception to the "universal custom" of lowering the flag at sunset.

But why 50 United States flags? Wouldn't it be better to display the official state flags, since it is the states they are said to be representing? Then one United States flag could be displayed in a position of honor, either on the pole to the far right of the ring of flags (which would place it flanking the main walkway, on the left of a person walking toward the monument) or on a staff situated somewhere above the ring of state flags, such as over the entrance or on top of the monument.

From 1961 until October 14, 1976, Alabama maintained this flag display on its capitol building. The Confederate and state flags were displayed on the Capitol tower staff, with the United States flag on a separate staff bordering the entrance walkway. (Photo by Bob Loeffelbein.)

There is a fine point of inference in this idea of having the American flag represent each individual state, which some states may resent, and, perhaps, should resent. After all, the federal government does not speak for the individual states in all matters. Sometimes, as in the instance of racial integration of public schools, the state and federal governments have strongly disagreed on which body has the final authority. It isn't always clear in Article I, section 10 of the Constitution, which limits the powers of the states in such matters as commerce and war; nor even in Amendment 10 of the Bill of Rights, where it is stated, "The powers not delegated to the United States by the Constitution, nor prohibited by it to the States, are reserved to the States respectively, or to the people."

The state of Alabama had an interesting way of showing its independence in interpreting the question of state *vs.* federal jurisdiction. From 1961 until 1976, the Confederate flag of the Civil War and the state flag were flown on the staff over Alabama's capitol building, with the stars and stripes displayed on a staff separate from the building entirely, fronting the main entrance.

The Confederate battle flag had replaced the stars and stripes atop the Alabama capital in 1961 to mark the Civil War centennial, at the order of Governor George Wallace. On October 14, 1976, the United States flag quietly reappeared atop the capitol, above the state and Confederate flags. That move came after a federal court (U.S. District Judge Robert E. Varner presiding) refused to order Wallace to make the switch, stating that it was a valid display, in spite of the lawsuit filed by Alvin Holmes, a black state legislator from Montgomery, who was seeking to force the state to fly the United States flag higher than the Confederate standard, in compliance with the Flag Code. Holmes stated that "the state-sponsored display of the confederate flag offended sensitive descendants of former slaves."

After Wallace won his point, he moved the national flag back on his own initiative. True, he put the state flag and the Confederate flag under the United States flag *on the same halyard*, which the Flag Code had originally forbidden. By then, however, President Nixon had made the May 5, 1972, Presidential Proclamation #4131, which allowed flags of states, cities, or localities, or pennants of societies, to be flown on the same halyard with the flag of the United States, so long as the United States flag was always flown at the peak and hoisted first, lowered last.

The controversy did not end with the restoration of the stars and stripes to the position of prominence. After all, the Confederate flag still flew. In 1988, Alabama NAACP president and state representative Thomas Reed and 13 other black legislators were arrested by state troopers and capital police while trying to climb an eight-foot fence around the capitol in order to tear down the Confederate flag. And in 1992, Governor Guy Hunt announced that it was his intention to continue flying that flag atop the capitol upon the completion of a $28.5 million restoration of the building. Alabama's 24 black legislators boycotted the rededication ceremony in protest. Stated Will Hill Tankersly, chairman of the Montgomery area Chamber of Commerce, "It's like going to church in your underwear.... It's not illegal, and it's not immoral, but it's just not appropriate." Later, Governor Jim Folsom (who replaced Guy Hunt in 1993) stated that he wouldn't put the Confederate flag atop the capitol (though he announced it would fly across the street at the first White House of the Confederacy). That left South Carolina as the last state still flying the Confederate flag over its capitol building.

Meanwhile, inside Alabama's capitol, a certain antagonistic feeling was long evident through a display in the building's lobby. There, enshrined on one wall, were replicas of the national seals of the countries to which the area incorporating Alabama has owed allegiance during its history: Spain, France, Great Britain, and the Confederacy. Missing was the great seal of the United States of America. When a state employee was queried concerning the absence, the answer was, "We don't have room for it," despite several blank wall areas nearby and space both above and below the display, which would have required only minimal rearrangement.

The flag of the Confederacy has caused a number of other confrontations in various southern states over the years. For example, at the Virginia Military

Institute, the New Market Day ceremony, commemorating ten VMI corpsmen who died in a Civil War battle there in 1864, was controversial from 1968 when black students were first admitted to the military school. In 1973 all but 2 of the 19 black cadets boycotted the ritual, which included an honor march past the Confederate flag. A student-run referendum showed a majority of the students favored changes in the ceremony designed to play down its Confederate symbolism, junking the tune "Dixie" and the Confederate flags in favor of VMI songs and flags. But the VMI board of visitors, which ran the 134-year-old school then, was unanimous in voting to keep the ceremony unchanged.

In April 1992 the government watchdog group Common Cause asked for the removal of the Confederate flag from the design of the Georgia state flag, claiming it was a racist symbol. It had been incorporated into the state's banner in 1956, more than 90 years after the end of the Civil War, to demonstrate the legislature's disdain for school integration.

In a poll by the *Atlanta Journal-Constitution*, 76 percent of white respondents stated they saw the Confederate battle flag as a sign of southern pride. Fifty-eight percent of blacks saw it as a symbol of racism and oppression.

The Georgia Civil Rights Network was coordinating a petition campaign to replace the 1956 flag with Georgia's original flag, the state seal on a field of blue. A flag incorporating the Confederate flag was "simply not representative of all the people in Georgia," stated Earl Shinhoster, the NAACP's southeastern regional director. "It would bring tears to the eyes of our grandmothers to change the flag," retorted Charles Lunsford, Georgia spokesman for the Sons of Confederate Veterans.

Governor Zell Miller introduced a bill to change the flag back, saying, "We need to lay the days of segregation to rest…. We need to do what is right." By March 1993, however, Governor Miller announced he was giving up his fight to remove the Confederate flag from Georgia's state flag "since extremists from both sides have complicated this issue beyond any immediate solution." Nevertheless, the Atlanta–Fulton County Recreation Authority went ahead and banned the state flag from County Stadium, which is the home of the Atlanta Braves baseball team and which served the 1996 summer Olympic Games.

In April 1988 there was another hoorah over the Confederate flag in Oklahoma. Governor Henry Bellmon signed a controversial resolution requiring the flag be flown over the state capitol. However, he said the flagpole would remain empty until he knew which kind of Confederate flag to display since there were three different ones used between 1861 and 1865. Senator Herbert Rozell authored the resolution.

EXAMPLE: In the December 1988 Holiday Bowl football game in San Diego, United States Marines unfurled a flag nearly covering the gridiron, holding it taut to display it flat.

In Waikiki, Hawaii, U.S. military personnel carry a giant flag in a parade sponsored by the Pearl Harbor Survivors Association. This display is in violation of the Flag Code, subsection 176(c), which states that "the flag should never be carried aloft or horizontally." (U.S. Navy photo.)

It wasn't the first time such a display occurred. In 1969 at an Army-Navy football game in Philadelphia a marching band unfurled two huge flags — a replica of the original 13-star one and the 50-star model — and proceeded to march down the field holding both flat-stretched flags by their hems.

Worse was the flat-stretched flag carried in the Delco 500 (auto race) parade in May 1996. Marchers poked their heads through holes in the flag and wore suspenders to hold the flag on their shoulders.

What, if anything, are these military units doing wrong?

ANSWER: For some reason it has become fairly common for parade and show bands or other marching units to carry a large Old Glory flat, flanked by members holding it by its edges. It's colorful, especially when they make it wave and billow.

Yet the Army-Navy game carriers were doubly wrong. First of all, flag regulations openly state the national ensign shall not be carried flat (U.S. Code Title 36, Ch. 10, sec. 176[c]). Secondly, even had it been okay to carry it flat, the band still gave the right-hand place of honor or precedence to the wrong (outdated 13-star) flag. The 50-star flag should have taken precedence in the order of presentation, with the blue field uppermost or at the highest part of the scene.

Since there are multiple sides for seating at a football game, the problem arises of deciding from whose point of view the blue field would be uppermost. Such nearly unsolvable problems may, in fact, be the reason for the regulation against flat display.

If such a display is to be pictured on television, flag etiquette would at least demand that it be shown from the viewpoint of the cameras and the millions of home viewers behind them. Otherwise it would be staged from the viewpoint of the "home" or host stands. All of which is academic, in view of the ruling.

The Army-Navy display poses another problem as well. In presenting a progression of flag history, the natural order is to work from first to last, or earliest flag to current flag. But this would be an error. Regulations state the current national flag must take precedence over all other flags, and no exception is granted anyone who wishes, for the sake of esthetics, to parade them in historical order.

Finally, all displays at sporting events raise the possibility that the flag is being used as "decoration," a practice frowned upon in the Flag Code. Section 176(d) forbids various decorative arrangements of the flag ("never ... festooned, drawn back, nor up, in folds...") and suggests that "bunting of blue, white, and red ... should be used ... for decoration in general." On the whole, anyone wishing to inject a patriotic spirit into some event can easily do so with splashes of red, white, and blue, eliminating the need to judge whether a flag display is intended as solemn and reverent or merely decorative.

EXAMPLE: In the 1992 campaign for United States president, incumbent George Bush, at a trade conference with Mexican president Carlos Salinas de Gortari and Canadian prime minister Brian Mulroney, was pictured with two Mexican, two United States, and two Canadian flags as background decor, all in the same display. Ross Perot was pictured by the Associated Press with 20 or so massed Star-Spangled Banners behind him at a speaker's podium in Olympia, Washington. And as election returns poured in, national television showed Bill Clinton outside the Arkansas state house with about 20 massed flags behind him as well. Were these displays in keeping with the spirit of the Flag Code?

ANSWER: A difficult question of flag display is whether more than one United States flag may be displayed simultaneously. The Flag Code has a great deal to say about how to display the stars and stripes with "other" flags. For example, in a display of two flags on crossed staffs, the United States flag should be on the right as it faces forward (the viewer's left), with its staff atop that of the other flag. But what if both flags are United States flags? The regulation becomes nonsense, impossible to follow. This is the case with many of the display regulations. Nowhere does the code describe how to display more than one United States flag at a time. Does this mean, by implication, that such displays are forbidden by the Flag Code? Or is the matter simply left to the discretion of the flag-waver?

A key word here might be "discretion." There is generally nothing discreet, nor dignified either, in the multiple flag displays perpetrated everywhere from political conventions to department stores. The atmosphere they create is pretty far from the solemnity and reverence of a patriotic observance. One flag, fluttering above an edifice of the United States government or standing solemnly to the side of the judge in a court of law, bespeaks the spirit of a nation. A hundred flags ringing a used car lot are reduced to the level of decoration — a use the Flag Code definitely rejects, in subsection 176(d). That subsection counsels the use of "bunting of blue, white, and red ... for decoration in general." If people followed this suggestion, the question of how many flags could be displayed at once might become a moot point.

EXAMPLES: The United States flag at the courthouse of Latah County, Indiana, was flown at half-staff in observance of the death of the county assessor (May 1989). In Virginia the United States flag was half-masted all over the state for four state patrolmen shot in the line of duty. And when Billy Carter, former president Jimmy Carter's brother, died from cancer of the pancreas (September 1988) the United States flag was flown at half-mast in his home town of Plains, Georgia. Were these half-mastings correct?

ANSWER: The Flag Code is strict on half-masting, even to enumerating what office holders can be so honored and for how long. Most of this was spelled out by Dwight Eisenhower in Presidential Proclamation #3044 (December 12, 1969). Eisenhower's proclamation was directed largely at federal agencies and prescribed rules for displaying the flag at half-staff on federal property. However, when Congress inserted the provisions of the proclamation into the actual text of the Flag Code (by Public Law 94-344 in 1976), they broadened both the guidelines and their application. The current code does not specify federal or any other property. It contains provisions for half-masting either "according to presidential instructions" or "in accordance with recognized customs."

Therefore there is nothing that specifically prohibits local officials or even private citizens from flying the flag at half-staff on appropriate occasions at their own choice (often decided by councils, groups). However, the use of organization, city, county, or state flags might have been better advised in the cases of the half-masting for a county assessor and would perhaps be more appropriate for the murdered state patrolmen. The officers were serving the state and so should have been honored by that state's flag. This would eliminate the risk of infringing upon long-standing custom of using the national flag only as a symbol of national unity.

In fact, free choice in half-masting the stars and stripes can work against the cause of unity. In 1970, Mayor John Lindsey of New York City ordered the flag half-masted to honor the four students shot by national guardsmen at Ohio's Kent State University. Lindsey's own citizenry were divided in their opinions of his proclamation. Workmen, angry at student anti-war groups, were pictured climbing up and raising the flag to full-staff outside New York's city hall.

Disagreements have been noted within states, too, on proper flag display. Tennessee governor Ray Blanton correctly ordered *state* flags flown at half-staff over state buildings upon the death of Elvis Presley. However, individuals all over Memphis, where Elvis spent his early years in a public housing project, half-masted the stars and stripes.

Other unusual half-mastings have occurred. In June 1977, San Francisco mayor George Mosconi ordered the city hall flag flown at half-mast for a homosexual man who was slain in a street attack. In August 1979, all flags at Dodger Stadium and Los Angeles city hall were lowered when Dodger baseball team owner Walter O'Malley died. Loyola-Marymount University put its flags at half-mast for the death of its star basketball player, Hank Gathers, in March 1990. Flags in Kokomo, Indiana, were half-masted for Ryan White, the teenager who publicized the discrimination suffered by victims of AIDS, in April 1990.

Unfortunately, some half-mastings symbolize little more than disrespect and ignorance of regulations. The flag at California State–Fullerton college suffered such an indignity when coach Augie Garrido conducted a full-fledged "funeral" to bury "the negative environment" of the start of the 1985 baseball season. Team captains served as pall bearers of an old equipment trunk. The team responded with four straight victories.

But it was left to Governor Meldrin Thomson of New Hampshire to order the half-masting that strayed farthest from the original intent of such an honor. In April 1976, he ordered flags flown on state buildings at half-mast to "memorialize the death of Christ on the Cross on the first Good Friday." The New Hampshire Civil Liberties Union called his action "an utterly inappropriate usurpation of power.... The lowering of flags, which are the symbols of the secular state, in this connection is ... in blatant disregard of the separation of church and state." And they were right.

EXAMPLE: Swim team members of the 1984 Olympics had slipovers made in the design of the United States flag, front and back. Is it okay to sport the flag as clothing?

ANSWER: The Flag Code emphatically states (sec. 176[d]) that "the flag should never be used as wearing apparel." Of course, the swim team members did not have actual flags cut up to make their outfits. Such an action would certainly have constituted desecration of the flag. In the matter of flag-design clothing, a lot depends on how closely the clothing resembles the genuine article. But the swim team members might still have been in violation of the code. Section 176[j] reads, "No part of the flag should ever be used as a costume or athletic uniform."

Worldwide athletic events like the Olympics and the Pan-American Games always furnish the news media with pictures of well-meaning, but misguided, United States fans trying to display their patriotism by flag waving. At the 1990 Goodwill Games in Seattle, the television camera several times picked out a fan waving a large American flag with a Russian flag sewn onto one side of it to produce a two-faced banner. This was a clever Goodwill Games gesture, but it was also a violation of the Flag Code, which prohibits attaching anything to a flag (sec. 176[g]).

Sports Illustrated magazine has been one of the worst offenders in playing up misguided patriotism. In February 1980 it pictured three ladies using an American flag as a lap robe. Another time it pictured one of the American hockey players with the stars and stripes wrapped around his neck. At the 1988 Olympic Games, there was *Sports Illustrated* again, picturing a lady hockey fan with the flag wrapped around her neck, on a two-page spread.

EXAMPLES: In the 1983 *Superman* movie sequel, in a scene where Clark Kent attends his high school reunion, the flag is displayed on a wall of the ballroom with the blue field to the right of the viewer. Even worse, in July 1986 when Alexander Haig, a former Army vice chief of staff and secretary of state (1980–82), spoke to 60 members of the Maritime Alliance of the Pacific Northwest, an American flag was posted on the wall directly behind his head with the blue-starred field to the right of viewers. Were these displays correct?

ANSWERS: Reversing the position of the blue field continues to be the most common flag display mistake. The blue field should always be at the top and always on "the flag's *own* right," not necessarily on the viewer's right. This depends on where the flag is flown.

Haig probably had nothing to do with placing the flag incorrectly on his podium. But, in his position as featured speaker and as former high-ranking military officer, he should have noticed it and had it corrected.

Examples of improper flag display abound in movies and television. In the ABC-TV drama *Ring of Thieves*, a flag was mounted on the wall behind a lectern as a colorful backing frame for a full close-up of actor Lex Barker emoting, and it was a photographic smash — except that the blue field was, again, posted backwards.

In *Fool's Parade* (1971), with James Stewart, a flag was displayed on a wall backwards again. Stewart, a general in the Army Air Force with the Air Medal and Distinguishing Flying Cross, should have noticed the gaffe.

In a courtroom skit on "Rowan & Martin's Laugh-In" (Oct. 30, 1971) the American flag was on the wrong side of the podium. On a podium or raised stage the flag, on a standing pole, is always on the right of the speaker, which is also its own right. If it were placed on the floor of the auditorium, however, it would be placed on the audience's right. This fine point is almost always misunderstood, but can be remembered if the flag is always given the place of honor, the right-hand side (the viewer's left) of the area it is in. It stands with no other flag to its right as it faces forward.

Have things gotten better lately? Don't be silly.

A wall flag was mounted backwards in *Izzie & Moe* (1985), another was mounted backwards in a courtroom scene in *Vengeance, the Story of Tony Cimo* (1986), and one was knocked over and left lying on the floor in one of Chevy Chase's "Saturday Night Live" pratfall introductions (1986). In a November 1989 segment of the "Paradise" television series, an Army colonel's flag-covered casket had the blue field over the wrong shoulder. In the 1990 movie *Sweet Revenge*, state and national flags are mounted from crossed staffs behind a judge in a courtroom scene with the American flag on the wrong side, and its staff placed incorrectly beneath the state flagstaff.

Driving around any city, on any day, one sees the United States flag incorrectly displayed, blithely disregarded, and badly treated. One day in Atlantic City I noticed a flag in front of a funeral home. It was correctly displayed, but in mid-afternoon the maintenance man came out and took it down, long before sunset. As he reeled it down, he allowed it to drag across the ground while he rolled it up in his arms like a bedspread coming out of a laundromat dryer, instead of correctly folding it into a triangle as designated by the Flag Code.

Of course, folding the flag in the manner prescribed for the uniformed services poses a problem for people like this maintenance man, since it cannot be accomplished properly by one person. In formal ceremonies the flag is usually folded as it is taken down. It involves two or more lengthwise foldings (depending on flag size), followed by triangular folds being rolled up from the trailing edge to eyelet edge. The blue field remains outermost. It is folded this way so it can be easily hooked back to the lanyard and raised so it unfolds freely.

For informal one-person lowering, it has become accepted procedure either to roll up the flag or to hang it in drapes across an arm as it comes off the halyard. But it should be folded as stated above before being put away, using a table as a folding aid if necessary, and no part of the flag should touch ground or floor.

1

Background to the Flag Code

Enough has probably been said for now about how *not* to display the stars and stripes. It is time to take a look at the positive aspects of display.

To bear the Star-Spangled Banner is an honor. To own one is a sacred trust, for it is an emblem of freedom, equality, and justice for all who have gone before and will come after. It is a symbol of the brotherhood of man, standing for courage, for chivalry, for generosity, and for honor. As such, it deserves the highest honor one can accord it.

Certain fundamental rules of heraldry (the study of genealogical insignias), established by long custom, indicate proper methods of displaying flags of allegiance. Some aspects of the United States Flag Code hark back to these. For example, the right hand and arm, by heraldic tradition, is the sword arm, the point of danger, and hence the place of honor. No ancient king in his right mind would allow anyone he couldn't trust to stand or ride by his right (sword-bearing) hand. It would be too easy to surprise and overpower him. (Heraldry has ignored the plight of the left-handed ruler.) So the custom arose of putting a friend or honored guest on one's right, and of reserving the right-hand honor place for the flag of allegiance as well. This custom explains why the blue field of the United States flag — the *union*, considered the honor point — is always to be displayed to the flag's own right as it faces forward.

All rules for flag display don't come directly from heraldic history, of course. On Flag Day, June 14, 1923, and again on Flag Day in 1924, representatives of 68 patriotic organizations met in a National Flag Conference in Washington, D.C., for the purpose of formulating regulations for the use and display of the flag of the United States of America. Public Law 623 of the Seventy-seventh Congress was the result, ultimately approved by the president on June 22, 1942. This resolution codified already existing customs and rules governing flag display. A slightly amended version was approved on December 22

13

that same year as Public Law 829. The text of PL829 was codified as Title 36, Ch. 10, secs. 173–178, and except for a 1953 act incorporating regulations concerning the flag of the United Nations, this part of the code remained unchanged until 1976. On July 7 of that year, President Gerald Ford signed legislation that revised the Flag Code. Submitted by Senator Birch Bayh (D-IN) "to clear up some misunderstandings over proper use of the flag," these Flag Code amendments were approved as Public Law 94-344, and entered into the appropriate sections of Title 36.

Other legislation dealing with the flag is codified as Title 18, Ch. 33, sec. 700 (including the Flag Protection Act of 1989) and Title 4, Ch. 1, sec. 3 (forbidding the use of the flag for advertising purposes in the District of Columbia).

The Flag Code has no specific connection to the Constitution. The flag, as a matter of fact, is not even mentioned in the Constitution. Both the flag and the Constitution have become accepted symbols of America, but too few people know what either the Flag Code or the Constitution actually says.

Most Americans know there is a code of flag etiquette, but they wouldn't know where to find it. And it's been shown that most of them aren't familiar with its provisions except very generally.

Yet the Flag Code is much more than etiquette. It is part of the United States Code of federal law. Though the code has never carried any penalties for violation of its provisions, its intent — to insure proper treatment of the flag by all persons — has been taken to heart at the state level. The provisions of the Flag Code have now been incorporated into the laws of most states, and in those states penalties have been attached. No longer is the code composed merely of patriotic custom.

The Flag Code is often wrongly thought to apply only to the military establishment. Section 173 of the code is titled "Display and Use of Flag by Civilians; Codification of rules and customs." The section reads in part:

> The following codification of existing rules and customs pertaining to the display and use of the flag of the United States of America is established for the use of such civilians or civilian groups or organizations as may not be required to conform with regulations promulgated by one or more executive departments of the Government of the United States.

Besides sections concerning display of (173–175) and respect for (176) the flag, the code provides regulations for conduct during flag-display ceremonies (177). Preceding these portions of the code are sections establishing the national anthem and outlining proper response to its playing (170–171), and a section setting forth the Pledge of Allegiance and advising on proper delivery thereof (172).

The Flag Code also contains provisions for its own modification (section 178), as follows:

§178. Modification of rules and customs by President

Any rule or custom pertaining to the display of the flag of the United States of America, set forth in sections 171 to 178 of this title, may be altered, modified, or repealed, or additional rules with respect thereto may be prescribed, by the Commander in Chief of the Armed Forces of the United States, whenever he deems it to be appropriate or desirable; and any such alteration or additional rule shall be set forth in a proclamation.

This is the catchall section which allows the president of the United States, as commander in chief of the armed forces, to change any portion of the Flag Code.

Of course, changes could cause problems between the federal code and state laws. The code as it exists has been widely copied into state laws, which of course the president cannot change. Therefore conflicting legislations could arise. In spite of this, however, it remains the contention of this author and the theme of this book that change in the Flag Code is necessary.

"America is not like a blanket — one piece of unbroken cloth," the Reverend Jesse Jackson has stated. "America is more like a quilt — many patches, many pieces, many colors, many sizes, all woven together by a common thread."

Throughout this book, many examples will be presented for nearly every section of the Code to illustrate how they need rewriting to bring them into the present. Section 178 gives the president the power to do it. The states would welcome clarification — could even help with it, since some have already modified the federal wording. These modifications were accomplished by and large through citizen pressure, and it was accomplished with flag-flying, under the guarantees of the Constitution, the right way for dissidents to create change.

There are, of course, always dissident factions in the United States who see the American flag as a symbol of "presidential" policy. They forget that the banner is really their own symbol every bit as much as that of a president or any member of any establishment. When they revile it, they revile themselves and their own beliefs, as well as the right that flag, and the constitutional government it represents, gives them.

Besides, it seems that members of the establishment the dissidents have been attacking would become more angry if the dissidents used and revered the flag, as their emblem that change is possible, than if they defiled it. Experience has shown that reigning politicians start thinking the flag represents only their beliefs, when the truth of the matter is that the American people decide what that flag shall stand for.

Members of both sides, dissidents and establishment (defined as all those believing in the status quo), might do well to study the United States Flag Code.

The first thing to remember about the Flag Code is that, like any body of law, it must be taken as an entity, each section having a bearing on every other one. And it must be read specifically, with care for the exact meaning of each word.

With these points understood, let us begin our section-by-section examination of the United States Flag Code.

2
Displaying the Flag

(United States Code Title 36, Ch. 10, secs. 174–175)

§174. Time and occasions for display
(a) Display on buildings and stationary flagstaffs in open; night display

It is the universal custom to display the flag only from sunrise to sunset on buildings and on stationary flagstaffs in the open. However, when a patriotic effect is desired, the flag may be displayed twenty-four hours a day if properly illuminated during the hours of darkness.

The original text of this section noted that the flag could be displayed "at night upon special occasions." The amendments of 1976 (Public Law 94-344) changed this to "twenty-four hours," struck the "special occasions" proviso, and added the instruction regarding illumination.

There are now at least 35 officially designated places where the flag flies, or has flown, 24 hours each day, not counting the flags left on six trips to the moon by NASA astronauts. Of these 35 sites, presidential proclamations have placed four, and Congress has established two others via public laws. The rest have been authorized by tradition, as local patriotic gestures, usually commemorating some event in the nation's history. The sites are as follows:

1. **Fort McHenry National Monument and Historical Shrine, Baltimore, MD** (Presidential Proclamation #2795, July 2, 1948, by Harry Truman).

   Fort McHenry has been commemorated as the birthplace of America's national anthem by a cacheted envelope issued by the postal service July 4, 1973. At one time a red, white, and blue buoy marked the exact spot in the bay where Francis Scott Key is thought to have been when he penned the anthem.

2. **The Flag House, Flag House Square, East Pratt St., Baltimore, MD** (Public Law #319, 83rd Congress, approved March 26, 1954). It read:

Baltimore's Flag House, located just off the waterfront, is honored as the home of the woman who made the immortal flag that flew over Fort McHenry the night of the battle during which Francis Scott Key penned the American national anthem. It is the only building in the U.S. allowed to fly *two* flags 24 hours per day — the current one and the 1814 one. The flag makers were Mrs. Mary Pickersgill and her daughter, Carolyn Purdy. The flag was made under U.S. contract for $405.90, size 42×30 feet, of cotton bunting. Today, the Flag House is a specialized museum in which everything pertaining to "The Star-Spangled Banner" is kept. A unique all-stone map of the United States is featured in its walled-in yard. (Photo by Bob Loeffelbein.)

> That notwithstanding any rule or custom pertaining to the display of the flag of the United States of America as set forth in the joint resolution entitled "Joint resolution to codify and emphasize rules and customs pertaining to the display and use of the flag of the United States of America," approved June 22, 1942, as amended, authority is hereby conferred on the appropriate officer of the State of Maryland to permit the flying of the flag of the United States for twenty-four hours of each day in Flag House Square, Albemarle and Pratt Streets, Baltimore, Maryland.
>
> Sec. 2. Subject to the provisions of section 3 of the joint resolution of June 22, 1942, as amended, authority is also conferred on the appropriate officer of the State of Maryland to permit the flying of a replica of the flag of the United States which was in use during the war of 1812 for twenty-four hours of each day in Flag House Square, Albemarle and Pratt Streets, Baltimore, Maryland.

3. United States Marine Corps (Iwo Jima) Memorial, Arlington National Cemetery, Arlington, VA (Presidential Proclamation #3418, June 12, 1961, by John F. Kennedy).

The last survivor of these flag-raisers on Iwo Jima in World War II, John Bradley, of Antigo, Wisconsin, died of a stroke at age 70 on January 11, 1994. It was Marine PFC Rene A. Gagnon who identified these men as the flag-raisers to Marine Corps headquarters in Washington: Marine PFC Franklin R. Sousley (killed in action) at far left; Marine PFC Ira H. Hayes of Bapchule, Arizona, with a slung rifle; Marine Sgt. Michael Strank of Conemaugh, Pennsylvania, barely visible beside Hayes; Navy Ph. M Second class John H. Bradley, then of Appleton, Wisconsin; PFC Gagnon, whose helmet is barely visible beside Bradley; and Marine Sgt. Henry O. Hansen of Somerville, Massachusetts, at the foot of the flagstaff. The statue design was taken from an oil painting by Tom Lovell, which he did from the Joe Rosenthal AP newsphoto.

This memorial is a statue inspired by a world-famous photograph by Associated Press war correspondent Joe Rosenthal. It depicts four Marines erecting a flag atop Mount Suribachi on February 23, 1945, when Iwo Jima was finally taken. It remains a symbol of the valor and courage of American fighting forces in that war. It has also been commemorated on a U.S. 3-cent stamp, issued as part of the Armed Forces series in October 1945. The memorial is located in Arlington National Cemetery and is the site of regular military drills that are open to the public. By proclamation of President Kennedy in 1961, the memorial is illuminated at night.

4. Mount Suribachi, island of Iwo Jima in the Pacific Ocean, honoring the American soldiers who succeeded, after one of the bloodiest battles in American history, in planting the flag there.

5. Marine Monument, Quantico, VA. Probably established by custom.

6. National Memorial Cemetery of the Pacific, Honolulu, HI. This military cemetery lies nestled within the crater of an extinct volcano. Informally known as the Punchbowl Crater, the site is entered on the National Register of Historic Places under its Hawaiian name, Puowaina, meaning "Consecrated Hill"

LEXINGTON, MA

Representing the Minutemen of the American Revolution, the statue of Captain Parker stands on Lexington Green, Massachusetts. The American flag, which flies 24 hours a day on this site is visible over the statue's left shoulder in this photo.

or "Hill of Sacrifice." The remains of some 13,000 World War II soldiers who saw action in the Pacific were the first burials in this cemetery, which was established by an act of Congress in 1948. Famed World War II correspondent Ernie Pyle, who was killed in 1945 by Japanese machine gun fire, is buried there.

7. **Battle Green, Lexington, MA.** (Public Law 335, Eighty-ninth Congress, approved November 8, 1965).

8. **Memorial Arch, Valley Forge National Historical Park, Valley Forge, PA.** Here a flag flies to honor the soldiers who served at Valley Forge during the winter of 1777-78. The arch was authorized by Congress in 1910 and dedicated in 1917.

9. **The White House, Washington, DC** (Presidential Proclamation #4000, September 4, 1970, by Richard Nixon). A floodlight was installed on the south portico of the executive mansion to illuminate it.

10. **United States Capitol, east and west central fronts, Washington, DC.**
    According to the architect of the Capitol's office, no record has been found for the earliest date the flag was flown over the east and west central fronts of the Capitol, but the custom of flying the flags continuously 24 hours a day over the east and west fronts was begun during World War I after requests to do so were received from all over the country.
    Early engravings and lithographs in the office of the architect of the Capitol show flags flying on either side of the original low dome above the corridors connecting the areas now known as Statuary Hall and the Old Senate Chamber. After the addition of the new House and Senate wings in

Flag flying day and night at Memorial Arch, Valley Forge National Historical Park. (Photo by John Ansley, courtesy of the Valley Forge National Historical Park.)

the 1850s, even before the great dome was completed in 1863, photographs of the period show flags flying over each new wing and the central east and west fronts.

An appropriation to provide flags for the east and west fronts was made in the Sundry Civil Appropriations Act (28 Stat. 393), approved August 18, 1894, as follows:

> To provide flags for the east and west fronts of the center of the Capitol, to be hoisted daily under the direction of the Capitol Police board, $100, or so much thereof as may be necessary.

11. Senate wing of the Capitol when the Senate is in session, and the House wing when it is in session.

12. United States Customs Ports of Entry (Presidential Proclamation #4131, May 5, 1972, by Richard Nixon).

13. Fifty flags at the base of the Washington Memorial, Washington, DC (Presidential Proclamation #4064, July 6, 1971, by Richard Nixon).

14. Mt. Sloven, Colton, CA (no longer flying).

When old Isaac Sloven, a pal of Kit Carson, came to the area of Colton, California, back in pioneer days, he gave his name to a peculiar mountain of natural cement. It became the cement works that has been mined continuously now for over 75 years, under the management of the California Portland Cement Co. Until modern mining methods suppressed the dust thrown up, the town could be located from miles away just by the dust cloud hanging over the open strip mining operation.

The flag came later, after plant manager Thomas J. Flemming saw a large American flag unfurled at night during a visit to Chicago. Impressed by its beauty, he thought of the possibilities of such a flag atop Mt. Sloven. Flemming, through a special dispensation granted by Congress, was given permission for the flag to fly 24 hours provided it was kept illuminated. He returned home, erected a 90-foot pole, and as a patriotic gesture on July 4, 1917, raised the flag. From the mountain's crest 1,509 feet above sea level, the large flag, 24 × 15 feet, flew day and night. Brilliantly flood-lighted at night, it could be seen for miles, since the mountain rises abruptly from a valley floor that is otherwise level for miles around.

In 1941 the Native Sons of the Golden West presented a state bear flag to the cement plant, and it was placed below the American flag and also flew day and night. The two flags flew continuously except for the period of World War II when blackouts were enforced. However, the top of this so-called "Vanishing Mountain" was sliced off for mining purposes in 1952, and the flag was removed. Experts say that the mountain has so much natural cement left that at the rate of 50,000 sacks per day it will still be 100 years before the supply gives out; as a historical site, however, it will long since have been forgotten. Indeed most area residents have already forgotten the flag once flew there. It is only from old newspaper records that the story came out.

15. Birthplace of Francis Scott Key, Terra Rubra Farm, Keysville, MD, in Manachosi Valley, Carroll County. The flag, maintained by the Kiwanis Club of Westminster, Maryland, has flown here since May 30, 1949.

16. Grave of Francis Scott Key, Mount Olivet Cemetery, Frederick MD.

Barbara Fritchie's grave is in the south part of the cemetery. Along the western border are the graves of over 400 Confederate dead from the battles of Antietam and Monocacy.

17. Castle of Death Valley Scotty, Death Valley, CA.

18. The Cemetery, Deadwood, SD. The 24-hour custom here was started during World War I, from Brown Rocks, overlooking the city. It was soon discontinued, but with the advent of World War II, it was reinstated and has continued.

19. Grave of Betsy Ross, Mount Mariah Cemetery, Philadelphia, PA. The city of Philadelphia commissioned Dr. Allen Mann, a University of Pennsylvania anthropologist, to dig up the legendary seamstress for re-burying in the courtyard of her house, which is now a national monument. Diggers found her third husband, then a box containing the remains of her grandson or great-grandson, but had to search around a bit in this southwest Philadelphia cemetery to find Mrs. Ross. ("I'm certainly relieved things worked out," stated Dr. Mann to reporters afterward. "I certainly wouldn't want to get blamed for losing Betsy Ross.")

20. Grave of Jennie Wade, the only civilian killed in the Battle of Gettysburg, Gettysburg Evergreen Cemetery, Gettysburg, PA.

21. Lafayette's Tomb, Paris, France. Though his grave is in the Cimitière Pipcus in Paris, the Marquis de Lafayette was able to fulfill his wish to be buried beneath American soil. Before his death, he had procured quantities of earth from the fields where he had battled on the side of the colonists in the American Revolution, and this soil was used in his grave. On July 4, 1834, six weeks after his death, a small ceremony took place at that gravesite. An American flag was placed by the grave, and a band played "The Star-Spangled Banner." Reports written at the time state that an American flag was to stand there "en permanence."

There are also several reports of the American flag flying here even during the German occupation of 1940–44. The cemetery, being far back from the streets and on the property of a convent, was not of any interest to the Germans. And the flag as shown in pictures did not extend above the walls around it, so it is very possible that it remained flying during that time.

22. Municipal War Memorial, Worcester, MA. This memorial was designed specifically to fly the flag 24 hours per day. The flag was raised November 11, 1933, on a 90-foot staff set into a bronze and granite base.

23. Northwestern State Bank, St. Paul, MN.

24. Riverdale Cemetery, Niagara Falls, NY.

25. Sunset Hill Cemetery, Jamestown, NY.

26. Pennsylvania Hall, Gettysburg College, Gettysburg, PA.
The flying of a 34-star flag commemorates the use of the hall as both a

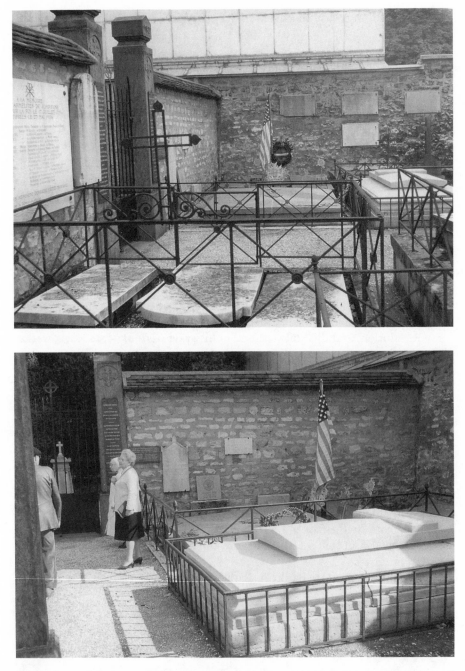

At the grave of the Marquis de Lafayette in Paris, France, a United States flag flies at all times.

Flag atop Pennsylvania Hall, Gettysburg College, Gettysburg, PA. (Courtesy Special Collections, Gettysburg College.)

lookout and a hospital during the Battle of Gettysburg, when that flag was in use.

It was in 1861, when the Civil War began, that a flagpole was placed on the building (then called Dormitory Hall) and a flag ceremoniously raised. Though the pole remained until October 1878, when a heavy storm knocked it down, the flag was flown there only sporadically thereafter, primarily on special occasions, and primarily because no one was willing to take on the chore of daily raisings and lowerings. In 1898 the building name was changed to Pennsylvania Hall.

Joe Carver, janitor there since 1914, when interviewed in 1970 recalled that the president of the college, sometime around 1923, had told him to let the flag fly 24 hours rather than climb to the building's peak twice a day. Sometime thereafter some unknown person started the story (unsubstantiated) that Congress had authorized the practice in recognition of the building's having been used as a military hospital in July 1863.

In 1961, after the 34-star flag was raised over the building during a Civil War centennial celebration, the business manager chose to continue flying that flag.

27. City Hall, New Bedford, MA.

28. State House, Boston, MA.

29. Flag Plaza, headquarters of the National Flag Foundation, Pittsburgh, PA.
Flag plaza, which also houses the Allegheny Trails Council of the Boy Scouts of America, was the gift of Vivian Lehman as a memorial to her husband, Chester Hamilton Lehman. Five different flags fly here, with the United States flag in the position of honor at the center. One of the four other flags is always a historic flag, a different one each day. Every day, a color guard of boy scouts performs a ceremony in which the historic flag is lowered and retired, and another one raised in its place.

30. The Plaza, Taos, NM.
The American flag was first flown in Taos in 1846 when the territories under Mexican rule were liberated by the United States Army under General Stephen Watts Kearney. In 1861, during the Civil War, the flag was repeatedly torn down from its pole in front of Army headquarters in Taos by Confederate sympathizers. Garrison officer Captain Smith Simpson, infuriated by these "rebel intrusions," devised a plan to prevent further violations. According to Margaret Simpson Gusdorf, his daughter:

> Father took some helpers to Taos Canyon and had them cut down the tallest cottonwood tree that they could find and take it to the Taos plaza. He then called Kit Carson, Col. St. Vrain and Lieut. Boggs to assist him, and he nailed the flag securely

Flag Plaza, Pittsburgh, PA.

to the pole which they set up in the plaza. Then they retired to St. Vrain's store, where the Taos Theater is now located, and kept a guard posted there for several days. Father told everyone within hearing distance that anyone who interfered with the flag would be shot. There was no further difficulty! Father kept the flag flying and, when the military officers heard what he had done, they permitted him to keep it up night and day. When the first flag wore out, father replaced it and continued to do so throughout his lifetime and asked me to continue to do so when he passed on.

Taos has kept a flag flying in the plaza night and day every since in honor of this heroic vigilance and as a symbol that citizens of New Mexico were loyal to the Union.

31. Flagstaff Mountain, Boulder, CO.

32. Pike's Peak, CO (no longer flying). Incidentally, Captain Zebulon M. Pike never succeeded in climbing to this peak when he tried it in 1806. Major Stephen Harriman Long was the one who planted the flag on the summit. It had 23 stars then.

There is no record in any literature of a 24-hour flag on Pike's Peak. After settlement of Colorado Springs in 1870, however, an Army Signal Corps unit was established there to observe weather conditions year-round to 1889. And there is a record of a huge searchlight being placed atop the peak in 1905. The 24-hour flag may have been flown then, but doubt remains.

33. Captain William Driver's Grave, Nashville, TN (according to the Library of Congress, 1966).

William Driver was a sea captain from Salem, Massachusetts. According to records, he was the first to give the United States flag the name "Old Glory." There are two different stories of how this naming came about.

Captain William Driver

The first story is that one day in 1831, he was able to sail for the South Seas on the brig *Charles Doggett* when a group of friends came aboard for a bon voyage party and presented him with a United States flag to fly on his ship. When it was hoisted and unfurled, he shouted, "I'll call her 'Old Glory,' boys, 'Old Glory'!"

The second and more poignant story has Captain Driver receiving the flag from his mother on his twenty-first birthday, March 17, 1824. Since she had made the flag, he was justly proud and exclaimed over it, "It's the most glorious flag I have ever seen, and 'Old Glory' I'll call her." He treasured and kept it many years. Later, in 1862 when Buell's army occupied Washington, DC, Driver personally hoisted his Old Glory over the Capitol building. From there, though, competing stories — neither one conclusively proven — are told of what happened to it.

Grave of Capt. William Driver, Nashville, Tennessee.

The most romantic story is that it was handed down from generation to generation within the family and finally presented to the Smithsonian Institution, where it is carefully displayed today. The most unromantic story is that it was given to the Sixth Ohio militia, where it waved proudly until October 1863, when it was eaten by a team of mules tethered to the quartermaster's supply wagon where it was kept each evening.

34. The Tombs of the Unknown Soldiers, Arlington Cemetery, Arlington, VA. "Known but to God" is the legend on the Tombs of the Unknowns. Changing of the guard draws crowds several times daily. Paradoxically, there are no flag displays over either a tomb of Civil War unknown dead, located just around the corner from the more famous tombs in Arlington Cemetery, or a tomb of a Revolutionary War unknown soldier, located in the Old Presbyterian Meeting House churchyard, 316 South Royal St., Alexandria, Virginia.

This photo shows the flag on display at the U.S.S. *Arizona* Memorial, honoring those whose lives were lost in the Japanese attack on Pearl Harbor on December 7, 1941. The ship in the foreground is the U.S.S. *Missouri*, arriving in port on Survivor's Day, which honors the sailors and Marines who fought in that battle. (U.S. Navy photo.)

35. Little Bighorn Battlefield, Crow Agency, MT.

Historian J.D. Young of the United States Department of the Interior's National Park Service at Custer Battlefield National Monument said the flag "does not and, according to records there, never did fly 24 hours per day over Custer Battlefield National Cemetery." Contrasting claims have appeared, however, and are believed in some quarters.

Taken together, including the "probables" and "maybes," these sites represent a total of 84 flags flying or having once flown at night. A surprising number? Remember, there are 50 at the Washington Monument alone! Even without those, however, Washington, DC, is the city most represented. Baltimore is next with two. Twelve states are known to be represented: Maryland, Massachusetts, and Pennsylvania with four each; Virginia with three; Colorado, New York, and California with two each; and Minnesota, New Mexico, South Dakota, Tennessee, and Montana with one each. What's most surprising is that 38 states have no historic all-night display.

Individual citizens who fly the flag outside their homes 24 hours per day must conform to the Flag Code. The flag must be night-lighted and, if flown in inclement weather, made of waterproof material.

Flag at the home of J.R. Simplot, Boise, Idaho. (Photo by J.R. Simplot Co.)

Individuals who don't conform to the code are apt to meet opposition. The neighbors of Ken Neiman in Burke Station, Virginia, got their Housing Development Control Committee to make him conform or remove his flag.

Among patriotic flag wavers who abided by the Flag Code regulations have been the late Edward Everett Horton, veteran actor of stage and screen into his 90s, and industrialist J.R. Simplot. Horton, who lived on an estate in Encino, California, flew his flag day and night, spotlighted, until his death. Simplot, at 85, was still flying probably the largest private residence flag — 55 × 30 feet — in front of his landmark home at 4000 Simplot Way in Boise, Idaho, night-lighted, as he had for years. In 1984 he had to call law enforcement officers when three young men were presumed attempting to steal it. It turned out they were only half-masting it, in honor of a buddy they were holding a bachelor party for.

In a flag-display controversy, Donald and Dorothy Seabeck of Uniontown, Ohio, declared war on the United States Army over their right to fly the stars and stripes outside their home (September 1981). The Army Corps of Engineers had decided it was, technically, on federal property, so if they wanted to continue flying it, they would have to pay a special $75 license. "I love my country and I love my flag," stated Dorothy. "Our young men in this country paid for that flag with their lives. The flag is part of our country. I'm proud to fly it. I'm going to fight this. I can't let the American people down." And they did keep flying it.

Astronaut Alan B. Shepard, Jr., commander of the *Apollo 14* mission, stands beside the deployed U.S. flag during the first extra-vehicular activity. Shadows of the lunar module, Astronaut Edgar D. Mitchell, LM pilot, and the Erectable S-band antenna can also be seen. (NASA photo.)

What about those flags planted on the moon by visiting astronauts? Shane Clift, 6, of Westminster, Maryland, asked NASA whether the flag is still on the moon. The reply was, "Yes, so far as it is known." However, the flag planted by Buzz Aldrin and Neil Armstrong in 1969 was made of ordinary cloth and though there is no wind on the moon (which is why a brace is seen across the top of the flag to keep it unfurled), it has been exposed to harsh sunlight.

If it is still flying, it is the one place where the United States flag flies at full-staff 24 hours a day without ever being raised or lowered and without ever being saluted.

(b) Manner of hoisting

The flag should be hoisted briskly and lowered ceremoniously.

Although the U.S. Marine Corps regulations call for "raising and lowering by hand," adding that it "should never be raised while furled," a company has now marketed an automated flagpole for the rest of the country that remains not so regulated, for those civilians who would like to fly the flag, but can't be on tap for raising and lowering, as well as for business or government buildings where it frees a maintenance man for other duties.

Electronic Flag Poles is listed on the Federal Supply Service by contract #GS-OOS-88951. The poles offered by this company are completely automatic,

Going ... going ... gone. An electronic flagpole may be short on ceremony, but it raises and lowers the flag when no one else is there to do it. This 50-foot pole is in Forest Park, Illinois. (Photo courtesy of Electronic Flag Poles, Inc.)

even to lowering the flag by themselves in inclement weather, and the flags are self-storing (inside the pole) as well. The poles operate by light-sensitive photoelectric cells, or, when wished, by manual switch. They can also be set to fly at half-staff for prolonged periods, and they have an anti-furling device to keep the flag from twining up in the halyard.

(c) Inclement weather

The flag should not be displayed on days when the weather is inclement, except when an all-weather flag is displayed.

The term "inclement" here has provoked some questions. What is meant by "inclement" weather? Does that mean at the first sign of raindrops, or only in the eventuality of a protracted "wetting" rain or snowfall? And if the flag is taken down when it rains, is it raised again when the rain stops? (That isn't covered anywhere in the code.) If so, flags might be going up and down like yo-yos all day during spring showers at thousands of installations across the country.

The first half of this segment of the Flag Code was written before flag materials could withstand whipping winds and mildew. Today, however, we have drip-dries and even plastic flags, so the code segment has been amended (1976) to specify that "all-weather" flags may be flown in "inclement" weather, whether that be spatterings or soakings.

This flag mount from the National Banner Company of Dallas, Texas, shows how a new idea in flag display might require revision of the Flag Code — for example, regulations concerning half-masting (since the position of the flag differs from a conventional pole mount) and display with the blue field next to the pole (since this one follows the wind, like a weathervane). The company calls it the Space Walker flag mount. (Photo courtesy of the National Banner Company.)

It isn't often that one of the general populace concerns himself or herself personally with this particular problem, but it does happen. Sometimes it is even duly reported so others may think about it next time. Such was the case of a young girl at a Phillies-Mets baseball game in Philadelphia. When a sudden thunderstorm struck, everyone ran for shelter — everyone but this girl. She ran, instead for the center field flagpole, where she proceeded to lower the stars and stripes.

She stuffed the flag under her coat and, dripping wet herself, ran for the dugout. Players, umpires, and fans alike gave her a resounding burst of applause from their nice dry hideouts.

(d) Particular days of display

The flag should be displayed on all days, especially on New Year's Day, January 1; Inauguration Day, January 20; Easter Sunday (variable); Mother's Day, second Sunday in May; Armed Forces Day, third Saturday in May; Memorial Day (half-staff until noon), the last Monday in May; Flag Day, June 14; Independence Day, July 4; Labor Day, first Monday in September; Constitution Day, September 17; Columbus Day, second Monday in October; Navy Day, October 27; Veteran's Day, November 11; Thanksgiving Day, fourth Thursday in November; Christmas, December 25; and such other days as may be proclaimed by the President of the United States; the birthdays of States (date of admission); and on State holidays.

This segment of the code has easily been the most changed of all. The reasons are that some of these dates are not official national holidays, some are official only in some places, and many have had their names or dates or both changed, sometimes more than once. Armed Forces Day has replaced Army Day, April 6, for example. For another, Washington's birthday was originally celebrated on February 22, but an act of Congress on June 28, 1968 (Public Law 90-363), changed George's birthday to the third Monday in February (though this change did not become effective until January 1, 1971).

Mother's Day, of course, is not an official holiday, and Father's Day is not even listed as a flag-flying day. But Mother's Day is one of the oldest of the designated days. In section 141 of Chapter 9 under Title 36, "Patriotic Societies and Observances," it states:

> The President of the United States is authorized and requested to issue a proclamation calling upon the Government officials to display the United States flag on all Government buildings, and the people of the United States to display the flag at their homes or other suitable places, on the second Sunday in May, as a public expression of our love and reverence for the mothers of our country. [May 8, 1914, No. 13, sec. 1, 38 Stat. 770.]

The instruction to fly the flag on Memorial Day has a special codicil explaining that the flag is to be flown at half-staff from sunrise until noon, honoring all those killed in service to the nation, then full-staff from noon until sunset. This means that, at sunrise, the flag is hauled first to the top of the halyard, then lowered to half-staff. At the noon changeover, the correct procedure is to take the flag down from half-staff, then hoist it to the top of the halyard again. It should *not* be taken straight up from half-staff.

Interesting feuds sometimes grow over commemorative holidays. One has grown up around Memorial Day. Some 106 years ago, General John Alexander

Logan, first commander of the Grand Army of the Republic, proclaimed May 30 as Decoration Day, or as it came to be known, Memorial Day. But also for over a hundred years now the populace of Waterloo, New York, has maintained the idea Decoration Day was theirs. At a social gathering in 1865, it was Henry Carter Welles, village treasurer, chief engineer of the fire department, vestryman of St. Paul's Episcopal Church, and instigator of the Waterloo Wright Guards (Company C of the Thirty-third New York State Volunteers), who remarked in no uncertain terms that while praising the living heroes of the war, it would be well also to remember the patriotic dead by decorating their graves.

Welles tried time after time to get people interested in this idea, but it wasn't until the early spring of 1866, when he talked to Brevet Brigadier General John Boyce Murray, prominent attorney and Seneca County Clerk, that Welles got the support he needed. General Murray soon formed a force of veterans and influential townspeople, and plans were developed for a complete observance. Thus Memorial Day was born in Waterloo on Saturday, May 5, 1866.

The heat was terrible that day, and records show that Welles never recovered from it. He died two years later, though not before he had seen the first nationally proclaimed Memorial Day on May 30, 1868. General Murray, on the other hand, lived until 1883, and it was he who reaped the glory as the founder of Memorial Day.

Both names faded with time, and they were largely forgotten until 1965 when the people of Waterloo were preparing for their annual parade. John C. Becker, a member of the local historical society and the Waterloo library, mentioned to the guest speaker, Congressman Samuel S. Stratton, that the following year would be the one hundredth anniversary of the first Memorial Day in Waterloo. The Congressman spearheaded Resolution 587, giving the community official credit. It passed the House of Representatives unanimously May 17, 1966, with the same approval from the Senate two days later: "Resolved that Congress of the United States, in recognition of the patriotic tradition set in motion one hundred years ago in the village of Waterloo, New York, does hereby officially recognize Waterloo, New York, as the birthplace of Memorial Day." Bronze plaques were affixed to the homes of General Murray and Henry Welles, and an attractive Waterloo mansion was set aside as the Memorial Day Museum and official permanent headquarters for the Memorial Day Committee.

In another feud, three states have claimed one of their own responsible for the borning of Flag Day: Wisconsin, New York and Pennsylvania. Everyone agrees that the date, June 14, was chosen because that was the date in 1777 when the flag was adopted by the Continental Congress as the official banner of the United States. And it is a matter of record that the national observance of Flag Day was proclaimed by President Woodrow Wilson in 1916. Beyond these facts, however, stories differ.

Two men credited with the idea of Memorial or Decoration Day are John Alexander Logan (left) and Henry C. Welles. (Photo of Henry Welles courtesy of Waterloo Memorial Day Centennial Committee.)

Bernard J. Cigrand (1866–1932), a school teacher in Waubeka, Wisconsin, spent years trying to get Congress to declare June 14 as National Flag Day. In 1877 they finally did request that all public buildings fly the flag on that date. This request was widely honored, but there was still no designation of an official holiday. The country school house of Stony Hill (or Schumacher's Hill), where Cigrand taught and where he reportedly founded Flag Day on June 14, 1885, was once preserved as a shrine by the National Fraternal Flag Day Foundation (now defunct).

George Bolch, according to New York's claim, first held Flag Day in 1889 at a free kindergarten for the poor. The state education department took note, and soon after, the state legislature passed a law making the state superintendent

General John B. Murray, whose efforts made the first Memorial (Decoration) Day a reality. (Photo courtesy of Waterloo Memorial Day Centennial Committee, from "The History and Origin of Memorial Day in Waterloo, New York" 1966.)

At extreme right stands Bernard J. Cigrand, whom the state of Wisconsin hails as the founder of Flag Day. Cigrand's family members, shown left to right, are Mrs. Art N. Cigrand; Dr. Art Cigrand; Mrs. M. Kornean, sister; Mrs. Bernard Cigrand; Mrs. Anna Miler, sister; and Mrs. Kate Regner, niece. (Photo #WHi [x3] 21449 by the State Historical Society of Wisconsin. Used by permission.)

of public schools responsible for preparing programs for observances of Lincoln's and Washington's birthdays, Memorial Day, and Flag Day (June 14) in the public schools. In 1897 the governor made the Flag Day proclamation official for public buildings.

William T. Kerr was credited as father of Flag Day by Pennsylvania while still a schoolboy in Pittsburgh in 1888. In 1893 the mayor of Philadelphia, in response to the Society of Colonial Dames, ordered a flag display on public buildings for June 14. Today, Flag Day is a legal holiday only in the state of Pennsylvania, where it was adopted on May 7, 1937.

Flag Day has become an individual community matter, each community or city preparing its own celebration, which has been everything from a rally in Minneapolis, Minnesota, to a "Patriotism Day" parade in Rochester, New Hampshire, to a combination flag raising, speech making, and prayer for peace ceremony in New York's Battery Park, on the edge of the financial district, which Wall Street workers attended on their lunch hour.

In many places Flag Day takes a week. In fact, on June 9, 1966, Flag *Week* was suggested by Congress, and President Lyndon Johnson signed a joint resolution introduced to the Congress by Rep. H. Allen Smith (R-CA) that month.

Records also show that President Richard Nixon also proclaimed Flag Week in June 1970, prescribing it as the week in which June 14, Flag Day, occurs.

Constitution Day, September 17, is only part of what Title 36, Ch. 9, sec. 159, refers to as Constitution Week. Day or week, however, it doesn't seem to be much observed anywhere.

Columbus Day, traditionally observing the anniversary of the discovery of America on October 12 (as of April 30, 1934, via Ch. 184, 48 Stat. 657) was changed to the second Monday in October by the Ninetieth Congress on June 28, 1968. The change took effect January 1, 1971.

Veterans Day was once known as Armistice Day because it commemorated the date — November 11, 1918 — that the fighting ended in World War I, when a German representative signed the truce between the Allies and Germany in Marshal Foch's railroad dining car in Forest Compiègne, France. But there have been other armistices signed since then, so in 1954, the day to honor all armistices and the men and women who made them possible was changed to Veterans Day.

In addition to the name change, this holiday underwent a short-lived change of date. Public Law 90-361, the same act of Congress that moved Washington's birthday, Memorial Day, and Columbus Day to Mondays, tried to do the same for Veterans Day. This law took effect January 1, 1971. However, by 1975 this change had proved unpopular, and the Ninety-fifth Congress passed Public Law 94-97 moving the holiday back to its original date. This law became effective January 1, 1978. The national change lagged several years behind the state of Virginia, which had restored the November 11 date for its own observance in 1973.

Part of the moving ceremony of Armistice Day since its inception by Congress in 1938 was the traditional period of silence, observed exactly at 11 A.M., when the fighting officially ceased (though the German fleet didn't actually surrender until November 21). This idea was carried over to the newer designated Veterans Day, but the moment of silence was changed to honor all American dead from all wars. The official American ceremonies are still conducted at the Tombs of the Unknowns in Arlington National Cemetery, across the Potomac River from the nation's capital.

The first unknown in the grave in Arlington Cemetery represents the many American soldiers unidentified in death with a simple inscription: "Here rests in honored glory an American soldier known but to God." This is how he was selected: This boy, or man, was one of four unidentified American soldiers whose bodies, by Congressional resolution, were disinterred in October 1921 from four white-crossed graves in United States cemeteries in France. These bodies were placed in caskets and taken to Chalonssur-Marne, where wounded and widely decorated veteran Sgt. Edward F. Younger selected one casket by placing on it a spray of huge white roses. This historic casket arrived in Washington November 9, 1921, on the cruiser *Olympia*, Admiral Dewey's flagship in the Battle of Manila Bay, and for a short time rested on the rotunda of the Capitol on the same catafalque on which had rested the bodies of the three martyred presidents, Lincoln, Garfield, and McKinley.

On Armistice Day, November 11, 1921, President Harding and other high officials, ranking officers of the Army and Navy, and Allied nation diplomats followed the patriotic caisson bearing the flag-draped casket through Washington's rainy streets to Arlington National Cemetery, where, after solemn ceremonies, it was placed to rest forever in the Tomb of the Unknown Soldier.

Armistice Day is still celebrated in Great Britain, though, as in the United States, both its name and date have been changed. Now the Sunday nearest November 11 is called Remembrance Day (or Poppy Day), commemorating the armistice signing for World War I, and special services and parades are held. The queen (or a representative from the royal family) lays a wreath on the Cenotaph, and at 11 A.M., the hour at which the armistice was signed, sirens go off to begin a two-minute silence. In earlier times everyone stopped and stood still during that period. Today this is less observed, though radio and television stations still stop broadcasting.

Most people wear an artificial poppy for the day, usually made by ex-servicemen and sold by them in the streets. Wreaths of poppies are laid and "gardens of remembrance," consisting of rows of small white crosses with poppies attached, are planted near war memorials and in churchyards where war dead are buried.

The origin of the use of poppies is probably connected with John McCrae's poem "In Flanders Field." Mythologically, poppies adorned Hypnos, god of sleep, as well as his son Morpheus, god of dreams (who gave his name to morphine, which is derived from poppies). In addition to sleep, poppies relate to death, as flowers sacred to the goddesses Demeter and Persephone, who were associated with "the mystery of death and the hope of a blissful immortality," according to *The Golden Bough* by James Frazer.

There have been, and remain, other nationally proclaimed flag-flying observances than those listed in the Flag Code, but they are lesser known, having lost their popular appeal or having never caught the interest of the public at all. As listed in Title 36, Chapter 9, they include Child Health Day, May 1 (sec. 143), National Maritime Day, May 22 (sec. 145), Gold Star Mother's Day, last Sunday in September (secs. 147–148), Thomas Jefferson's birthday, April 13 (sec. 149), Aviation Day, August 19 (sec. 151; in 151[a], this was changed to Pan-American Aviation Day, but in sec. 152 it was repealed), Citizenship Day, September 17 (sec. 153), and Loyalty Day, May 1 (sec. 172). It begins to appear there may soon be no more "special days" available for displaying the flag. It will be one long reminder, not of love of country, but of publicity gimmicks promoting various causes. Worthy as these causes may be, they might be better recognized with symbols other than the national flag. We risk getting too far away from the true meaning of flag display.

(e) Display on or near administration building of public institutions

The flag should be displayed daily on or near the main administration building of every public institution.

The term "public institution" means publicly-owned, not those simply used by the public such as stores. However, many business concerns find it to be excellent public relations to fly the flag daily.

Many families like to fly the flag in front of their homes, too. If such a gesture determined true patriotism, then Mellott, Indiana, would be the most patriotic community in the whole United States. As of January 1973 all but six homes there were flying the American flag daily.

The phrase "on or near" offers an interesting loophole. From 1961 until 1976, under Governor George Wallace, the state of Alabama displayed the state flag and the Confederate flag atop its capitol building, while the American flag was flown from a ground-level staff flanking the entranceway, but not attached to the building. This display captured the attention of the media when Alvin Holmes, a black state legislator, filed suit in an attempt to force the state to give the national flag prominence over the other banners. A federal court ruled the display was valid and not in violation of the Flag Code. However, Wallace later placed the national flag atop the capitol on his own initiative (though he did not remove the state or Confederate flag).

It is true that the regulations of the Flag Code always state the national flag be given precedence over the state flag in displays. But that "on or near" regulation, and the fact the the state and federal flags were not in the same immediate display, made the argument academic, merely a matter of the taste of the interpreter. The news media were arguing that Alabama had an "intent" to belittle the national flag because of the state's stand on racial desegregation. However, without the power to read minds, intent is always hard to prove.

There is a code section (175[e]) stating that the American flag should be flown at the highest point of any display of flags. But, again, the state's interpretation that the two flags were not in the same display had some validity.

(f) Display in or near polling places

The flag should be displayed in or near every polling place on election days.

This regulation does not say how the flag will be displayed, but it must be remembered that each separate item in the flag regulations is meant to incorporate every other item that is pertinent in any way as well. Evidently no one knew this when Jack Kemp, the former pro quarterback, making his bid for New York state political office in 1971, arrived at a Buffalo precinct to vote. He reenacted voting several times as various television camera crews arrived to shoot this earth-shattering event. All the while, no one noticed the American flag leaning against the voting booth, upside down — the international distress signal — except a sportswriter from *Sports Illustrated* magazine, who mentioned it in his story.

Another writer came up with an even more unusual report. On a speech-making foray into Florida in February 1972 when vote-gathering for his presidential bid, George Wallace spoke below an American flag which had 56 stars, by actual count. And the writer of that information missed a good feature story by not following up or finding out where it came from and why.

(g) Display in or near schoolhouse
The flag should be displayed during school days in or near every schoolhouse.

The subject of flag displays at schoolhouses is usually associated with a more sensitive and volatile issue: whether students should be required to recite the Pledge of Allegiance as was once the daily custom in many classrooms.

The United States Supreme Court ruled in 1943 (*West Virginia Board of Education vs. Barnette*) that public school authorities could not compel students to recite the pledge or even stand during it. The court held that a West Virginia law mandating flag salute and recitation of the pledge was unconstitutional. Yet the argument in favor of reciting the pledge has continued. The Philadelphia Board of Education, for example, voted in November 1976 to begin the school day with the Pledge of Allegiance and a moment of silent prayer. Those of the 260,000 students who did not wish to participate did not have to. The resolution was introduced by an outspoken board member named Felice Stack, who said she was shocked to learn the prayer and pledge were not practiced throughout the school system.

The Pledge of Allegiance has its own place in the Flag Code, section 172, which is presented — with a complete history of the pledge — in Chapter 4.

§175. Position and manner of display
The flag, when carried in a procession with another flag or flags, should be either on the marching right; that is, the flag's own right, or, if there is a line of other flags, in front of the center of that line.

Seattle has a city regulation that has real merit, and fits into this law in a positive manner. It forbids a parade on city streets unless the procession is headed by an American flag at least 52 × 66 inches in size.

(a) *The flag should not be displayed on a float in a parade except from a staff, or as provided in subsection (i) of this section.*

This ruling is almost universally ignored in the big parades that have been the vogue for New Year's, Thanksgiving, and Christmas in recent years. The 1973 Pasadena Rose Festival parade included two floats that ignored this ruling. Knott's Berry Farm, the California amusement park adjacent to Disneyland, sponsored a float featuring a huge American flag backdrop with the stars blinking off and on electronically. Meanwhile, the WGN–Continental Broadcasting float featured a flag design covering the entire float, with a very militant

Top: A staffed United States flag in a marching unit like this joint services color guard must be on the marching right (its own right) or front-and-center of the line of attendant flags. In the display shown here, all six military services are represented, complete with battle streamers, during an observance of the fiftieth anniversary of the Japanese attack on Pearl Harbor. This observance took place at the U.S.S. *Arizona* Memorial. (U.S. Navy photo.) *Bottom:* Illustration from Marine Corps pamphlet shows the two correct positions for the United States flag in procession with other flags.

looking eagle perching protectively with wings enfolding the back end of the float. The central portion opened and closed to show various broadcast celebrities inside.

The annual King Orange Jamboree parade and the Rose Festival Parade, both held over New Year's, have had their share of flag-displaying errors, like

These floats in the 1973 Tournament of Roses parade look patriotic, but Flag Code regulations forbid display of the flag from a float in a parade except from a staff, which the float in the top picture might arguably have.

most parades over the years. For examples, in the 1975 (Dec. 31) Miami parade a group of costumed cuties, the Patriots of (Arlington) Northern ·Virginia, pranced throughout the route clutching the sides of their huge flat-displayed flag. The Orange Queen's float featured a rumpled flag coming out of a horn of plenty. The only bright spot for Flag Code purists was the Groton, Connecticut, Nutmeg Volunteer Junior Fife and Drum Corps, who carried a mass of outdated flags in correct reverse historical order, from the present back.

(b) *The flag should not be draped over the hood, top, sides, or back of a vehicle or of a railroad train or a boat. When the flag is displayed on a motorcar, the staff should be fixed firmly to the chassis or clamped to the right fender.*

Until the amendments of 1976, this section of the code instructed readers that flags should be clamped to "the radiator cap" instead of the right fender. Of course, cars haven't had outside-the-hood radiator caps since the 1930s. However, in classic and antique auto shows, it isn't unusual to still see some of the old flag clamps fitted to radiator caps.

The 1942 version of the Flag Code directed that flags displayed on cars could be "clamped to the radiator cap." The antique Ford pictured here sports a typical radiator flag bracket of its era. (Photo by Bob Loeffelbein.)

The Flag Code doesn't specifically cover a latter-day fad, so what is the regulation concerning painting an entire vehicle into a flag replica? This is not a move our forebears could have imagined, but in the 1970s the flag design was busting out all over. Young people were painting their cars for fun, and

The driver of this U.S. mail delivery truck clamped his flag on the right side of the vehicle, though not on the right fender as specified by the Flag Code. (Photo by Bob Loeffelbein.)

Trucks of Larry Campbell's Excavation Construction, Inc., of Hyattsville, Maryland, were painted in red, white, and blue because he "felt visitors would expect such a truck in the nation's capital." (Photo by Bob Loeffelbein.)

companies were painting up their dump trucks for eye-catcher advertising. So long as they didn't paint an actual configuration of the flag, it would be impossible to prove "intent" to desecrate the flag in these cases.

Autos, trains and boats are mentioned in this section, but not airplanes. Who would have thought it would be needed? But of course, human ingenuity and love of novelty has brought about the painting of the flag and various designs of its segments and colors on both commercial and private airplanes. With this new display of the flag, a problem has arisen. The Flag Code calls for the flag to be mounted with the blue field on the flag's own right, which is fine for the left side of an airplane, but looks odd from the right-hand side, because it appears the flag is defying the laws of physics by streaming against the wind. Perhaps the Flag Code needs an addition to cover airplanes — and rockets. Meanwhile, the International Civil Aviation organization has stepped in and decreed, with no official sanction, that flags painted on aircraft must face the direction of flight, so as to be aerodynamically and aesthetically correct.

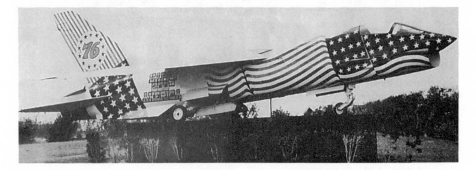

A military jet decked out in flag-like splendor for America's Bicentennial.

(c) *No other flag or pennant should be placed above or, if on the same level, to the right of the flag of the United States of America, except during church services conducted by naval chaplains at sea, when the church pennant may be flown above the flag during church services for the personnel of the Navy. No person shall display the flag of the United Nations or any other national or international flag equal, above, or in a position of superior prominence or honor to, or in place of, the flag of the United States at any place within the United States or any Territory or possession thereof: Provided, That nothing in this section shall make unlawful the continuance of the practice heretofore followed of displaying the flag of the United Nations in a position of superior prominence or honor, and other national flags in positions of equal prominence or honor, with that of the flag of the United States at the headquarters of the United Nations.*

The rule for the church pennant includes a Jewish worship pennant for Jewish services, which pictures the tablets of law, the Star of David, and the

A church service aboard ship shows correct display of church pennant above U.S. flag. (U.S. Navy photo.)

uniform insignia of Jewish chaplains superimposed on a white pennant. These became available through the military supply system in 1977. The British version of the church pennant has horizontal stripes of red, white, and blue, with the Union Jack at the hoist.

There is no explanation of how the church pennant gets above the stars and stripes, however, and this raises questions. First, if the flag is lowered in order to raise the church pennant above it, is it then handled as though it were being half-masted, or not? And how does one conform to the code section stating the flag doesn't come down until sunset, if it must be taken down to attach the church pennant before being raised again? The easiest solution, as some chaplains have found, is to use separate halyards, and ignore the regulation about half-masting.

The significance of raising the church pennant over the flag — which is done for nearly all the free world's navies, but not in communist countries — is that God shall have precedence in the hearts of all, even over love of country. Why the Navy was singled out over the other branches of the Armed Forces is not documented. The church pennant display is, however, an old Navy and Marine Corps custom, and it prevailed despite some strenuous arguments against it. Those arguments came during the 1923 conference in which many patriotic groups met to discuss rules for the proper display of the national emblem. This conference, which ultimately led to the passage of the Flag Code regulations, looked with disfavor upon the Navy display of the church pennant over the national emblem. This disapproval was also found among members of the Congress. On January 28, 1924, Commander J.H. Sypher, superintendent of Naval Records and Library, wrote to the chief of naval operations on the subject:

> The recent National Convention held in this city on Flag Day to draw up rules for the uniform observance of proper flag etiquette throughout the country, made a rule that no flag *or pennant* should be hoisted above the National Ensign. I am informed that this rule was aimed particularly at the Navy custom of half-masting the colors and hoisting a pennant over them whenever the crew is at church.
>
> Some years ago, this matter was taken up in Congress and the following resolution was passed by the United States Senate:
>
> "That the Secretary of the Navy be, and he is hereby, directed to inform the Senate whether or not at any time or under any circumstances any flag, emblem or banner is raised above the Stars and Stripes on any vessel, building, or ground under the jurisdiction of the Navy Department of the United States."

In the discussion of this subject, the senator from Idaho stated:

> It is claimed to be the practice of the United States Navy to raise a flag above the Stars and Stripes. I do not believe that any considerable portion of the people understand that this is the practice in the Navy of the United States, but I do speak with confidence when I say no senator will approve of any such act. No flag, church or state, has a right to be placed above the Stars and Stripes. We do not recognize the precedence or prominence of the flag of any church above the Stars and Stripes.

Commander Sypher recommended that in view of the "dislike of this practice both in the Navy and throughout the country, as is indicated in the last Flag Convention ... the Navy practice be modified so that it may show honor to God without at the same time degrading out National Emblem." There is, however, little evidence to indicate that there was much "dislike" of the custom within the Navy. The old tradition continued to be followed both on ships and at many shore installations, and was eventually recognized and sanctioned in the Flag Code.

The regulation states that the church pennant may be flown above the flag during services "conducted by naval chaplains." But what if the chaplain is not from the Navy, or what if the service is not conducted by a chaplain at all? Only the larger ships have officially designated chaplains among their complement, so the commanding officer, the executive officer, or some other volunteer often takes over these weekly duties on smaller vessels. During time of war, the Navy ships also often carry Army and Marine Corps personnel. Army and Marine chaplains are then pressed into Sunday duties for all aboard. The Flag Code does not specifically address these circumstances.

The regulation also specifies services "at sea." But the church pennant flies at all Navy establishments during church services, regardless of whether those services are afloat or ashore. Is it incorrect procedure to fly the church pennant above the national flag on shore? Somewhere in history is a forgotten reason for the "at sea" wording. It should be modernized, along with other out-moded or confusing phrasing.

As originally passed in 1942, this section of the Flag Code contained only the first sentence, ending with "personnel of the Navy." The second sentence, addressing the issues of other nations' flags and the flag at the United Nations, was added by an act of the Eighty-third Congress (Public Law 107) on July 9, 1953.

The first time the United Nations flag caused a problem was in July 1950, five years after the signing of the United Nations charter, when General Douglas MacArthur was named supreme commander of the U.N. forces in the Far East and President Harry Truman ordered him to hoist the U.N. flag in Korea. The tricky point was whether the United States flag or that of the United Nations would take precedence.

The Flag Code of the United States, passed into law five years before the U.N. was established, consistently held that no other flag (except the church pennant in the circumstances described above) should take precedence over the stars and stripes. Much of section 175 — subsections c, d, e, f, g, and k — deal specifically with keeping the American flag in the place of honor relative to other flags. But in 1947 the U.N. issued this order: "The Flag of the United Nations shall not be subordinated to any other flag." Impasse!

Further complicating the picture was the U.S.S.R. looking on. If MacArthur hoisted the American banner in the honor position, the Soviets would likely claim it showed evidence of United States imperialism. But if the U.N. flag was placed in the position of honor, there would be sharp objections from home. MacArthur could be damned if he did and damned if he didn't.

There was still one further complication. President Truman had also included in his order of July 8, 1950, the wish to have the flags of all the nations fighting the North Korean forces — Great Britain, Canada, Australia, New Zealand, and the Netherlands — displayed "concurrently." What did that mean?

What did General MacArthur do? No one seems to really know for sure. Queries to the Truman Library and MacArthur Memorial and to the Department of Defense failed to elicit any knowledge. However, since the general was acting in behalf of all those countries and the United Nations, and since the conquered area was not an American possession, the only logical move was to follow U.N. procedure, with the U.N. flag taking precedence and all other flags displayed as equals. This probably meant flying the U.N. flag either higher than or in front of all the national flags involved, then displaying the national flags according to international usage, that is, alphabetically. Alphabetically, at least to Americans, means starting at the far right of the display itself.

One reason it is presumed MacArthur handled the flag display problem this way is that later the United Nations, at its then-headquarters at Lake Success, New York, flew the U.N. flag on top and the national flags in alphabetical order.

Indeed, the U.N. has continued with this method ever since.

Sometimes an organization works out a variation of the display rules to suit its particular circumstances. For example, the Shriners (Masons) follow another version of the Flag Code, one decreed in a booklet for their Legions of Honor, as promoted by their Patriotism Committee: "All nations name the position on the right as the honored one.... All Temples shall display the flags of the three countries in which temples have been chartered, the United States, Canada and Mex-

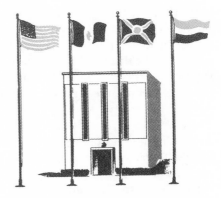

United States flag properly displayed to the right (as flag faces forward) of other flags.

ico.... EXCEPT that the flag of the country in which the flags are being posted or paraded shall have the honored position on the right."

An incident that passed unnoticed by the press during President Richard Nixon's February 1972 trip to China showed a meticulous sense of honor on the part of the Chinese. When the Nixons dined at the head table with their

For this dinner celebrating Richard Nixon's visit to China in 1972, Chinese officials placed the American flag in the position of honor, that is, on the right as the flag faced forward. (National Archives photo.)

hosts, the huge wall space directly behind and above the Chinese and American heads of state was covered by the Chinese and American national flags. According to international usage, if two countries' flags are displayed, the host flag should be displayed in the position of honor, the right-hand position as the flags face forward. But, knowing the American code, the Chinese had given the American flag the right-hand position of honor. Not one reporter caught this political nicety.

The U.S.S.R., in dealing with United States presidents, was not so giving. Soviet Premier Gorbachev, in his November 1985 meeting with President Ronald Reagan in Geneva, Switzerland (a neutral site), got the best of the honored position, with the Soviet banner on the right. According to United Nations flag etiquette, they should have been displayed alphabetically from the right, which would put the U.S.A. flag before the U.S.S.R. one (at least if one is going by English acronyms).

The United States Flag Code does not mention any exceptions for Americans displaying the flag in foreign countries. Naturally, however, it cannot control United States flag display by foreign nationals in their countries. Our U.S. protocol people do make our flag code regulations available for state visits, etc., but they are impossible to enforce. For example, during the 1970 international ski races in France the ski course was lined with mattresses wrapped around tree tunks, to soften collisions by errant skiers. To add a little color, the sponsors crudely wrapped and tied these pads with the flags of competing nations. A huge picture of the tree wrapped with the American flag, all in color on a foldout cover, was run by *Life* magazine on its March 6, 1970, issue. It caused hardly a stir. Nor does the code attempt to regulate the use of foreign flags in the United States. For example, in January 1992 a security guard at the Westinghouse-run Hanford atomic products operation in Richland, Washington, was suspended for refusing to raise a Japanese national flag over the facility. Since the fast flux test facility had already done research for Japanese interests

Crossed-staff display shows United States flag in position of honor.

(and Japanese investors were being wooed to provide more research money to keep the atomic reactor open), the Japanese flag had been raised there before. But not by this particular guard, who refused because his upbringing had instilled in him a strong conviction that it was not proper to raise a foreign flag on United States soil, except to honor an official leader or representative of that government. Nevertheless, such a raising is not forbidden by the Flag Code.

A United States flag is raised in Denmark as a display of respect and celebration. Every July 4 since 1912 (except for the periods of the two world wars), Danes have gathered in the hills of Rebild to celebrate United States Independence Day. The festival is an expression of gratitude to the United States, which has welcomed more than 300,000 Danish immigrants to its shores. (Photo courtesy of the Tourist Association of Aalborg.)

(d) *The flag of the United States of America, when it is displayed with another flag against a wall from crossed staffs, should be on the right, the flag's own right, and its staff should be in front of the staff of the other flag.*

On January 5, 1974, the United States Postal Service came out with a 10-cent stamp showing two American flags with crossed staffs. The theme was an American Revolution Bicentennial observance, so one of them was a 13-star flag in use in 1777 and the other was the present 50-star banner. The Postal Service correctly took the position that the current flag is "the" flag of the United States, and the outdated banner "another flag." Therefore, the 50-star flag was pictured on its own right, with its staff in front.

(e) *The flag of the United States of America should be at the center and at the highest point of the group when a number of flags of States or localities or pennants of societies are grouped and displayed from staffs.*

(f) *When flags of States, cities, or localities, or pennants of societies are flown on the same halyard with the flag of the United States, the latter should always be at the peak. When the flags are flown from adjacent staffs, the flag of the United States should be hoisted first and lowered last. No such flag or pennant may be placed above the flag of the United States or to the right of the flag of the United States.*

United States flag in center and highest position, as directed by code subsection 175(e). Yet subsection 175(f) states that no other flag shall be placed on the right side of the United States flag. There appears to be a conflict between these two subsections.

There is an apparent conflict between these two subsections of the code. Subsection 175(e) directs that the flag should be placed in the center when grouped with other flags; yet 175(f) decrees that no other flag may be placed to the United States flag's right. These two subsections would benefit from some rewriting for clarity, perhaps combined with an and or clause.

Nowhere does the code specifically treat the problem of what to do with other flags and pennants when the American flag is flying at half-mast in mourning. However, both 175(c) and 175(f) state that no other flag or pennant shall be placed above the United States flag. Thus the solution is that other flags would, out of respect, also be half-masted, remaining below the American flag.

Subsection (f) mentions city flags, which is interesting, because until relatively recently, United States cities did not fly individualized banners. Cities of Europe, however, have used city banners for centuries. They usually began as the coats-of-arms of the ruling nobles, coming into acceptance as they were carried where the nobles and their retinues traveled or warred. Some of these banners were huge. The citizens of Milan, Italy, in A.D. 1035, carried their banner on a red cart on which a mast had been constructed with a cross pole and a large gilded ball on top. The banner floated from the cross pole on this mast.

In Pamplona, Spain, today there remains an annual event called "the running of the bulls" where part of the celebration is a competition among city flag bearers in twirling their staffed flags.

Such competition might be one way for American cities to get their flags publicized too. Although some cities have had their own flags for a number of years, even those cities' own citizens usually don't know about them. There are at least four city flags in California alone, and it would be a safe bet that a poll in any of the four — Los Angeles, San Diego, Inglewood, or Fresno — would not find one out of ten residents who could describe the city flag.

More people ought to find out about their city flags, because their backgrounds are quite interesting. The Los Angeles flag, for example, was first raised on the special flagpole on the south side of the Spring Street steps of the City Hall on April 5, 1937. Mayor Shaw raised the flag while a police honor guard stood at attention. This flag had been adopted by ordinance on July 15, 1931, and that ordinance described it as bearing the Los Angeles circular seal on a background of green, orange, and red. The green symbolized the olive groves which dotted the countryside in the early days; the orange, the orange groves there; and the red, the vineyards. It was also noted that green and red are the dominant colors in the flags of Mexico and Spain, the two nations who owned the area. The raising of the flag commemorated the eighty-seventh anniversary of the city as an incorporated area. Ratification was April 4, 1850.

Other cities known to have their own flags include New York, Philadelphia, Chicago, Baltimore, and Pittsburgh.

(g) *When flags of two or more nations are displayed, they are to be flown from separate staffs of the same height. The flags should be of approximately equal size. International usage forbids the display of the flag of one nation above that of another nation in time of peace.*

The United States Flag Code calls for the stars and stripes to be on its own right, however, and other nations that do not have this stipulation for their flags usually adhere to this as a political nicety, as China did on the Nixon visit.

At present, if the United States flag is displayed with other national flags, the display is usually arranged alphabetically, as in United Nations usage. Parades for the Olympic games also follow this practice. However, another Olympic Games tradition conflicts with both the United States Flag Code and the international practice described here. Winners of the first three places in each event are awarded their medals on a three-tiered victory stand, while the national anthem of the winner's country is played and that nation's flag is raised. The problem is that the second and third place winners' national flags are raised to lesser heights, violating the rule of not displaying one country's flag above another. A solution might be to raise the winners' flags to an equal level, with first place to the flag display's right (the viewer's left), the traditional place of honor. Even then, if all three medalists were American, the code on no flag to its right would be violated. The United States Flag Code would have to be amended to include such exceptions.

(h) *When the flag of the United States is displayed from a staff projecting horizontally or at an angle from the window sill, balcony, or front of a building, the union of the flag should be placed at the peak of the staff unless the flag is at*

Correct displays according to subsection 175(h).

half-staff. When the flag is suspended over a sidewalk from a rope extending from a house to a pole at the edge of the sidewalk, the flag should be hoisted out, union first, from the building.

Perhaps the wildest display of this general type was hung by Byron B. Lenius of Renton, Washington, in 1970. He hung 27 United States flags, each one different, from the eaves around his home, topping off the display with a large current stars and stripes streaming from a flagpole. He claimed his collection was the only complete 3 × 5 foot one available for public display, and had plans to mount them all on poles in his yard, hoping to later incorporate as Flag City, U.S.A.

But even this imaginative display may have been upstaged during the bicentennial year. James A. White, living in Phoenix's Sun City development, claimed his house had lost value because he was forced to live next door to "a bicentennial celebration." The Maricopa County board of supervisors took a look around and reduced his assessed value to $14,000.

What they had found was the Lewis Singer home with, among other things, 13 flagpoles 8 to 16 feet high, painted red, white, and blue; an American flag 8 × 16 feet painted on the roof of the house; a 70-foot water tower erected on the front lawn, also painted red, white, and blue; a front yard palm tree painted red, white, and blue; flags strung from the palm tree to the house; a cattle trough in the front yard painted red, white, and blue, of course; a fountain shooting water 20 feet into the air; with the entire scene night lighted by "thousands of lights," and music played through outdoor speakers day and night.

(i) *When displayed either horizontally or vertically against a wall, the union should be uppermost and to the flag's own right, that is, to the observer's left. When displayed in a window, the flag should be displayed in the same way, with the union or blue field to the left of the observer in the street.*

The 1942 version of this subsection directed that a flag not flown from a staff "should be displayed flat." Misinterpretation of this wording has no doubt led to the belief that it is appropriate to carry the flag flat, by its edges, or to display it rolled out on the ground or other flat surface. However, both these assumptions run contrary to other segments of the Flag Code. Subsection 176(c) states that "the flag should never be carried flat or horizontally," while 176(b) reads, "the flag should never

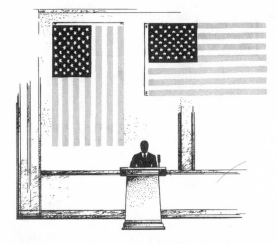

This drawing shows proper positioning for a flag displayed against a wall, either vertically or horizontally. Note the position of the blue field.

touch anything beneath it, such as the ground, the floor, water, or merchandise."

When the authors of the original 175(i) referred to displaying the flag "flat," they meant a flag hanging against a wall or in a window. The original intention is made clear by the 1976 revision of the subsection, which addressed the issue with much more

Flag hanging vertically over a street. The blue field hangs north or east, depending on the direction of the street.

specific wording.

The 1942 version described another correct display of an unstaffed flag: "suspended so that its folds fall free as if it were staffed." But what if the folds are falling *up*? The official Army parachuting team, the Golden Knights, who

The United States Army Golden Knights jump team won first United States team gold medal in International jumping at the 1969 World Meet. (Question: How do they keep from dragging the flag in the dirt when they land? No flag code regulation covers this.) (U.S. Army photo.)

won the United States' first gold medal in the World International Jumping Meet in 1969, have a spectacular little stunt they use in their performances. They jump with three of them holding onto straps sewn to the bottom edge of a large American flag, so that it streams out above them as they free-fall. It's striking, but possibly at odds with official flag etiquette. Besides, it can be dangerous. A similar free-flying United States flag at a jump demonstration at a Munich, West Germany, summer festival (June 1978) tangled a soldier's parachute lines, and he fell into a cemetery to his death.

 (j) *When the flag is displayed over the middle of a street, it should be suspended vertically with the union to the north in an east and west street or to the east in a north and south street.*

 This reads clearly enough, except not all streets run due east-and-west or north-and-south. The code obviously needs rewriting to include diagonals.

 An inspiring sight is the world's largest free-flying flag (correctly installed), the 60 × 90 foot stars and stripes hanging 160 feet above the roadway from the New Jersey tower of the George Washington Bridge across the Hudson River,

Dusk view of George Washington Bridge tower with 60 × 40-foot flag flying. (Port of New York Authority photo by P. Eckel.)

which separates New Jersey from New York. The stars on this flag are four feet in diameter, the stripes are five feet wide, and two miles of nylon thread were used in its construction. During the 1964-65 World's Fair it was flown almost daily, but now it is raised only on legal holidays, weather permitting, which means having a wind velocity under 10 mph in addition to no rain or snow.

The reason for this restriction is that the flag weighs 250 pounds, and the various pulleys, supporting cables, and hoisting ropes 550 pounds more, so this mass takes 14 to 20 men, depending upon the amount of wind, a half-hour to raise, even with the aid of hand winches.

The flag in the photograph was the fourth of its size to be flown in this location. The first was put on display in 1946, and each has had an active life of four to five years. Each new one takes 36 persons about three weeks to complete, according to Annin and Company of Verona, New Jersey, the makers.

An even larger flag was attempted for the Bicentennial Fourth of July — weight 1½ tons, 1½ times the size of a football field, with stars 11 feet high and stripes 15 feet wide. Unfortunately, winds whipped it into pieces while it was being installed.

These may not be the first large flags nor the largest, however. During a reunion of the Grand Army of the Republic 50 years after the end of the Civil War, a flag so big it took 60 veterans to carry it was marched up Pennsylvania Avenue in Washington, D.C. During World War I, mill workers in a Manchester, New Hampshire, factory made a flag four stories high, 50 × 90 feet, weighing 200 pounds. That was probably the largest mounted flag until years later when Dettra Flag Company made one 66 × 96 feet, to hang in New Jersey's Atlantic City Convention Hall. It covered the entire end wall of the building.

The last showing of what was then the largest flag ever made — 235 by 104 feet was for the 1976 United States Bicentennial, on the J.L. Hudson Company Store in Detroit. The flag has since been donated to the Smithsonian Institution. (Photo courtesy of the J.L. Hudson Company.)

Two huge flags have been flown by the J.L. Hudson Company of Detroit. The first one, made by Annin and Company for display on Armistice Day, November 11, 1923, was 90 × 200 feet. It was unfurled for display once per year for 23 years. When it finally wore out, a second, even larger one, 104 × 235 feet, was made and was first displayed on Flag Day, June 14, 1949. Covering seven stories of the downtown Hudson store, it also was displayed only once per year, though it was loaned out for special displays. Once it was displayed on a specially rigged nine-story scaffold on the Capitol in Washington, D.C., in 1929, and it was an exhibit at the 1939 World's Fair in New York. Once recognized as the world's largest flag by the Guinness Book of World Records, the flag was donated to the Smithsonian Institution in 1976.

That flag took the George P. Johnson Company of Detroit six months to make. It included 2,038 yards of wool, 5,500 yards of thread, 57 yards of heavy canvas, and more than a mile of strong rope to hold it to the building. Each star was six feet tall, each stripe eight feet wide. The material involved would make 611 regular-sized 5 × 8 foot flags. It took a crew of 55 men to handle the ¾-ton weight. The packing case itself weighed 250 pounds.

That no longer is the Guinness record, though. On June 14, 1980, an even larger flag — the largest ever made, at 210 × 411 feet — was rolled out onto the Washington Monument lawn. ("We can't even talk about flag etiquette," said organizer Len Silverfine in acknowledgment of the code violation. However, reporters noted that the flag did rest on a two-acre ground cover.) Then it was sent on a tour of the country to raise $550,000 so it could be erected to replace the one destroyed by the wind during the Bicentennial on New York's Verrazano Narrows Bridge. This flag is the size of two football fields — 21 stories high, if hung — and weighs seven tons. The stars are 13 feet in diameter, the stripes 16 feet wide. It took 25 workers, two forklifts, and a crane three hours to unload it from its custom-made transport truck.

Silverfine, president of the Great American Flag Fund, as he called his project, planned to put the flag in place for July 4, 1981. He told reporters, "It took me two years just to raise the initial $25,000 needed to get the project started. I took my proposal to businesses around the country with a slide presentation on the first flag display [on the Verrazano Bridge]." Revlon president Paul Woolard agreed to underwrite it.

(k) *When used on a speaker's platform, the flag, if displayed flat, should be displayed above and behind the speaker. When displayed from a staff in a church or public auditorium, the flag of the United States of America should hold the position of superior prominence, in advance of the audience, and in the position of honor at the clergyman's or speaker's right as he faces the audience. Any other flag so displayed should be placed on the left of the clergyman or speaker or to the right of the audience.*

A half-dozen times a year, on the average, an error from this section seems to jump out from the television screen. The mistake is usually fleetingly seen, but the stars and stripes is so eye-striking in color and design that it is always noticeable. For example, in the "Mannix" television series in April 1972, the flag was pictured on the wrong side of the judge in a courtroom scene.

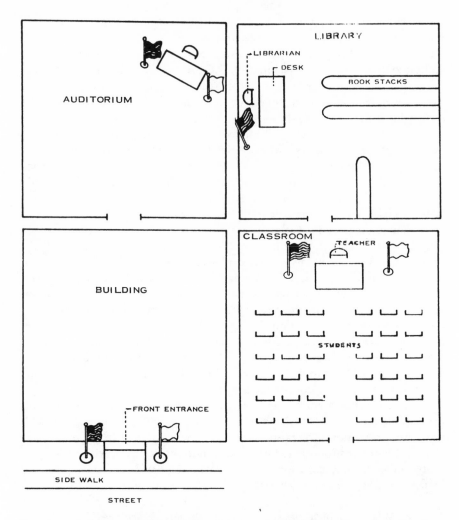

Drawings show proper display of flags in or outside buildings. Note that other flags are always to the United States flag's left.

Some civic organizations have their own flag codes, which usually incorporate all the federal provisions while adding details to cover the use of various flags unique to these societies. The Masons, for example, publish a flag etiquette booklet that includes all sorts of variations in positioning the United States flag relative to other flags, depending on who is being represented or honored by each banner. (See examples on pages 63 and 64.)

(1) *The flag should form a distinctive feature of the ceremony of unveiling a statue or monument, but it should never be used as the covering for the statue or monument.*

The flag should never be allowed to fall to the ground or floor, but should be carried aloft to form a highlight of the ceremony as it swings from in front of the item being unveiled. It should never be allowed to brush against objects, which might soil it.

(m) *The flag, when flown at half-staff, should be first hoisted to the peak for an instant and then lowered to the half-staff position. The flag should be again raised to the peak before it is lowered for the day. On Memorial Day the flag should be displayed at half-staff until noon only, then raised to the top of the staff. By order of the President, the flag shall be flown at half-staff upon the death of principal figures of the United States Government and the Governor of a State, territory, or possession, as a mark of respect to their memory. In the event of the death of other officials or foreign dignitaries, the flag is to be displayed at half-staff according to Presidential instructions or orders, or in accordance with recognized customs or practices not inconsistent with law. In the event of the death of a present or former official of the government of any State, territory, or possession of the United States, the Governor of that State, territory, or possession may proclaim that the National flag shall be flown at half-staff. The flag shall be flown at half-staff thirty days*

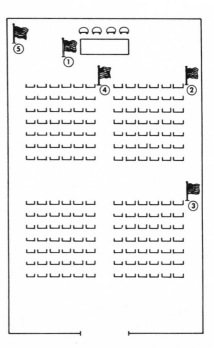

A flag display booklet published by the Masons shows positioning rules developed by their organization. These do not contradict the federal Flag Code but only add more variations for the organization's needs. For example, the figure above shows flags (1) displayed by or for speaker or lecturer; (2) displayed by or for a representative group of the audience; (3) displayed by or for a second representative group of the audience; (4) displayed by or for a third representative group of the audience; and (5) alternate location for (1) above, generally used when the position (1) would obscure the speaker's vision of the audience or vice versa.

from the death of the President or a former President; ten days from the death of the Vice President, the Chief Justice or a retired Chief Justice of the United States, or the Speaker of the House of Representatives; from the day of death until interment of an Associate Justice of the Supreme Court, a Secretary of an executive or military department, a former Vice President, or the Governor of a State, territory, or possession; and on the day of death and the following day for a member

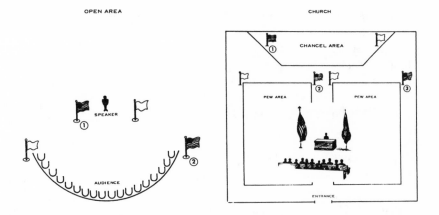

Flag display variations developed by the Masons and published in their flag etiquette book. *Figure on left*: (1) Flags displayed by or for the speaker (speaker standing or sitting in the open, conducting instruction, giving a lecture, etc., to an assembled group of individuals or to a representative element of a society, etc. (2) Flags displayed by the assembled group or by the representative element of a society, etc., while in attendance at a function. *Figure on right*: (1) Flags displayed by the minister or by the church in behalf of a featured or visiting speaker. (2) Flags displayed by an organization, society, etc., (BSA troop; Key Club; Tri-Hi-Y) in attendance in the church. (3) Flags displayed by an organization in attendance other than the organization represented by the flags indicated in (2). Flags displayed by the organizations would be located in a manner that would place the national flag to the right of their location in the pews.

of Congress. The flag shall be flown at half-staff on Peace Officers Memorial Day, unless that day is also Armed Forces Day. As used in this subjection —

(1) the term "half-staff" means the position of the flag when it is one-half the distance between the top and bottom of the staff;

(2) the term "executive or military department" means any agency listed under sections 101 and 102 of Title 5; and

(3) the term "Member of Congress" means a Senator, a Representative, a Delegate, or the Resident Commissioner from Puerto Rico.

The custom of lowering the flag to half-mast or half-staff is a carryover from the old, old military practice of "striking the colors" as a sign of submission in time of war. As early as 1627, however, the flying of the flag at half-mast had become a sign of mourning.

This honor is supposed to be reserved for persons who have done great service for the country. Half-masting of the national flag for persons other than those listed in the code may occur by order of the president; state governors may proclaim half-masting on the death of state government officials.

The most unusual half-masting in the history of the American flag took place in 1973. For a period of nine months the flags over the Capitol were dipped in mourning on the average of one day out of every four: 76 days out of 295. The deaths of former presidents Harry Truman on December 26, 1972, and Lyndon Johnson on January 22, 1973, kept flags lowered for an un-precedented 51 straight days. Even then they were raised again a week early, to honor returning Vietnam prisoners of war. President Nixon signed the reverse proclamation raising the half-masted flags after a telephone conversation with widow Lady Bird Johnson. "Mrs. Johnson and I agreed that for the American flag to be flying high for the

Flag at peak of staff (left) and at half-mast (right).

prisoners' return to American soil would be the finest possible tribute both to her husband's memory and to the heroism of the prisoners and their families, as well as to the missing men, the men who gave their lives and all who helped to win peace with honor in Vietnam," Nixon said.

The specifics of half-masting, describing for whom the flag would be low-ered and for how long, were first spelled out by Dwight Eisenhower in Presi-dential Proclamation #3044, March 1, 1954. These directions were formally incorporated into the Flag Code as part of the 1976 revisions (Public Law 94-344). The flag is lowered for 30 days for a president or former president, and ten days for a vice president, chief justice (active or retired) or house speaker. For the death of a senator or congressman the flag on most Washing-ton buildings remains at half-staff only on the day of death and the following day, but by tradition, flags in the senator's state or the congressman's district — as at the Capitol itself — stay at half-staff until the burial. The directive to half-mast the flag on Peace Officers Memorial Day was added by Congress on Sep-tember 13, 1994.

The administration at the University of Pennsylvania had a fight on its hands about half-masting during the Vietnam era. A group of students demanded that the United States flag at the school be flown at half-mast to protest the Vietnam War. The American Legion, against the idea, asked Gov-ernor Raymond P. Schafer to intervene, but he refused. He did make a speech, however, saying, "I cannot condone the actions of anyone who would use the flag as a political toy, especially when that very flag protects those who attempt to use it for such purposes."

The administration then solved their own problem. To avoid an angry stu-dent confrontation, the flag was just not flown at all during a cooling-off period. That, of course, was contrary to the code, just as the student demand for half-masting without the required Presidential approval was, but better than having people hurt. Perhaps an easier and more effective method of drawing attention to American dead in Vietnam would have been for the students involved to petition President Nixon, through the congressman for the district, to proclaim an official half-masting of *all* flags in the country for a short period of time. It would have been a logical request, lawfully made, and all the bad feeling generated between students and university administration might have been converted into a widespread cooperative labor of love, a patriotic gesture.

One flourish of patriotism once covered by subsection 175(m) was the use of streamers. From 1942 until the 1976 revisions, this subsection included the directive that "crepe creamers may be affixed to spear heads or flagstaffs in a parade only by order of the President of the United States." The streamers referred to were battle streamers and commendation pennants such as are flown by the United States Navy, Marine Corps and Army in formal parades. They are, however, flown on the staffs of the official flags of the service branches, not the staff holding the stars and stripes. The Navy flag, for example, carries 27 battle streamers (with 23 silver stars and 33 bronze stars attached) symbolizing 157 campaigns and major battles, and 899 unit citations and commendations, from the American Revolution through the Vietnam conflict.

Those were official battles, though there were more "wars" the United States had been in, according to Senator Barry Goldwater. He stated on the Dick Cavet television show that Americans had fought in 192 wars, of which only five were declared. This figure, he explained, included the number of times federal troops were ordered into action, both overseas and domestically.

Since the revisions of 1976, the Flag Code no longer contains any mention of streamers.

(n) *When the flag is used to cover a casket, it should be so placed that the union is at the head and over the left shoulder. The flag should not be lowered into the grave or allowed to touch the ground.*

If a man or woman dies during a period of military service, the flag for

A flag covering a closed casket is draped so that the blue field lies at the head and falls over the left shoulder.

the casket is furnished by the service branch. If he or she dies as an honorably discharged veteran, however, the flag is furnished by the Veteran's Administration in Washington, D.C., and may be procured from the nearest post office by using Veteran's Administration Form 2008.

In filling out the application, the person signing for the flag must state whether he or she is the next of kin or, if another relative, state that kinship. Postmasters will also require proof of honorable discharge before issuing the flag.

With the application comes a sheet offering the following additional instructions for draping a flag over a casket:

(a) *Closed casket.*—When the flag is used to drape a closed casket, it should be so placed that the union (blue field) is at the head and over the left shoulder of the deceased.

(b) *Half-Couch (Open).*—When the flag is used to drape a half-couch casket, it should be placed in three layers to cover the closed half of the casket in such a manner that the blue field will be the top fold, next to the open portion of the casket on the deceased's left.

(c) *Full-Couch (Open).*—When the flag is used to drape a full-couch casket, it should be folded in a triangular shape and placed in the center part of the head panel of the casket cap, just above the left shoulder of the deceased.

This sheet further states that "during a military commitment ceremony, the flag which was used to drape the casket is held waist high over the grave by the pallbearers," then folded immediately after the sounding of "Taps." The sheet includes detailed instructions for correct folding of the flag (below).

Families of servicemen missing in action didn't originally get flags, until

CORRECT METHOD OF FOLDING THE UNITED STATES FLAG

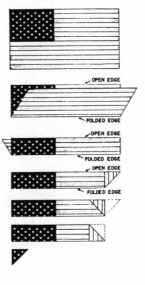

(*a*) Fold the lower striped section of the flag over the blue field.

(*b*) Folded edge is then folded over to meet the open edge.

(*c*) A triangular fold is then started by bringing the striped corner of the folded edge to the open edge.

(*d*) Outer point is then turned inward parallel with the open edge to form a second triangle.

(*e*) Triangular folding is continued until the entire length of the flag is folded in the triangular shape of a cocked hat with only the blue field visible.

Form approved.
Budget Bureau No. 76-R049.7.

VETERANS ADMINISTRATION
APPLICATION FOR UNITED STATES FLAG FOR BURIAL PURPOSES

SECTION I—APPLICATION (*Postmaster: Be sure to submit both the original and duplicate to the nearest VA Regional Office.*)	BRANCH OF SERVICE (*Check*) ☐ ARMY ☐ NAVY ☐ AIR FORCE ☐ MARINE CORPS ☐ OTHER (*Specify*)
LAST NAME—FIRST NAME—MIDDLE NAME OF DECEASED (*Print or type*)	VETERAN'S SERVICE (*Check*) ☐ WW I ☐ WW II ☐ SPANISH AMERICAN ☐ AFTER 1-31-55 ☐ OTHER (*Specify*)

CHECK THE CONDITION UNDER WHICH DECEASED WAS SEPARATED FROM SERVICE

☐ 1. VETERAN OF A WAR, MEXICAN BORDER SERVICE, OR OF SERVICE AFTER 1-31-55, DISCHARGED OR RELEASED FROM ACTIVE DUTY UNDER CONDITIONS OTHER THAN DISHONORABLE.

☐ 3. BY DEATH IN ACTIVE SERVICE AFTER MAY 27, 1941, AND FLAG NOT FURNISHED BY THE SERVICE DEPARTMENT.

☐ 2. DISCHARGED FROM, OR RELEASED FROM ACTIVE DUTY IN U.S. ARMED FORCES UNDER CONDITIONS OTHER THAN DISHONORABLE, AFTER SERVING AT LEAST ONE ENLISTMENT, OR DISCHARGED FOR DISABILITY INCURRED IN LINE OF DUTY.

☐ 4. SEPARATED FROM PHILIPPINE MILITARY FORCES, UNDER CONDITIONS OTHER THAN DISHONORABLE, AFTER SERVING UNITED STATES IN SUCH FORCES UNDER PRESIDENT'S ORDER OF JULY 26, 1941, AND DIED ON OR AFTER APRIL 25, 1951.

NAME, ADDRESS, AND RELATIONSHIP OF PERSON ENTITLED TO RECEIVE FLAG (*If none, indicate "NONE." See par. 7 of the attached Instructions.*)

SECTION II—PERSONAL DATA OF DECEASED (*To be filled in if possible*)	CLAIM NO. C-	SOCIAL SECURITY NO.
SERVICE SERIAL NO.	DATE OF ENLISTMENT	DATE OF DISCHARGE	DATE OF BIRTH
DATE OF DEATH	PLACE OF DEATH (*Address*)	PLACE OF BURIAL (*Address*)	DATE OF BURIAL

CERTIFICATION: I CERTIFY THAT, to the best of my knowledge and belief, the statements made above are correct and true, the deceased is eligible, in accordance with attached Instructions, for issue of a United States flag for burial purposes, and such flag has not previously been applied for or furnished.

| SIGNATURE OF APPLICANT SIGN HERE IN INK | ADDRESS | RELATIONSHIP TO DECEASED | DATE |

PENALTY.—The law provides that whoever makes any statement of a material fact knowing it to be false shall be punished by a fine or by imprisonment or both.

VA FORM MAY 1966 **07—2008** SUPERSEDES VA FORM 07-2008, MAY 1955, WHICH WILL NOT BE USED.   16—60962-12   **ORIGINAL**

Form approved.
Budget Bureau No. 76-R049.7.

VETERANS ADMINISTRATION
APPLICATION FOR UNITED STATES FLAG FOR BURIAL PURPOSES

SECTION I—APPLICATION (*Postmaster: Be sure to submit both the original and duplicate to the nearest VA Regional Office.*)	BRANCH OF SERVICE (*Check*) ☐ ARMY ☐ NAVY ☐ AIR FORCE ☐ MARINE CORPS ☐ OTHER (*Specify*)
LAST NAME—FIRST NAME—MIDDLE NAME OF DECEASED (*Print or type*)	VETERAN'S SERVICE (*Check*) ☐ WW I ☐ WW II ☐ SPANISH AMERICAN ☐ AFTER 1-31-55 ☐ OTHER (*Specify*)

CHECK THE CONDITION UNDER WHICH DECEASED WAS SEPARATED FROM SERVICE

☐ 1. VETERAN OF A WAR, MEXICAN BORDER SERVICE, OR OF SERVICE AFTER 1-31-55, DISCHARGED OR RELEASED FROM ACTIVE DUTY UNDER CONDITIONS OTHER THAN DISHONORABLE.

☐ 3. BY DEATH IN ACTIVE SERVICE AFTER MAY 27, 1941, AND FLAG NOT FURNISHED BY THE SERVICE DEPARTMENT.

☐ 2. DISCHARGED FROM, OR RELEASED FROM ACTIVE DUTY IN U.S. ARMED FORCES UNDER CONDITIONS OTHER THAN DISHONORABLE, AFTER SERVING AT LEAST ONE ENLISTMENT, OR DISCHARGED FOR DISABILITY INCURRED IN LINE OF DUTY.

☐ 4. SEPARATED FROM PHILIPPINE MILITARY FORCES, UNDER CONDITIONS OTHER THAN DISHONORABLE, AFTER SERVING UNITED STATES IN SUCH FORCES UNDER PRESIDENT'S ORDER OF JULY 26, 1941, AND DIED ON OR AFTER APRIL 25, 1951.

NAME, ADDRESS, AND RELATIONSHIP OF PERSON ENTITLED TO RECEIVE FLAG (*If none, indicate "NONE." See par. 7 of the attached Instructions.*)

SECTION II—PERSONAL DATA OF DECEASED (*To be filled in if possible*)	CLAIM NO. C-	SOCIAL SECURITY NO.
SERVICE SERIAL NO.	DATE OF ENLISTMENT	DATE OF DISCHARGE	DATE OF BIRTH
DATE OF DEATH	PLACE OF DEATH (*Address*)	PLACE OF BURIAL (*Address*)	DATE OF BURIAL

CERTIFICATION: I CERTIFY THAT, to the best of my knowledge and belief, the statements made above are correct and true, the deceased is eligible, in accordance with attached Instructions, for issue of a United States flag for burial purposes, and such flag has not previously been applied for or furnished.

| SIGNATURE OF APPLICANT SIGN HERE IN INK | ADDRESS | RELATIONSHIP TO DECEASED | DATE |

PENALTY.—The law provides that whoever makes any statement of a material fact knowing it to be false shall be punished by a fine or by imprisonment or both.

VA FORM MAY 1966 **07—2008** SUPERSEDES VA FORM 07-2008, MAY 1955, WHICH WILL NOT BE USED.   16—60962-12   **DUPLICATE**

a program called Operation Hero Flag was launched on Flag Day 1973. A flag was flown over the Capitol on the birthday of each person listed as missing in action, then sent to his family.

The details of veterans' eligibility for casket flags are spelled out in the U.S. Code, Title 38, "Veterans' Benefits," Ch. 23, "Burial Benefits," Sec. 901, "Flags." That section reads as follows:

The flag-draped casket of United States president John F. Kennedy begins its ceremonial ride to the burial site. The casket rests on a military caisson, which is accompanied by the symbolic riderless horse, with boots turned backwards in the stirrups. This caisson ceremony is one of a number handled by the crack "Old Guard" unit, which also furnishes the guards at the Tombs of the Unknowns in Arlington National Cemetery.

(a) The Administrator shall furnish a flag to drape the casket of each deceased veteran who—

> (1) was a veteran of any war, or of service after January 31, 1955;
> (2) had served at least one enlistment; or
> (3) had been discharged or released from the active military, naval, or air service for a disability incurred or aggravated in line of duty.

(b) After the burial of the veteran the flag so furnished shall be given to his next of kin. If no claim is made for the flag by the next of kin, it may be given, upon request, to a close friend or associate of the deceased veteran. If a flag is given to a close friend or associate of the deceased veteran, no flag shall be given to any other person on account of the death of such veteran.

(c) For the purpose of this section, the term "Mexican border period" as defined in paragraph (30) of section 101 of this title includes the period beginning on January 1, 1911, and ending on May 8, 1916.

(d) In the case of any person who died while in the active military, naval, or air service after May 27, 1941, the Administrator shall furnish a flag to the next of kin, or to such other person as the Administrator deems most appropriate, if such next of kin or other person is not otherwise entitled to receive a flag under this section, or under section 1482(a) of Title 10, United States Code.

(e) The Administrator shall furnish a flag to drape the casket of each deceased person who is buried in a national cemetery by virtue of eligibility for burial in such cemetery under section 1002(6) of this title. After the burial, the flag shall be given to the next of kin or to such other person as the Administrator considers appropriate.

Most of the provisions of sections 174 and 175 describe the "do" of flag display. Proper display demonstrates respect by placing the flag in a position of honor, at appropriate times and under the proper circumstances. By the time the Flag Code was written, however, members of Congress had seen numerous uses of the flag to which the rules of formal display did not apply. Accordingly, they felt it necessary to include the "don't" side of flag use to further promote respect. These are covered in section 176, "Respect for flag," discussed in the following chapter.

3

Respecting the Flag

(United States Code Title 36, Ch. 10, secs. 176–177)

§176. Respect for Flag

No disrespect should be shown to the flag of the United States of America; the flag should not be dipped to any person or thing. Regimental colors, State flags, and organization or institutional flags are to be dipped as a mark of honor.

There is one exception. Navy vessels, upon receiving a salute of this type from another vessel (one registered by a nation formally recognized by the United States), must return the compliment. This is international law. Merchant ships do not trade honors.

An international incident that caused a slight flap at the time, with some little continuing reverberations, happened at the 1908 Olympic Games. The United States Olympic team arrived at the London stadium to discover that their national banner was the only one missing. British officials claimed they could find no United States flag suitable for flying. But when the opening parade unfolded, Ralph Rose, a burly shotputter, led the United States contingent carrying an American flag they had procured. Flag bearers from all other nations obeyed the protocol of the games, dipping their flag to King Edward VII, as head of state of the hosting country. But not Rose. He held the flag proudly erect, saying to those around him, "This flag dips to no earthly king." The American flag has never again been dipped to honor a foreign head of state.*

In 1968 Harold Connolly, a veteran hammer thrower, was selected to carry the banner in the Mexico City Olympics opening day parade. His reply was, "I would be honored, but I'd better tell you that I intend to dip it when I pass the presidential box." Harold Connolly didn't carry the flag that day. United States

---

*Some sources state that the United States' flag bearer at the 1908 summer games was John C. Garrels. However, the Encyclopedia of American Olympians lists Ralph Rose as the flag bearer and credits him with beginning the American tradition of not dipping the flag in this ceremony.

The Battle Color of the U.S. Marine Corps is dipped during one of the famous Friday evening parades at historic Marine Barracks, Washington, D.C. The Barracks is entrusted with the custody of the Battle Color by virtue of its position as the "Oldest Post of the Corps." The Battle Color, which bears 47 streamers representing all honors bestowed on Marine Corps units, as well as all the military campaigns in which Marines have participated, is carried by the Color Guard of the Marine Corps. (Defense Department photo by Master Gunnery Sgt. R.H. Mosier.)

Ralph Waldo Rose (left), who won gold (with a world record shot put), silver and bronze medals in the 1904 Olympics, was the United States flag bearer in the 1908 summer Olympic Games when he set the precedent for not dipping the American flag to any person (others in the picture: Whitney and McDonald, center and right). (Photo courtesy of U.S. Olympic Committee.)

team members always vote on who will carry the flag into the stadium, and Connolly's teammates simply voted against his selection.

Four years later, the Connolly name was resurrected by another vote, but this time the Connolly in question was Harold's Czechoslovakian-born, shot-putting and discus-throwing wife, Olga. The issue, once again, was who would bear the flag, and super-heavyweight weightlifter Ken Patera, who was given a chance against the perennial Russian superheavy world champion this time, was some team members' choice. Selected instead, by only two votes, was Olga Connolly, who had already antagonized the United States Olympic Committee by publicly blasting them for trying to supervise her press interviews.

All held their breaths as Olga neared the reviewing stand where Dr. Gustav Heineman, the president of the hosting Federal Republic of Germany, stood acknowledging the salutes of the competing countries' teams. Olga, like her husband, wanted to break with what they considered stiff-necked tradition, but earlier in the day of the parade she and the fellow athletes who had selected her to lead them had reached a compromise. So, as it happened, Olga marched the flag past Germany's president without a hint of a dip, but lowered it later during the reading of the Olympic oath.

The no-dip tradition still holds. Skier Bill Koch, who carried the flag in the 1992 Winter Olympics, had earlier said he intended to dip the flag to President Mitterand of France "to improve world relations," but teammates asked him not to, and he didn't.

(a) *The flag should never be displayed with the union down except as a signal of dire distress in instances of extreme danger to life or property.*

An upside-down American flag has long been an SOS message. It is mentioned twice in the 1898 book *Our Country's Flag and the Flags of Foreign Countries*, though no history of how the idea started is presented.

Whitney Smith's *Flags Through the Ages and Across the World* (New York: McGraw Hill, 1975) reports that "as a symbol of mourning or of protest against some political event or situation, such as a military defeat or a state visit by an unpopular foreign leader, a flag is sometimes flown upside down. Very rarely, an inverted flag is a symbol of distress (such as a shipwreck or fire). The custom has never been widespread because many inverted flags appear the same as when flown normally." This work, reporting on all countries' flags, also has no explanation of the origin of the practice.

In a light-hearted parody of the idea, yachtsmen may now buy the cocktail pennant, a flaglet employed by boatmen everywhere to indicate that drinks are being served aboard. It's usually a red-and-white flag with a cocktail glass in the center. If a boat's liquor supply runs out, the pennant is flown upside-down as a distress signal meaning "Who has a drink?"

It was around the time of the Vietnam war that flying the American flag topsy-turvy became a favorite form of protest, especially by young people opposed to the nation's involvement in Southeast Asia. The rock group Canned Heat seemed to cap off this trend with the cover of its LP "Future Blues," which pictured a group of space-garbed astronauts on a moon landscape, reproducing the famous Iwo Jima flag-raising pose from World War II, but with the American flag upside-down. The idea had pretty much run its course by the end of 1970, helped along by courts taking a harder line on such displays. The general citizenry got more uptight about flag misuse, too. For example, in November 1970 students at Skyline College in San Bruno, California, impeached their 28-year-old student body president for using an upside-down flag as a bulletin board in his office. The vote was 394 to 189.

Elizabeth Hubner, a 26-year-old Long Island housewife and mother of two, who had won an Americanism award at 16, ended up in court for flying a flag upside-down in her yard over police objections. "I think the nation is in distress because of the war," she explained to the press. "It's dividing us and wasting our money. For years I've been one of these living room liberals, complaining about the war but doing nothing. I just wanted to say to my neighbors that suburbia should get more involved."

One of her neighbors did get involved, reporting her to the police. She was convicted for breaking a state law, 136-D of the General Business Law, prohibiting casting "contempt, either by word or act, upon the flag." Conviction carried a sentence of up to one year and a fine of $1,000. However, her husband paid her bail of $500 after she had spent one day in Nassau County Jail, and her sentence was later suspended.

Pundits, off and on over the years (usually during a recessionary period), have noted that the flag atop the Treasury Building on the United States $10 bill is in the upside-down SOS position. The Treasury Department maintains that this is an optical illusion.

(b) *The flag should never touch anything beneath it, such as the ground, the floor, water, or merchandise.*

This regulation seems clear as stated. If the flag is not to touch anything beneath it, it cannot rest upon anything. But each regulation must carefully be taken in context with each other regulation. By itself, the statement above would make the draping of a veteran's casket illegal. However, an exception in this case is implied by subsection 175(n). Like most laws or regulations, flag codes must harken to "intent" in the use of the flag.

The only problem with this rule of thumb is that intent is usually pretty easy to see, but extremely difficult to prove, since it more or less involves mind-reading.

For example, a Navy chaplain used the flag as an altar covering, with his Bible resting upon it. Obviously it was not his intent to desecrate the flag. Does the Flag Code allow this exception, since the church pennant is sometimes allowed to fly above the stars and stripes to show that God takes precedence over Country?

The code does not allow this exception. There is no subsection stating or implying it, as happens with the casket-covering issue. Here the question needs to be asked: "Why does the American flag need to be used this way?" It is not religious in significance, so it really has no place on an altar.

Another case study question is, "Should a flag bearer carry any portion of the flag against the staff?" The flag is supposed to fly free at all times (subsection 176[c]). But intent enters into the question here too. How else would the bearer keep the flag from dragging the floor or ground in going through a low doorway or under low overhanging obstructions? This is one time even dipping of the flag is allowed, since it isn't being dipped *to* anyone or anything.

It is also expedient sometimes during very windy parade days for flag bearers to hold the trailing flag end against the staff, as the best choice between bending the code or having the flag whipped away by the wind and possibly damaged.

In August 1970, a flag incident caught a lot of publicity and raised questions of intent. When actress Sharon Tate was brutally murdered by the Charles Manson "family," one of the court photographs showed the body on the floor in front of a flag-draped couch. The flag draping turned out, through testimony, to be a protest.

A psychiatrist who didn't want his name used suggested it was a lazy person's protest. "It became a fad, and like all fads was followed slavishly by those persons too lazy, or possibly too stupid, to be individualistic. Thinking for oneself seems to be becoming a lost art in our young," he commented.

Many people believe that a United States flag that has touched the ground must be destroyed, but this is not the case. The intent of subsection 176(b) was to prevent the flag from becoming soiled or torn. True, it is disrespectful to deliberately allow the flag to touch anything beneath it. However, if it should become soiled by accidentally touching the ground, one only needs to have it cleaned. In fact, many of the nation's dry cleaning establishments, in cooperation with the American Legion, will dry clean any flag for free between June 1 and 12 if the owner will promise to fly it on Flag Day, June 14.

(c) *The flag should never be carried flat or horizontally, but always aloft and free.*

Some years back the Louisville, Kentucky, Junior Chamber of Commerce members paraded with a flag so large it took 11 men around its perimeter to stretch it taut. Parade-goers were asked to toss coins onto the flag, and the Chamber of Commerce thus collected $93 for a servicemen's relief fund. This was an admirable activity, but spoiled by misusing the flag two ways. Subsection 176(c) above states that the flag is not to be carried flat, and 176(h) states it is never to be used as a receptacle for anything.

Another flag faux pas happened at the April 1972 Cherry Blossom Festival parade in Washington, D.C. The Patriots of Arlington, Virginia, 400 marchers strong, featured a 12-girl drill team using a large flat-carried flag as a canopy, whipping it into the air while the girls marched under it.

As part of the pre-game ceremony at the 1973 Cotton Bowl a large flag was paraded flat also, by 14 uniformed band members. It was tastefully done, as part of a scene outlining the Capitol building, but no less incorrect.

The Rose Bowl that same year displayed a shield design of historical stars and stripes that was just as spectacular, *and* correct. It ended with the anthem being played as the 50-star flag was raised over the stadium.

The traditions of flag display are often based on more than attractiveness or ceremony. The American Flag and Banner Company once reported that a midwestern city engineer decided to erect two flagpoles and suspend state and national flags between them, anchored at top and bottom. The idea was to show them in full effect at all times. But a gale wind sprang up and, with the flags filling like sails, they pulled the flagpoles right out of the ground.

(d) *The flag should never be used as wearing apparel, bedding, or drapery. It should never be festooned, drawn back, nor up, in folds, but always allowed to fall free. Bunting of blue, white, and red, always arranged with the blue above, the white in the middle, and the red below, should be used for covering a speaker's desk, draping the front of a platform, and for decoration in general.*

The wearing of the flag, simulated flag, or close approximation of the flag got to be quite a fad during the late 1960s and early 1970s, and carnivals and "head" shops made many fast bucks, especially in cities like San Francisco and resort areas like Laguna Beach, California, and Virginia Beach, Virginia, where young people congregated.

Authorities eventually began clamping down. Even though the Flag Code did not have specific wording against using the flag as wearing apparel until 1976, anyone opposed to the practice could cite numerous violations of other segments of the code, including 176(e) (forbidding the use of the flag "in such a manner as to permit it to be easily torn, soiled, or damaged"), 176(d) (specifying that the flag should not be "drawn back, nor up, in folds, but always allowed to fall free"), and the first words of section 176: "No disrespect should be shown to the flag of the United States."

Actually, it is questionable whether the Flag Code can be called "law." Several court decisions over the years, including State of Delaware ex rel. *Trader vs. Hodson* (District Court of Delaware, 1967), *Lapolla vs. Dullaghan* (Supreme Court of Westchester County, N.Y.), and *Holmes vs. Wallace* (District Court of Alabama, 1976) have held that the Flag Code is intended as advisory rather than statutory. However, most states now have laws based upon or taken directly from the federal Flag Code, and these laws carry penalties for violation.

So it was that in 1970 in Charlotte, North Carolina, a 17-year-old boy paid a $15 fine and court costs for wearing an American flag on his jacket, with the peace symbol and the legend "Give peace a chance" superimposed. That same year in Wichita, Kansas, a 20-year-old Wichita State University student was busted and jailed for having the seat of his pants sewn (attached) to a flag.

An 18-year-old Virginia Tech student from Boston received a 30-day jail sentence and a $200 fine for the same stunt. His lawyer tried for both a preliminary and a permanent injunction against his prosecution, but the United States District judge presiding said, "Injunctive relief may not be granted by a federal court against such a state law (the Virginia Uniform Flag Act)." He said the first amendment to the Constitution does not protect flag desecration.

A 19-year-old Detroit girl who tried the same thing while holidaying in Virginia Beach, Virginia, was fined $250 and sentenced to 30 days in jail. The 30 days was suspended providing she leave town immediately. The arresting officer was a retired Marine captain, who had seen a lot of buddies die through a series of campaigns during World War II, Korea, and Vietnam. "Of all the guys in the department," he said, "she shouldn't have done it in front of me."

It was the same judge, a month later, who sentenced a 21-year-old Fort Story, Virginia, soldier to 45 days in jail and fined him $250 for wearing a flag on the seat of his jeans. His crime was enhanced by his arrest for selling L.S.D., but that charge was treated separately. In court, he removed the flag and tried to hide it under a desk. When questioned, he stated, "I've fought for the flag. No matter where I wear it, I love my country."

In 1983 sex magazine publisher Larry Flynt was arrested by a squad of F.B.I. agents on a charge of desecrating the American flag. He had been hauled into court earlier, but refused to give the source of a videotape crucial to the John Z. DeLorean drug trafficking case — and he showed up clad in an American flag as a diaper, a bullet-proof vest adorned with a purple heart medal, and a combat helmet.

Flynt's behavior was clearly disrespectful, but what about the actions of Congresswoman Patricia Schroeder when she draped an American flag around her shoulders for a *Ms.* magazine cover portrait in February 1988? At least one group, the American Legion, found this use of the flag just as unacceptable as Flynt's display. "It's inexcusable that a member of Congress would do this," stated John Minnick, spokesman for the American Legion's national office. Whatever the congresswoman's intent, her behavior was a violation of the Flag Code.

However, prosecuting flag-wearers on desecration charges has made for some difficult legal battles. For example, when Valarie Goguen, who was arrested for wearing a 4 × 6-inch flag sewn to the seat of his blue jeans (under a 70-year-old Massachusetts state law making it a crime to mutilate, trample upon, deface or "treat contemptuously" the American flag) and sentenced to six months imprisonment (half the maximum possible sentence), but his conviction was overturned by a federal court. The grounds were that the concept of "contempt" was too vague. The Supreme Court upheld the ruling 6–3 in March 1974 and voided Goguen's conviction without him ever testifying.

Justice Powell, who wrote the majority opinion, affirmed that Goguen's arrest and conviction violated the due process of the fourteenth amendment because the word "contemptuously" did not provide a "readily ascertainable standard of guilt," which is to say that one man's contempt may be another's joke.

But, as Justice White wrote in the majority opinion on First Amendment grounds, "It should not be beyond the reasonable comprehension of anyone … to realize that sewing a flag on the seat of his pants is contemptuous of the flag." There is something about the positioning that inescapably leads one to the conclusion that Goguen had in mind a vulgar connotation, a connotation that would not apply had he chosen to affix the flag to, say, his shoulder.

And as Justice Rehnquist stated in his dissenting opinion, a person who purchases an American flag is not just buying a piece of "cloth dyed red, white, and blue" but "the one visible … manifestation of 200 years of nationhood."

Yet, no matter how much one may deplore Goguen's tasteless and impertinent act, one comes to the conclusion, after reading the four Supreme Court briefs on the case, that the majority was legally correct in invalidating the Massachusetts statute on grounds of vagueness.

It is not enough to forbid using the flag with contempt without defining precisely what constitutes contempt, for men of common intelligence must not be forced to guess at the meaning of the criminal law. If they do have to, due process is breached.

It is interesting to note that when the United States Bicentennial rolled around in 1976, the citizenry seemed to forget about its war on the flag defilers of just a few years before. Suddenly manufacturers were putting the flag on *everything*, with no complaints from the populace. In fact, people all over the country were sporting flags on every surface without thought of prosecution, and the novelty sellers went right on salting away fortunes from illegally flag-covered goods.

No doubt those parading their star-spangled clothing in 1976 would have argued that their behavior was not "contemptuous" because their intent was to show their love for the flag. It seems that the question of intent lies just below the surface of any discussion about proper use of the flag. Nevertheless, ignorance of the law has never been allowed as an excuse for breaking it, and a law against flag defilement must be upheld in the halls of justice with the same respect accorded to laws against robbery and manslaughter.

Another legal question is provoked by the fact that the United States flag has changed over time. In fact, it has been altered more than any other national flag. Congress has made 27 changes in the national banner since its first formal adoption on June 14, 1777. One reason for the many changes is the flag's complexity, with 64 parts — 50 stars, 13 stripes, and the blue field — to be arranged according to the country's needs. (In contrast, many nations' flags have only two or three elements, such as the three-stripe designs favored by France, Italy, and many others.) So many parts and so many changes have resulted in numerous outdated American flags, which in turn have left courts with the question of whether it is legal to wear or to otherwise defile a flag other than the current 50-star model.

A ruling by the Army Institute of Heraldry makes the point that stars-and-stripes flags "are never obsolete." This might be brought out by the fact several historical sites still fly outdated flags. For example, an 1812 flag flies daily at the Flag House in Baltimore, Maryland, where the Star-Spangled Banner that flew over Fort McHenry was made. A 15-star, 15-stripe banner flies in front of the Frederick, Maryland, city hall, ever since a city vote was held to determine whether citizens approved of its use. "More people voted on it than voted in the general election," according to Mayor Gordon. (This was the so-called "Key" flag.)

The lack of official guidance on historical flags has been interpreted two ways by judges: (1) as an oversight, since there can obviously be only one official flag at a time; or (2) as meaning *any* flag which has been an official one at any time.

Since the question remains whether all past American flags are covered under the code, some police officers have become aware of court problems arising from the distinction. Earlier a case was mentioned where a young woman from Detroit was arrested on vacation in Virginia Beach for wearing a flag on the seat of her pants. It's interesting to note that the arresting officer, as angry as he was both at the deed and the flip attitude of the woman, took time to count the stars in her flag before he made the arrest ... even though the Virginia State code does not specify any number of stars, the thought being that the American flag never becomes obsolete.

In October of 1970, five young men in Philadelphia *won* an interesting case in court which points up this and other problems inherent in deciding actual and intentional desecration. Police brought charges after finding the five having a picnic on a flag. Two of the boys admitted they had used it also as a beach blanket at Atlantic City, New Jersey, and around the house as a poncho (since it had a hole in it). Their plea was that since it had only 48 stars they thought it was no longer an official flag. In court, their defense attorneys produced pictures of Raquel Welch in her flaglike bikini costume from the movie *Myra Breckenridge* and asked, "Is it worse for Raquel Welch to have the stars and stripes next to her bare anatomy than to sit on it? Do we condone that and prosecute these defendants? When she cloaks herself in the flag is she glamorizing the flag or desecrating it?" The municipal judge thought they had a point — proving he wasn't up on his flag regulations, either.

For Miss Welch's costume was not a flag. It was only suggestive of the flag because it was composed of colors and designs used in the flag, which are so striking that it becomes easy to "see" the flag in any combination of stars and stripes in red, white, and blue.

The auto-racing team of champion Cale Yarborough was pictured both on national television and in the pages of *Sports Illustrated* magazine in 1971, all wearing coveralls much more flaglike in appearance than Miss Welch's costume. Except for Miss Welch's remarkable anatomy, these jumpsuit costumes were even more eye-shocking. Yet there was no hue and cry about them at all. There seems to be some sort of double standard at work.

None of this settles the question of whether a 48-star flag is official.

The defense attorneys in this case had other trump cards to play, however. They produced cups, plates, and napkins bearing an American flag portrait.

"Technically, when we pour ketchup on a hot dog and eat it off that plate (with the flag imprint), we're desecrating the flag," admitted the judge. "This is startling."

The judge was incorrect, however, if he believed that two wrongs made a right. Because these implements were illegally imprinted (subsection 176[i] expressly forbids printing the flag on paper napkins and other dispensable goods) does not let the boys off the hook for also being wrong —*if* using a 48-star flag as they did *is* wrong.

Finally, the defense displayed an 1862 photo showing President Abraham Lincoln and General George McClellan sitting in a battlefield tent at a flag-covered table, and proclaimed their defendants as innocent as Abe Lincoln.

Here both lawyers and judge exhibited true ignorance of Flag Code history. True, Lincoln's table was improperly covered by present-day standards. (Flag Code subsection 176(d): "The flag should never be used as ... drapery.... Bunting ... should be used for covering a speaker's desk...." Subsection 176(b): "The flag should never touch anything beneath it....") But the Flag Code did not exist in Lincoln's day. The military code under which he operated was different in many respects and could not be applied to civilian use occurring more than 100 years after the Civil War.

The judge ended this confrontation on a positive note, however. "Whatever the number of stars, the flag is still the official standard," he warned. "From the facts before me, what you did was not malicious, perhaps more playful, and may have been done to bring about an issue. That's the court's suspicion. The next time, however, you may not be so lucky." Case dismissed.

Another judge, this one in Indiana, treated a flag law offender differently. The youth's crime was to use an American flag as a curtain for his minibus. His court-meted punishment was to stand for three hours holding an American flag, while enduring the harassment of an angry crowd of onlookers. Some got so irate that he finally had to be moved inside for his own protection.

There were others, however, who considered the judge's decision outrageous, given out of prejudice. A newspaper editorial on the matter, in fact, called it "a good example of the bad uses to which we sometimes put the laws regulating the use and treatment of the flag. These laws might make some sense if they were equally and dispassionately enforced, but they are not," continued the editorial writer. The complaint was that for every unlucky person punished, several hundred suffer no legal consequences for misusing the flag, and what makes the difference is the attitude or prejudice of the judge — against long hair, an anti-war bumper sticker, or something else even less easy to define. The point seems well taken.

Probably the best way to avoid all these questions of intent, official flags, etc., is to follow the recommendation of code subsection 176(d) and use bunting, rather than flag replicas, for decoration. After all, the colors themselves have a proud heritage. Red, white and blue have been used in the flag throughout the years since the original establishment of the design. By tradition, red stands for hardiness and valor, white for purity and innocence, and blue for vigilance, perseverance, and justice. (Two other nations have flags with alternating red and white stripes and a blue union. Malaysia, with the same number of stripes, has a crescent in its blue field. Liberia, with only 11 stripes, sports one star in its blue field.)

Even bunting has produced bungles. At the reopening of historic Ford's Theater in Washington, D.C., where President Abraham Lincoln was fatally shot, a "Festival at Ford's" show was televised for a vast Thanksgiving audience. And there, on Lincoln's box, were festooned decorations of bunting that was decidedly more flaglike than the code describes. To compound the Flag Code breach, the blue field was on the wrong side. The television producers were as much to blame as the directors of the theater and every government official who sat in the audience and failed to bring the error to the network's attention.

(e) *The flag should never be fastened, displayed, used, or stored in such a manner as to permit it to be easily torn, soiled, or damaged in any way.*

There is one correct way to fold and store the stars and stripes. (See page 67.) When completed, only a triangle is left, with the hasp connecting holes emerging beyond. Some sources state that the flag is folded into a triangle to symbolize the tricorner hats worn by soldiers of the American Revolution. Actually it is done as a matter of expediency. With the flag folded this way the hasp may be easily attached without fumbling through the folds of the flag. Then, as the halyard raises the flag, the folds fall free with no chance of fouling. With large flags it allows the honor guard to hold the triangle as it unfolds so it never drags the ground.

(f) *The flag should never be used as a covering for a ceiling.*

One used to see large flags suspended across the ceilings of gymnasiums and community centers during sporting events or social events. It no longer seems to be done. This ruling against the practice is actually unnecessary because hanging a flag to cover a ceiling would require that the flag be pinned up in a manner that would violate subsection 176(d). But the English language being easy to misunderstand, Congress chose to clarify the code with this ruling pinning down the pinning up of the flag.

(g) *The flag should never have placed upon it, nor on any part of it, nor attached to it any mark, insignia, letter, word, figure, design, picture, or drawing of any nature.*

Federal law (Title 15, §1052[b]) even provides that a trademark cannot be registered for use which "consists of or comprises among the flag or coat of arms or other insignia of the United States ... or any simulation thereof," "simulation" meaning close resemblances.

(h) *The flag should never be used as a receptacle for receiving, holding, carrying, or delivering anything.*

Could this ruling be interpreted as "holding/carrying" a person? If you were a judge, what would be your ruling if Yippie cult leader Abbie Hoffman was brought before you for having wrapped his new 6 lb., 9⅓ oz. son (named america — small a) in an American flag for the trip home from New York's Mt. Sinai Hospital? Father even posed with son for Associated Press photographers, so your case could be documented.

Subsection 176(g) is very clear about advertisements like this one: "The flag should never have placed upon it, nor any part of it, nor attached to it, any mark, insignia, letter, word, figure, design, picture, or drawing of any nature." The code also states (subsection 176[i]) that "the flag should never be used for advertising purposes in any manner whatsoever."

Several points would have to be considered: The federal Flag Code, which *is* being broken; New York state law, which is probably being at least bent out of shape; intent, which would probably be considered obvious in light of Hoffman's 42 arrests as a Yippie movement revolutionary; and even the baby's behavior, i.e., whether the flag was actually desecrated from involuntary release of waste materials.

(i) *The flag should never be used for advertising purposes in any manner whatsoever. It should not be embroidered on such articles as cushions or handkerchiefs and the like, printed or otherwise impressed on paper napkins or boxes or anything that is designed for temporary use and discard. Advertising signs should not be fastened to a staff or halyard from which the flag is flown.*

The first people taken to court for desecration of the United States flag were not 1960s radicals; they were salesmen in the early twentieth century.

In the late 1800s, use of the American flag to advertise products was common. The flag was seen on whiskey bottles, tin cans, and sides of barns advertising everything from cough syrup to chewing tobacco.

The first flag misuse bill was drafted in 1880, but it never got to Congress. In 1897 a group of patriotic societies founded the American Flag Association and declared war on flag exploiters. Though the organization is now defunct, it was a prime mover at that time. In spite of its hard work, though, the first flag desecration case didn't come before the United States Supreme Court until 1907. It involved two beer salesmen who sold bottles picturing the United States flag. They were accused of violating a Nebraska state law (passed on April 8, 1903) against flag desecration.

In this court case of *Halter vs. the State of Nebraska*, Justice John Marshall Harlan handed down this decision on March 4, 1907:

> From the earliest periods in the history of the human race, banners, standards and ensigns have been adopted as symbols of the power and history of the peoples who bore them. It is not then remarkable that the American people, acting through [the] legislative branch of the Government, early in their history, prescribed a flag as symbolic of the existence and sovereignty of the Nation. Indeed, it would have been extraordinary if the Government had started this country upon its marvelous career without giving it a flag to be recognized as the emblem of the American public. No American, nor any foreign born person who enjoys the privileges of American citizenship, ever looks upon it without taking pride in the fact that he lives under this free Government. Hence, it has often occurred that insults to a flag in the presence of those who revere it, have been resented and, sometimes, punished on the spot.... So, a state may exert its power to strengthen the bonds of the Union and patriotism and love of Country among its people. When, but its legislation, the State encourages a feeling of patriotism towards Nation, it necessarily encourages a like feeling towards the State. One who loves the Union will love the State in which he resides, and love both of the common country and of the state will diminish in proportion as respect for the flag is weakened. Therefore, a State will be wanting in care for the well-being of its people if it ignores the fact that they regard the flag as a symbol of their Country's power and prestige, and will be impatient if any open disrespect is shown towards it. By the statute in question the state has in its substance declared that no one subject to its jurisdiction shall use the flag for purposes of trade and traffic, — a purpose wholly foreign to that for which it was provided by the nation. Such a use tends to degrade and cheapen the flag in the estimation of the people, as well as to defeat the object of maintaining it as an emblem of national honor....
>
> ...[W]e are of the opinion that those who enacted the statute knew, what is known to all, that to every true American the flag is the symbol of the nation's power, — the emblem of freedom in its truest, best sense.
>
> It is not extravagant to say that to all lovers of the Country it signifies government resting on the consent of the governed; liberty regulated by law; the protection of the weak against the strong; security against the exercise of arbitrary power; and absolute safety for free institutions against foreign agression [*sic*]. As the statute in question evidently had its origin in a purpose to cultivate a feeling of patriotism among the people of the State, we are unwilling to adjudge that, in legislation for that purpose, the State erred in duty or has infringed the constitutional rights of anyone. On the contrary, it may reasonably be affirmed that a duty rests upon each State in every legal way to encourage its people to love the Union with which the State is indissolubly connected.

In the midst of World War II, however, President Franklin Roosevelt saw a need for some exceptions to rules against use of the flag on merchandise. On February 18, 1944, he set forth those exceptions in Presidential Proclamation #2605:

> The flag of the United States of America is universally representative of the principles of justice, liberty, and democracy enjoyed by the people of the United States; and

People all over the world recognize the flag of the United States as symbolic of the United States; and

The effective prosecution of the war requires a proper understanding by the people of other countries of the material assistance being given by the Government of the United States:

NOW, THEREFORE, by virtue of the power vested in me by the Constitution and laws of the United States, particularly by the Joint Resolution approved June 22, 1942, as amended by the Joint Resolution approved December 22, 1942, as President and Commander in Chief, it is hereby proclaimed as follows:

1. The use of the flag of the United States or any representation thereof, if approved by the Foreign Economic Administration, on labels, packages, cartons, cases, or other containers for articles or products of the United States intended for export as lend-lease aid, as relief and rehabilitation aid, or as emergency supplies for the Territories and possessions of the United States, or similar purposes, shall be considered a proper use of the flag of the United States and consistent with the honor and respect due the flag.

2. If any article or product so labeled, packaged or otherwise bearing the flag of the United States or any representation thereof, as provided for in section 1, should, by force of circumstances, be diverted to the ordinary channels of domestic trade, no person shall be considered as violating the rules and customs pertaining to the display of the flag of the United States, as set forth in the Joint Resolution approved June 22, 1942, as amended by the Joint Resolution approved December 22, 1942 ... for possessing, transporting, displaying, selling, or otherwise transferring any such article or product solely because the label, package, carton, case, or other container bears the flag of the United States or any representation thereof.

It is, however, against the law to use a representation of the United States flag (or the flag of any nation or state) as part of a registered trademark. Title 15, sec. 1052, of the U.S. Code states that any such trademark will be refused registration.

Returning to the Flag Code, consider the last line of 175(i): "Advertising signs should not be fastened to a staff or halyard from which the flag is flown." Around 1971 or 1972 McDonald's hamburger chain started flying their company's Golden Arches flag on the same staff

The Katy-Parsons Golf Club in Parsons, Kansas, sports a novel golf club as its flagpole. (Photo courtesy of the Katy-Parsons Golf Club.)

as the stars and stripes at all its stands. A concerned citizen finally queried the Washington (D.C.) *Star* newspaper's "Action Line" columnist about it. Action Line contacted a spokesman for McDonald's and printed his answer: "So long as the [McDonald] flag is below the national banner it's neither illegal nor in violation of the U.S. Flag Code. It is 'good business.'" Writing in the capital city for one of the United States' largest newspapers, the Action Line columnist apparently never questioned this answer. Nevertheless, anyone reading the code immediately recognizes McDonald's action as a violation of subsection 176(i). Sometime later, McDonald's quietly changed to separate halyards.

The Katy-Parsons Golf Club at Parsons, Kansas, went even further in using the flagpole as "good business." Their flagpole was built to the exact scale of a number two iron (June 1972). The head of the 36-foot club turned on a pivot to also act as a flag-weathervane.

The argument in their favor is that the ruling states, "Advertising signs should not be fastened to a staff or halyard from which the flag is flown." It doesn't mention a flagpole which is in itself advertising, though the intent of use seems pretty clear. However, the opposite side might argue that each is "fastened" to the other, thus the advertising *pole* is "fastened to the halyard from which the flag is flown," so it is a flag code violation. Besides, the first line of this code section states, "The flag should never be used for advertising purposes in any manner whatsoever," and that seems pretty clear.

If we were to take our flag regulations literally (and really, what other way is there?), the Postal Service has made some classic blunders too.

In July 1970 the department came up with a best-seller item. It was an 11 × 14-inch poster, a full color reproduction of the United States flag with the legend, "This Is Our Flag — Be Proud of It" added. Originally produced for display in area post offices, it received so much interest that it was selected by the Government Printing Office for public sale. In the first three weeks 17,000 copies were sold at 25¢ each, 25 for $3, and 50 for $5. In less than six months 100,000 had been sold.

Which flag regulation did both the Post Office Department and the Government Printing Office break? Subsection 176(i) again. That subsection states that the flag "should not be ... printed or otherwise impressed upon ... anything that is designed for temporary use and discard."

If these posters were violations of the code, how about the decals Humble Oil Company and *Reader's Digest* magazine gave away by thousands for people to put on their back auto windows, but which ended up pasted everywhere? *Reader's Digest* is generally credited with the boom in flag decals, since the increased demand seems to have closely followed the magazine's sending 18 million free decals to subscribers. Flag manufacturers reported record sales of 50 million decals by the end of 1969. Under the code, however, a flag decal is another misuse of the flag.

If posters and decals are a misuse, then what about a painting of the flag?

There was nothing else added. It was just a rendition of the flag on canvas, in paint. It was entered and shown in the 1970 Virginia Beach Annual Boardwalk exhibit, which draws artists and sculptors from all over the East Coast. Answer? Incorrect again, even though the painting has one saving grace in its favor: It is of a more permanent nature, not for "temporary use and discard."

By logical progression, working through posters, decals, and paintings of the flag, we arrive at the most costly question of all. Should the Post Office have been allowed all these years to print and sell stamps depicting the United States flag? The Post Office had no immunity from the code, even if it was a branch of the government. Should it be allowed to continue printing the flag on stamps in violation of the code? (Or should the code be revised to allow such use?) If it continues to use flag stamps, or is given special dispensation to do so, especially now that it is ideally a profit-making corporation, what is to deter other delivery companies now coming onto the commercial scene from doing the same thing?

The first United States stamp to picture the stars and stripes was a 30-center in 1869. It showed two staffed flags, one on each side of a shield, topped by a spread-winged eagle. The flags, however, were rather incidental in the design. An American flag was used in such background designs for other stamps also in 1898, 1903, 1909, 1919, 1926, 1931, 1933, 1935, 1936, and 1944.

It wasn't until 1945, though, that the flag was used as part of the central figure on a stamp. This was three years *after* the codifying of the flag regulations. It was used that year as part of the famed Iwo Jima flag-raising picture, one of the first Armed Forces series of stamps, and was also used on a stamp to commemorate Texas statehood. The Texas commemorative pictured the stars and stripes with a ray of light shining from the twenty-eighth star onto the lone star of a Texas state flag.

There were other incidental flag displays on 1946, 1947, 1952, and 1958 stamps. In 1952 a Betsy Ross commemorative depicted her working on the 1776 13-star flag, a bit of history that has now been pretty much disproved. The first use of the flag as a central figure by itself was on the 1957 American Flag commemorative issue. It brought up a very interesting dilemma: How do you commemorate a flag on a stamp if the Flag Code disallows such printed representation?

Following in order came the 49-star flag 4-cent stamp in 1959, the 50-star 4-cent stamp in 1960, another in 1963, the "Register and Vote" commemorative in 1964, and a 6-cent flag and White House issue in 1968, changed to an 8-cent denomination and later, in 1973, to a 10-cent denomination. Other stamps with incidental flag displays were printed in 1962, 1965, 1966-67, 1969, and 1970.

In 1968 a set of stamps picturing 10 American historical flags was issued. Nine of the flags came from the Revolutionary War period and one from the War of 1812. Of these, only three used any combination of stars and stripes.

They included the first stars and stripes of 1777, the United States flag from 1798 to 1818 (known as the Fort McHenry flag, which inspired the "Star-Spangled Banner" anthem), and the 1777 Bennington flag (carried by the Bennington Militia).

Flag presentations on postage stamps make good history lessons but are still incorrect flag usage. There was in fact an officially recorded complaint against the stamps. The South Carolina delegation to the seventy-first convention of the Veterans of Foreign Wars put forth a resolution to stop putting the American flag on postage stamps. "They are constantly hit upon and stamped, causing a severe and horrible defacing," the delegation spokesman

Opposite and above: The most-used United States stamp image is the Star-Spangled Banner, as shown here by 31 different designs ranging from the 3-cent stamps of 1945 to the 32-cent stamps issued in 1995. Such depictions are incorrect flag usage according to the federal Flag Code, which states that the flag "should not be … printed or otherwise impressed on … anything that is designed for temporary use and discard."

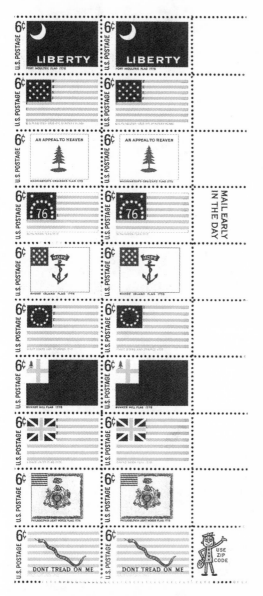

This set of United States postage stamps was issued in 1968. Nine of the flags depicted were flown during the Revolutionary War; the remaining flag, second from top, was flying over Fort McHenry during the War of 1812 and inspired Francis Scott Key to compose the poem that later became the national anthem.

said. Nothing much ever came of it, though. As a matter of fact, both the Amvets and the Elks have put out flag stamps of their own, as advertising, and nothing has ever been done about those either. The Amvets stamp looked so authentic that it was used on a letter and was stamped and delivered on one occasion without question by the Postal Service.

The United States Flag Code cannot, of course, regulate what foreign countries print on their stamps. Many nations have commemorated the United States flag.

In about 1970, Edith Buckley and Col. Lloyd Dockal, authors of the 1950 book *Old Glory Around the World*, searched out all the stamps issued by foreign nations that had featured an American flag somewhere in their designs up through 1969.

The first they found were dated 1893. Issued by the independent city of Shanghai, these included a regular-issue stamp plus several overprints and envelopes, wrappers, and postal cards. The next was issued in 1896, on a smaller scale, then another — a set of eight Australian postcards, and two Japanese cards — in 1908. In 1918 Panama printed a regular stamp. Altogether, Buckley and Dockal found 70 countries had issued 399 stamps of various kinds and denominations with the Star-Spangled Banner pictured somewhere on them. Some of them had to be perused with a magnifying glass, however, to be made out.

Primarily the stamps commemorated various home-

Unofficial flag stamps, issued by Amvets (left) and Elks Lodge (right). Amvets' one was so realistic it went through the mail.

nation and international events. For example, some honored Olympic Games winners with their pictures and home countries' flags, or member nations of the United Nations organization, or nations attending events like the International Fair, held in Valencia, Spain. Some, though, commemorated United States events, like the six San Marino stamps honoring the centenary of the first postage stamps in the United States (picturing the 5-cent Ben Franklin and 10-cent George Washington ones issued in 1847 and the 90-cent one of Abraham Lincoln issued in 1869). Two stamps also from San Marino commemorated the first anniversary of JFK's assassination, and a 1938 airmail commemorative from Tunisia noted the 150th anniversary of the United States Constitution.

Countries included in the Buckley-Dockal study were Afghanistan, Ajman, Algeria, Argentina, Australia (including New South Wales, Queensland, South Australia, Tasmania, Victoria and Western Australia), Belgium, Bhutan, Bolivia, Brazil, Bulgaria, China, Colombia, Costa Rica, Cuba, Curacao, Czechoslovakia, Dominica and the Dominican Republic, Dubai, Ecuador, Egypt, Ethiopia, France, Ghana, Gilbert & Ellis Islands, Great Britain, Guatemala, Guinea, Haiti, Honduras, Hungary, Italy, Japan, Jordan, Jugoslavia, Korea, Lebanon, Liberia, Luxembourg, Malta, Manama, Mexico, Monaco, Netherlands Antilles, Nicaragua, Niger, Nigeria, Pakistan, Panama, Paraguay, Peru, the Philippines, Poland, Portugal, Quatar, Romania, Russia, Saar, Salvador, San Marino, Shanghai, Sharjah, Siam (Thailand), Spain, Surinam, Syria, Togo, Trieste, Tunisia, Turkey, Umm Al Quwain, Uruguay, Venezuela, Vietnam and Yemen.

Since then, of course, there have been more, such as those shown on page 92.

Having come this far in probing the Flag Code, try a little more supposing. If the Flag Code makes it wrong to print posters and stamps, doesn't it also then make it wrong to print *any* flag picture, as in a magazine or this book? Carrying this thought to its ultimate conclusion, wouldn't it make it wrong even to print flag pictures in the booklets outlining the Flag Code itself, as well as in historical textbooks?

Then how closely must these regulations be adhered to? Does the code refer to a printed picture with the flag as a central theme, or any picture with the

Stamps from other nations sometimes feature the United States flag. Above, the two from the Republic of Guinea-Bissau commemorate the Los Angeles Olympic Games of 1984, while the Laotian stamp notes the 1992 World Soccer Games in San Francisco. One stamp from Afghanistan memorializes that country's fortieth anniversary of the victory over fascism, while the other notes the fortieth anniversary of the United Nations. The Dominica stamp is probably the most unusual of all. Showing a 13-starred flag (getting history a bit mixed up) it commemorates the bicentennial of the American Revolution.

flag in it? And are the millions of people who have taken pictures of the flag guilty of breaking this regulation? Or are only the photographic workers who actually "printed" their flag pictures guilty?

Spill a can of worms and every worm will have in mind a different direction to go. So it is with the Flag Code interpretations at the present time. The writers of the code didn't foresee how the printing, photographing, and duplicating arts would complicate interpretation in a future world. The Code needs to be updated to conform to today's technology and thinking. Times change and perfectly good laws turn "blue." Without rewriting to allow for logical and legitimate use of the flag, the Flag Code could turn into a code of blue laws.

(j) *No part of the flag should ever be used as a costume or athletic uniform. However, a flag patch may be affixed to the uniform of military personnel, firemen, policemen, and members of patriotic organizations. The flag represents a living*

The American Basketball Association's world champion Utah Stars wore American flag patches on their uniforms in the 1971-72 season. Later, in 1983-84, the New Jersey Nets team sported uniforms with star-spangled side panels flanked with white and red stripes, perhaps the gaudiest display ever seen on court. (Photo courtesy of the Utah Stars.)

country and is itself considered a living thing. Therefore, the lapel flag pin being a replica, should be worn on the left lapel near the heart.

Some countries have a relaxed attitude about bedecking their athletes with their national flags. For example, Briton Ron Hill wore a pair of track shorts made from a British flag in winning the fourteenth International Marathon race in the Netherlands in 1973 and no one raised an eyebrow.

In America, however, when the professional ABA champion Utah Stars showed up for the 1971-72 season in new uniforms sporting American flags sewn on the legs of the players' shorts, they heard about it from the ladies of the Daughters of the American Revolution. They were right to complain, of course, but the well-meaning owner of the basketball team — whose mother is also a member of the D.A.R.— was dumbfounded. He had been a flag-waver forever. His Denver boxing team was wearing flags on their uniforms, and his red, white, and blue Indianapolis race car had been christened "The Silent Majority Special" two years earlier.

Ignorance is no excuse, however. From its first draft in June 1942, the Flag

Code has forbidden the use of the flag on athletic uniforms. This regulation was originally part of Subsection 176(i) but was incorporated into a new subsection 176(j) in the revisions of 1976.

The Motion Picture Production Code (the movie censoring body) at one time watched for violations of the Flag Code, as well as for unacceptable material. One scene they ordered cut was in an MGM film being produced by William Wright just after World War II. The scene cut was a child's ballet number in which, as a finale, the dancer whirled out her cape to show it as an American flag. The Motion Picture Production Code administrators ruled out the scene because it conflicted with the regulation about the flag not being part of a costume.

The 1976 revision of the Flag Code inserted the wording regarding flag patches on "the uniform of military personnel, firemen, policemen, and members of patriotic organizations." This insertion was in keeping with the goal of the revision, which according to Senator Birch Bayh was "to clear up some misunderstandings over proper use of the flag." The regulation forbidding the use of the flag as part of a costume or athletic uniform had certainly provoked its share of misunderstandings. Did "costume" include the clothing worn by police and fire officials? Since only "athletic uniforms" were specified, were other uniforms free to bear replicas of the flag? The wearing of a flag replica to designate the United States' representation in worldwide programs, such as the space program, was not considered to be in violation. This would seem to clear the way for other uniforms. Yet astronauts are serving the United States on the international scene, whereas police and fire officials are local employees. It was difficult to point to any legal precedent for the wearing of flag patches or pins on most uniforms. However, many local officials felt strongly about the issue.

By 1970 police in more than a thousand towns and cities across the United States — out of an estimated 18,300 uniformed police departments in the nation — had added American flags to their uniforms, usually as shoulder patches or lapel pins. Many police bought these emblems with their own money, but about 800 departments bought patches through the American Federation of Police, and hundreds of others ordered them from commercial emblem makers. The head of A-B Emblem Company of Weaverville, South Carolina, the company that produced uniform patches for the Apollo astronauts, reported more than a million flag patches sold in eight months. In Muskegan Heights, Michigan, 32 police officers went so far as to replace their regular police badges on the front of their winter coats with flag patches.

Sometimes individual officers wore flags in the face of regulations forbidding it. Bronx patrolman Patrick Doland, a Korean veteran with 15 years on the force, faced departmental charges in January 1971 for wearing an unauthorized flag on his lapel, above two rows of citations. In a happy ending, the department rescinded the rule and authorized city police to wear a 1 × 1½-inch metal flag above their badges and a flag patch in place of a badge on the front of their winter coats. Doland even received a letter from President Nixon congratulating him on his firm stand "to honor our flag."

Nixon had supported the trend from its beginning, consistently wearing a half-inch American flag on a gold base on his coat lapel. In a letter to the American Federation of Police, Nixon wrote:

> In my view, the display of the American flag on the uniforms worn by law enforcement officers is appropriate, both as an indication of respect for the flag itself and as a reminder that our flag symbolizes the American freedoms which peace officers of our country have dedicated their lives and their energies to preserve.

Because President Nixon endorsed the wearing of the flag pin did not make it correct flag code procedure, of course. (But evidently he wasn't very up on his flag etiquette, anyway; when he called an "Honor America Day" on July 4, 1971, he had Billy Graham preach from the steps of the Lincoln Memorial over a large flag stretched flat out, over a platform, a violation of code subsection 176[b].) However, he could have made the wearing of flag pins entirely correct by amending the Flag Code with a presidential proclamation, as provided in section 178 of the code.

Ronnie Thompson, mayor of Macon, Georgia, in the late 1960s, is the man credited with starting the flag-wearing idea back in July 1969. He says he did it because so many officers were being attacked on the job — 29 within six months. After the men had flag patches sewn on their blue uniforms, there was only one such assault in a like period of time. Mayor Thompson then extended his plan to the Macon Fire Department, also with good results.

When the Philadelphia Police Department permitted the wearing of small flag pins, the city firemen followed suit with flag decals on their helmets and patches on their uniform shoulders. Their commissioner, James J. McCarey, took a dim view of this display. "Department regulations permit firemen to display only the Hero award and certain service pins," he stated. "We would look like a motorcycle club if everyone wore something different."

Most of the small police departments, which didn't have to cut through regulatory red tape, adopted patches or pins quickly once the idea was publicized. The two-man department at Chilmark on the Massachusetts island of Martha's Vineyard was soon sporting the flag, as were officers in the frozen village of Valdez, Alaska, and on the island town of Langley, Washington (population 448).

With flag patches, decals, and pins working so well as an assault deterrent for police and fire personnel, it wasn't long until individuals, then entire departments started placing flag insignia on their vehicles. It happened in Austin, Texas, where decals were donated by a savings and loan association; San Diego, California, where a bank supplied the decals; and the two Kansas Cities, where police car antennae flew tiny flags also supplied by local banks. Highway patrol cars in Minnesota and Montana started sporting flag decals, as did the state police cars in Indiana, where decals were furnished by the American Legion.

In Detroit, where police cars carried flag decals on both front fenders, patrolman Fred Williams said, "Somebody's got to uphold the old flag. It's been taking a beating."

St. Petersburg police captain B.J. Atkins said one factor in his department's adoption of the patches was a news picture from the 1968 Democratic Convention in Chicago showing a policeman guarding the flag at a demonstration. "This officer was standing there with tears in his eyes defending the flag," Atkins said.

In Chicago the flying of the flag was going even further afield. Some post office mail delivery trucks started flying small staffed flags from side brackets.

The Jane L. Sparks Crusade for a Red, White and Blue America was an individual effort to promote the use of flag pins and decals. In a rather hard-sell approach, she nagged or needled people or groups in person, by phone, and by mail until they displayed flag decals or pins or some form of the stars and stripes. And she didn't let the fact she was a semi-invalid deter her zeal.

She worried at policemen in her precinct in Norfolk, Virginia, for weeks before they gave in and started wearing flag pins on their uniforms. Then she started in on the firemen. Then the police chiefs of the surrounding cities of Virginia Beach, Chesapeake, Portsmouth, and Hampton Roads all heard from her. "Look at the state of the nation," she said. "It's distressing. We need to display the flag to remind ourselves what the flag stands for — freedom."

Her dream was to have everyone in the United States wearing the flag by 1976. She and husband W.G. Sparks, who shared her project, gave out hundreds of flag decals, along with "Support Your Local Police" bumper stickers.

W.G. was a strong vociferous spokesman for police and fire departments. "The police have been cussed and fussed at enough," he told reporters. Both the Sparkses got mightily upset at stories of dissidents abusing policemen and firemen wearing flag patches or pins, or bombarding official vehicles showing flag decals. "Firemen and policemen are the soldiers of the home front," said Mrs. Sparks. "They ought to work under the U.S. flag just as soldiers in Vietnam do."

As well-meaning and patriotic as the wearing of the flags may be, it takes on an entirely different context for some civil rights workers. "The flag becomes the banner of the powerful white establishment," was the way Charles Morgan, an Atlanta lawyer for the American Civil Liberties Union, put it in 1969. He repeated a remark he'd heard by a black civil rights worker in the South: "Find the city that flies the most flags and you've found the city where we have the most trouble."

Syndicated columnist Mary McGrory, an avowed antagonist of Nixon supporters everywhere, also found this kind of flag display threatening and offensive. She wanted to ban the wearing of lapel flag pins because Nixon and his close associates wore them.

"The flag pin vogue was originated by our departed president," she stated (mistakenly). "I believe that it was in its way as serious and willful a desecration as sitting on the Star-Spangled Banner." She went on:

> The flag on the posterior was supposed to tell Middle Americans what some young people thought of a country that waged the Vietnam War for ten years. The flag on the lapel was meant to say that some Americans are more American than others, specifically more so than those who declined to endorse the burning and bombing of peasant villages in Asia.
>
> Richard Nixon began wearing the flag about the same time the war protesters began to mass against him. The suggestion was that he was not only its custodian, but its embodiment.

This is a harsh personal judgment. If true, however, it would certainly be a flagrant misuse of the flag, as a public relations political tool. Opponents to this view say, "If the president of the United States can't wear the flag, who can?" But the answer is simple: No one can. Not even the president, unless he changes the Flag Code, which he is empowered to do.

At any rate, flag pins did eventually make their way into the Flag Code, though the change was originated by Congress some years after Nixon's departure from office. The 1976 revision of the code inserted the remark that "the lapel flag pin ... should be worn on the left lapel near the heart." (This remark is another example of confusing wording. The code still does not specifically state that flag pins are permissible, but only implies permission by decreeing how such pins should be worn.)

Over the years, the wearing of flag replicas has been the breach of flag code most often inspiring controversy, and not always in the way one might expect. For example, in March 1980 the L.K. Comstock Company, a sub-contractor at a nuclear power plant in North Perry, Ohio, fired ten electricians for wearing flag decals reading "Free the Hostages" (meaning the American hostages being held at the time in Iran) on their hard hats. Company policy forbidding anything other than the company logo on hats was well known. However, the hostages' cause was such an emotional issue nationwide that the company had to back down, rehire the ten (minus pay for off time), and publicize how decals — which the company decided to distribute to workers — could be worn on hats so they would not be distracting. Still, public sympathy notwithstanding, Flag Code subsection 176(j) made the display incorrect.

Another unusual controversy erupted in Spokane, Washington, when county sheriff Mike Hirst refused his boss's blanket order to wear American flag patches on uniforms in the wake of the 1991 Gulf War. Hirst said he supported wearing the flag, but felt complying with such a department-wide order amounted to "making a political statement" on his boss's behalf (supporting the war). "I just don't like being forced to say something for somebody else," he explained. His reprimand made waves in the media, and his boss changed the order so deputies could choose to wear either a flag or a sheriff's department emblem on their right sleeves. Then Hirst sewed on his flag.

Back in the sports arena, in 1990 the Cincinnati Reds and Oakland Athletics professional baseball teams displayed flag patches on their uniforms "as a show of support for the U.S. troops in the Persian Gulf." As a further show of support, Reds owner Marge Schott had their stadium decked out with orange ribbons for the playoffs and World Series. The mother of a serviceman from Cincinnati had started the orange ribbon campaign locally when troops were first sent to the Middle East. The wearing of American flag patches was also initiated on sports officials' uniforms on February 2, 1991, when men's basketball referees for the Carolinas Junior College Conference started sporting them to honor two of their peers, Marshall Irby and Randy Oler, who were Army reservists called to duty during the Gulf War.

(k) *The flag, when it is in such condition that it is no longer a fitting emblem for display, should be destroyed in a dignified way, preferably by burning.*

Most people believe burning is the only approved method of destroying a flag. As you see, however, the code says "preferably by burning." Burning has probably become the accepted method because no one has been able to think of another way of destroying it. Destroying, according to the dictionary, means "to put out of existence," which signifies *completely.*

If burning is the accepted method of destroying the flag, then why all the hubbub about burning of flags in political demonstrations? Is it because demonstrators are burning flags in good condition? Well, where does it say who is to judge a flag's condition? A flag can be bought, so it can have an owner. The owner then decides when it is time to incinerate it. At least that is logic.

The problem lies not in the burning, but in the intent, which can often be inferred from the ceremony leading to or surrounding the burning. "Destroyed in a dignified way," the regulation states. The Armed Services have very specific and dignified ceremonies surrounding flag burnings. Demonstrators, on the other hand, have torn the flag, walked upon it, spit upon it, and dragged it through the streets before burning it. Then, during the burning, they have acted like high school kids at a football bonfire rally.

The unwritten message of the Flag Code is that the condition and treatment of the national emblem is a public concern. The code makes every flag subject to its regulations, regardless of ownership.

Since the code doesn't designate an inspecting or overseeing body to enforce its regulations, it puts the responsibility on every American citizen, and his elected judicial protectorate.

For years there has been talk of amending the United States Constitution specifically to outlaw flag burning, in order to counteract the 1990 Supreme Court ruling (*U.S. vs. Eichman*) that flag burning as a political statement is protected by the constitutional guarantee of free speech. In January 1995 four Washington state representatives — Larry Sheahan (R–Rosalia), Mark Schoesler (R–Ritzville), Bill Grant (D–Walla Walla), and Dave Mastin (D–Walla Walla) — presented a memorial, for the third time, urging President Bill Clinton and the United States Congress to propose an amendment to the Constitution giving Congress and the states more power to prevent flag burning and other desecration. The state house passed it with a 76–19 vote.

"There are certain symbols that should be protected and the flag is one of them," Mastin stated. "The flag, for a vast majority of the country, means greatness and unity of the country."

Rep. Pete Kremen (D–Bellingham) agreed, saying, "Flag burning is a hate crime against the nation." But Rep. Brian Hatfield (D–Montesano) put things into perspective with the comment, "Banning flag burning won't prevent flag burning. It will just punish it."

Neither side in the argument seemed to remember that the federal Flag Code calls for burning as the only preferable way of destroying a worn-out or damaged American flag. That ignored facet to this argument inspired a joke being passed around one community: A man, standing over a pile of raked leaves in his yard, was complaining to a neighbor: "Legally, I can burn the flag, but not the leaves!"

A Boy Scout in Goldsboro, North Carolina, had his own method of helping retire old flags. The local *News-Argus* printed a letter from him stating he would, as his Eagle Scout project, collect and retire flags no longer fit for service. Allen York received his Eagle Scout rank from the National Council B.S.A. in 1991 after collecting 266 flags and burning them at the Seymour Johnson Air Force Base.

An even more inspiring story is the one about baseball player Rick Monday of the Los Angeles Dodgers. A player with a lifetime .264 batting average, he nevertheless had a "Rick Monday Day" proclaimed by the Illinois State Legislature. It was earned at a game between the Chicago Cubs and the Dodgers in Los Angeles on April 25, 1976. Monday, then a Cub, was in shallow left field when two men raced onto the diamond. "One of them had an American flag tucked under his arm," Monday told reporters later. "And the next thing I knew they were sprinkling the contents of a can on the flag. I realized they were going to burn it, so I took off. They couldn't see me coming from behind, but I could see one had lighted a match. The wind blew out the flame, and as he lighted another one I grabbed it." Monday deposited the rescued flag in the Dodger bullpen, and the crowd gave him a standing ovation. He walked back to center field, and 25,000 fans sang "God Bless America."

The Flag Code mentions nothing about cleaning a flag. Neither dry cleaning methods nor flag materials were much advanced at the time of the code writing. Today, however, cleaning is commonly accepted — careful cleaning, to insure non-fading and no running colors.

Flags on public buildings, monuments, and the like actually wear out so quickly they seldom last to be cleaned. But privately owned flags, which would be quite expensive to replace every few months, must be cleaned periodically. (Sadly, much of the grime accumulation comes simply from poor storage practices and could be eliminated by using a flag storage box.) Since relatively few people display the flag daily because of the bother of putting it up and taking it down at specific times each day, a home flag will last a good while in most areas of the country. Exceptions are the heavy industry areas and mining areas where pollutants and dust fill the air daily.

Shortly after World War II the Public Buildings Administration undertook a research project to make the Star-Spangled Banner wave longer. The administration was then buying flags for over 1,500 buildings, at a cost of $15,000 a year.

The cotton and wool bunting flag then in use lasted just 27 days. In windy San Francisco at least one new flag had to be installed every day. When the first nylon flag was tested, the flying time increased to 76 days. Of course, the nylon cost was double, but the saving was still 22 days per flag, or 1,374 flag days per year on the 1,500 buildings.

Either nylon or cotton cam be washed or dry cleaned, though dry cleaning is less subject to accident. The National Institute of Dry Cleaning, in fact, cooperates with local dry cleaners and the American Legion to offer free flag cleaning if flag owners will promise to fly the stars and stripes on Flag Day, June 14. The Boy Scouts of America also help promote this idea with a "New Glory for Old Glory" program.

Some projects, however, are too big even for the Boy Scouts. A gigantic Old Glory, measuring 411 × 210 feet and weighing seven tons, was given a cleaning (after gathering dust in a Washington, D.C., warehouse for eight years) in time for a troop support rally in March 1991. Four hundred volunteers from the Wilson Sporting Goods Golf Ball factory in Humboldt, Tennessee, pitched in on the showering in the company parking lot.

Two fire department pumpers, six flatbed trucks, and two tankers filled with thousands of gallons of soapy water were required. The polyester flag was dried after being placed on huge rollers.

The flag's creator, Vermont marketing consultant Len Silverfine, claimed it was the world's largest flag (at that time). However, the 1991 *Guinness Book of World Records* stated China had that record, with a 413 × 275 foot flag.

Other enterprises have come up with their own solutions for keeping the stars and stripes bright. To cut down handling soilage and wear and tear on flags, especially those large 6 × 10 and 12 × 8 foot convention room flags that are displayed flat against the wall behind the speakers' podium or hung from the ceiling, Draper Shade and Screen Company of Spiceland, Indiana, has marketed a special mounting with cords and pulleys that will roll the flag down for display and roll it back up for storage and transport, rather like a rollup window blind.

The Draper Shade and Screen Co. marketed this flag on a roller, with pulleys that lower and raise it into the carrying tube. (Photo courtesy of the Draper Shade and Screen Co.)

The Ross-Atkins Stores in California solved the problem another way. They sell flags encased in see-through lucite. These, however, are limited in size. The idea was instituted for desktop displays.

The regulation concerning the destruction of worn-out flags should not pertain to flags of historical interest, of course. Nowhere does the code state that such exceptions are to be made, but perhaps a change to this effect should be considered by the President, who has the power to change the code. A change is necessary because localized museums across the country have already made their own historical exceptions, enshrining flags flown in local battles or carried by regiments of local citizens, without benefit of federal approval.

There are, in fact, people who work as professional flag restorers. Among them are Mrs. Josephine Roser of Fort Montgomery, New York, and Mrs. Eugene Klein of Sun City, California.

Mrs. Roser inherited her career from her parents, who had taken it over in 1943 from Mrs. Katherine Fowler Ritchey of Brooklyn. Mrs. Roser's father was a master tailor at the United States Military Academy when he heard about it, so he took it on at first as extra work, to fill in the slow spots in tailoring.

Mrs. Roser's children weren't interested in carrying on the family tradition, so she trained a sister-in-law. They went on to work for several state departments, as well as doing contract jobs for museums. In 14 years Mrs. Roser restored more than 350 flags and banners representing Rhode Island, Missouri, New Hampshire, South Carolina, Pennsylvania, New Jersey, Michigan, New York, and Maine. She worked 10- to 16-hour days, six days a week, and as long as 10 to 12 days on each restoration.

Mrs. Roser always used the netting method of restoration, in which the original flag is encased between layers of nylon netting. The three are painstakingly sewn together. The outward appearance of the old flags is not materially altered, and it is possible to display or store a flag restored this way. Carefully handled, it can even be safely carried in ceremonies.

Portions of some flags are so deteriorated they disintegrate to the touch. But Mrs. Roser developed a chemical that prevented the disintegration process. Basically, she placed nylon netting, pre-dyed to match the basic color of the flag, under and over the tattered material. Then she basted the layers together with a diagonal zigzag stitch, with special features and designs hand-stitched.

Mrs. Klein, the other so-called "modern-day Betsy Ross," whose husband was commander of Sun City's local American Legion Post, has done her work only locally and on a volunteer basis. For example, when the desert community suffers one of its occasional Santa Ana wind storms that rips up the flags flying over City Hall, schools, the post office, and other public buildings, she mends them.

Vandalism is another problem faced by flag flyers. It leads to solutions that are not always correct. For example, the Social Security office in Lewiston, Idaho, was flying the flag 24 hours per day. When someone complained, the director answered: "We decided to display the flag at our office in this manner because vandals persisted in cutting the rope used to raise and lower it. Therefore, the end of the rope was mounted higher on the pole, out of reach, and a light was installed to shine on the flag." Unfortunately, the flag wasn't all-weather. This solution poses a problem for half-mastings, too.

The Allied Flag Company of Cambridge, Massachusetts, came to the rescue of people with the problem in 1975. They invented a new flagpole that protected against flag theft and normal vandalism. Wire is used in place of rope for long halyard life, and an enclosed pulley at the top of the pole keeps the wire on track. The wire halyard is inside the aluminum pole, reached via a locked porthole near the bottom.

§177. Conduct during hoisting, lowering or passing of flag

During the ceremony of hoisting or lowering the flag or when the flag is passing in a parade or in review, all persons present except those in uniform should face the flag and stand at attention with the right hand over the heart. Those present in uniform should render the military salute. When not in uniform, men should remove their headdress with their right hand and hold it at the left shoulder, the hand being over the heart. Aliens should stand at attention. The salute to the flag in a moving column should be rendered at the moment the flag passes.

REFLECTIONS: Respect for the flag, service to the Nation, a deep sense of professionalism and pride in one's self are depicted in this photo of a Navyman saluting as the ensign is hoisted. Photo by PH2 Milt Putnam.

The question that often bothers people, at parades most especially, is not answered here. The last line is clear: Salute as the flag passes you. However, whereas early-day parades had only one American flag leading the whole thing off, today every marching unit has its own honor guard carrying the stars and stripes. The Orange Bowl or Rose Bowl parades on New Year's Day, for example, would have several dozen en route. So, the question: Does this mean everyone stands and salutes every time the flag passes?

A Navyman salutes at a flag-raising ceremony, which is mirrored in his glasses. (Photo by PH2 Milt Putnam, from *All Hands* magazine.)

That seems to be what the regulations say. But this practice would soon drive everyone to distraction along the parade route. There would be one continual wave-like motion along ten miles of roadway. So common sense dictates the salute at attention is rendered only for the first honor guard to pass. Thereafter only common courtesy need be noted, i.e., quiet attention at each passing.

It is probably to be expected, but it is a sad commentary nonetheless that Armed Forces bases, shipyards, and other areas where the rendering of the colors in the mornings and evenings should receive the most respectful attention seem instead to be the most lax. Rules are enforced for the military, of course, but civilian workers, for the most part, seem either to duck under cover to avoid coming to attention for the 8 A.M. flag-raising, or to blithely ignore the ceremony. (A solution could be dawn-to-dusk flag display.)

Part of this is undoubtedly because workers still abroad at that time are either late or about to be late for work. Another part of it is that nearly everyone shortcuts routine eventually. Still another part is "monkey see, monkey do." Doing things the easy, the careless way, especially if a lot of others are also doing it, is catching.

None of this, of course, excuses such lax and unpatriotic behavior. It just explains some of it: human nature.

Incidentally, the Flag Code makes no differentiation in flag etiquette for Americans in the United States or abroad. An American citizen defiling the flag while in another country could be held liable for his actions just as if the action had taken place in the United States. The arrest might have to await his or her return to the homeland, however, depending upon the feelings of the government in the country where the acts occurred.

This particular problem has not arisen yet, not because there have not been such acts perpetuated by Americans overseas, but because the United States government has not made an issue of any such acts.

Mostly such desecration of the American flag has been on the part of foreign nationals, which is another matter entirely. The United States government can file official protests over such actions to the government(s) involved, and has. The usual result is an apology via the offending country's ambassador.

Special cases take special solutions. During the track and field competition of the 1972 Olympics, held in Germany, two black Americans mounted the winners' stand and raised clenched fists as the American anthem was played to honor their victories. They were barred from Olympic competition for life. Explaining this action, the American Athletic Union and the Olympic Committee stated that they did not want any country's flag or anthem, or the Olympics themselves, to become a political tool.

A lot of people, however, think it is hypocritical to say that. They think the Olympic Games have already become too political to change.

4

Anthem and Pledge

(United States Code Title 36, Ch. 10, secs. 170–172)

§170. National anthem; Star-Spangled Banner

The composition consisting of the words and music known as The Star-Spangled Banner is designated the national anthem of the United States of America.

There are many misconceptions surrounding "The Star-Spangled Banner," including when it was written and what its title was originally. Fortunately, not everyone is as confused as the CBS-TV announcer who twice referred to the national anthem as "America, the Beautiful" in introducing Charley Pride to sing it at the Super Bowl VIII football game on January 1, 1974. Pride, of course, correctly sang "The Star-Spangled Banner."

Francis Scott Key, a lawyer who charged Richard Lawrence in the Andrew Jackson assassination attempt and who was three times appointed a United States district attorney, wrote the words to the anthem, but he did not name his song "The Star-Spangled Banner." The fact is, he didn't even write a song. He wrote a poem. And it was called "Defence of Fort McHenry" (or, as it was later published, "Bombardment of Fort McHenry").

It went like this:

Oh, say can you see by the dawn's early light
   What so proudly we hailed at the twilight's last gleaming?
Whose broad stripes and bright stars, thru the perilous fight,
   O'er the ramparts we watched were so gallantly streaming?
And the rocket's red glare, the bombs bursting in air,
   Gave proof through the night that our flag was still there.
Oh, say does that star-spangled banner yet wave
   O'er the land of the free and the home of the brave?

Oh the shore, dimly seen through the mists of the deep,
   Where the foe's haughty host in dread silence reposes,
What is that which the breeze, o'er the towering steep,

As it fitfully blows, now conceals, now discloses?
Now it catches the gleam of the morning's first beam,
    In full glory reflected now shines on the stream:
'Tis the star-spangled banner! O long may it wave
    O'er the land of the free and the home of the brave!

And where is that band who so vauntingly swore
    That the havoc of war and the battle's confusion,
A home and a country should leave us no more!
    Their blood has washed out their foul footsteps' pollution.
No refuge could save the hireling and slave
    From the terror of flight, or the gloom of the grave:
And the star-spangled banner in triumph doth wave
    O'er the land of the free and the home of the brave!

Oh! thus be it ever, when freemen shall stand
    Between their loved homes and the war's desolation!
Blest with victory and peace, may the heav'n rescued land
    Praise the Power that hath made and preserved us a nation.
Then conquer we must, when our cause it is just,
    And this be our motto: "In God is our trust."
And the star-spangled banner in triumph shall wave
    O'er the land of the free and the home of the brave!

Francis Scott Key. (National Archives illustration.)

Many people think that this poem, set to the now-familiar music, was adopted immediately as the national anthem of the United States. Actually it wasn't established as such by congressional decree until 1931—117 years after it was written—even though President Woodrow Wilson had, in 1916, ordered it played as the national anthem by the military services. (By the time of the anthem's official recognition, the flag wasn't even the same one Key had written about. That flag had 15 stripes and stars.)

It is common schoolbook knowledge that lawyer Key jotted down the first stanza of his poem on the back of an envelope while aboard a boat held by the British fleet as it attacked Fort McHenry and Baltimore. He had gone, as an official emissary, seeking Admiral Cockrane of the British fleet, to obtain the release of a friend, Dr. William Beanes, who was held prisoner. The release was secured before the bombardment started, but by then both Key and Beanes knew that the fleet was sailing to attack Baltimore, so the admiral had to put them in protective custody to prevent his plans being leaked to the Americans. The night when Key wrote the first part of the anthem was September 13, 1814.

On September 5 Key departed Baltimore Harbor aboard a Chesapeake Bay sloop, a one-time Norfolk packet owned by the brothers Benjamin and John Ferguson, who had leased it to the government for use as a cartel or flag-of-truce vessel. Exhaustive research has failed to reveal its name, though it probably

was the *President* and not the *Minden*, as many writers have suggested. Key transferred to the *Surprise*, which took the cartel in tow. Before the battle Key moved back aboard the cartel. He wrote the remaining three stanzas of his poem the next day, during his return to Baltimore, and the entire poem was revised that night while he was staying at the Fountain Inn (now the site of the Southern Hotel).

The feelings that

Shown here are three photos of Fort McHenry today. The historic flagpole — which isn't the original — stands in the inner courtyard. (Photos by Bob Loeffelbein.)

inspired the poem are best described in Key's own words, from a speech he delivered years later before a hometown audience in Frederick, Maryland (he was born at Double Pine Creek, Frederick County, August 9, 1780):

> I saw the flag of my country waving over a city — the strength and pride of my native State — a city devoted to plunder and desolation by its assailants. I witnessed the preparation for its assaults, and I saw the array of its enemies as they advanced to the attack. I heard the sound of battle; the noise of the conflict fell upon my listening ear, and told me that the brave and the free had met the invaders.

In the same speech he described how his tense emotions were suddenly released at the sight of the American flag still waving defiantly over the fort at dawn on September 14.

Key showed his verses, when completed, to his wife's brother-in-law, Judge Joseph H. Nicholson of Baltimore, who was so moved that he had the poem printed on handbills and distributed throughout the city, under the title "Defence of Fort McHenry." Two of these are known to survive today, along with two handwritten copies by Key, one in the Library of Congress, the other with the Pennsylvania Historical Society.

The first dated publication, under that same title, was September 20, when the poem was reprinted in the *Baltimore Patriot* newspaper. It was shortly thereafter that the title was changed to "The Star-Spangled Banner."

Today the memory of Francis Scott Key is honored by the Francis Scott Key Park and Star-Spangled Banner Monument, dedicated September 14, 1993 (for the 150th anniversary of Key's death). The park and monument are located next to Washington's Key Bridge, near the site of Key's Georgetown home.

Designed by noted landscape architect James van Sweden as an impressive combination of sculpture, architecture, and landscaping, the park features as

This back-lighted display in the Fort McHenry Museum presents the first stanza of "The Star-Spangled Banner" in Francis Scott Key's own handwriting. (Photo by Bob Loeffelbein.)

its symbolic centerpiece a wisteria-covered circular arbor showcasing views of the Potomac River and other Washington historical landmarks. A lighted replica of the 15-star, 15-stripe flag that inspired Key's verses flies from a 60-foot flag-pole at the heart of the site 24 hours each day. A bronze bust of Key by sculptor Betty Mailhouse Dunston graces the site, along with various displays to inform visitors of Key's life and times.

The Francis Scott Key Foundation, which has made this park a reality, was formed in 1983, with the purpose of fostering greater public awareness of Francis Scott Key's life and values. Its future goals are threefold:

(1) To expand the Star-Spangled Banner Monument by establishing a museum and home for the Honor America! Roll, a voluntary registration of people pledging to follow Key's example and get involved in their home communities;

(2) To work with community and national organizations to redefine and restore the historic Georgetown waterfront to create an inspiring gateway to the nation's capital; and

(3) To develop and support educational programs promoting Francis Scott Key's legacy of civic responsibility, community involvement, and appreciation of national heritage. Plans include a Flag Day poetry contest, photographic exhibits, and awards honoring persons who serve their communities in some outstanding manner.

There have been other memorials to Key and his poem. For a short time, a marker called "The Star-Spangled Buoy" marked the exact spot where Key wrote the first verse of the anthem. This buoy was a tall nun type, painted with 16 alternate red and white stripes, vertically, topped with a blue field and 15 white stars. It was moored in Baltimore Harbor September 5, 1914, but was removed November 2, 1914, because it was labeled a navigational hazard.

The actual flag which flew over the fort during the British attack, repaired by expert seamstresses, is now in the Smithsonian Institution in Washington, D.C. It is large, 42 feet long by 30 feet wide—140 square yards of red, white, and blue. It was made to order for Fort McHenry. The flagmaker, Mary Pickersgill, and her 14-year-old daughter worked on their hands and knees stitching together the banner on the malthouse floor of Claggett's Brewery.

The Pickersgill home, in Baltimore, is now a national monument and museum under the management of the Department of the Interior, called the Flag House. It was built in 1793, and Pickersgill lived in it from 1807 until her death in 1857.

KEY'S POEM SET TO MUSIC

Papers of a music publisher named Thomas Carr in Baltimore have established him as the first to release the words and music to "The Star-Spangled

Banner" under that title, in 1814. A Baltimore actor named Ferdinand Durang is said to have been the first to sing it in public, though a conflict appears to this claim. Everyone is in accord that the first public singing was Wednesday, October 19, 1814, at a theater on Holliday Street in Baltimore. It was announced on the playbill of the Warren and Wood Company production "Count Benyowsky" that the "new patriotic song" would be rendered by "Mr. Hardinge" following the evening's play. On the playbill, both Mr. Hardinge and F. Durang are listed in the cast. Hardinge's name, however, is crossed out and another name inserted, apparently by the playgoer. This has led to speculation that Hardinge was ill that night and was replaced by a substitute for both the play and the featured song spot. However, his name was *not* crossed out on this same playbill in the song spot, so it is equally likely he was only replaced in the play.

For years the tune was credited to Britain's John Stafford Smith, in effect making an Englishman the co-writer of the American anthem. Smith was born in 1750 and spent his life in London as a composer, choir director, organist, and music scholar. His most remembered work was transcribing many old manuscripts into modern notation for Sir John Hawkins' *History of Music.* As late as 1940, in the fourth edition of Bakers' *Biographical Dictionary of Musicians,* it was stated: "The tune of his [Smith's] song 'Anacreon in Heaven' was used by Francis Scott Key for 'The Star-Spangled Banner.'" However, the fifth edition (1958) reports: "In his [Smith's] fifth collection of glees (1799), he published an arrangement of 'To Anacreon in Heaven' ... which led to his being mistakenly regarded as the composer of the tune, though actual origin is unknown."

Smith's credit for the tune of "The Star-Spangled Banner" may die hard, since so many old sources used by scholars list him as the tunesmith. One collector's item, a rare single-faced 78 rpm record of "The Star-Spangled Banner," bears a label reading, "Composed by J.S. Smith," with no mention of Key at all. Many older published editions of the song report, "Music by John Stafford Smith."

Anyone who wants to make up his or her own mind is referred to the scholarly writings of Oscar Sonneck and Richard S. Hill. According to Hill, a musicologist at the Library of Congress, the tune "To Anacreon in Heaven" was sung to at least 100 different sets of words in this country, most of them patriotic. It was originally composed shortly after 1770 for the Anacreontic Society of London, a musical and social group, with words by Ralph Tomlinson, as a tribute to one of the legendary imbibers of all time, the Greek poet Anacreon (pronounced Uh-NACK-ree-on). Anacreon was born around 1560 B.C. and died at about age 85 (from choking on a grape, by one account) and was noted for his light-hearted verses celebrating wine and love. None of his poems survive, though a number of later imitations do. One by William Oldys (1606–1761) goes:

Busy, curious, thirsty fly,
Drink with me, and drink as I;
Freely welcome to my cup,
Couldst thou sip and sip it up.
Make the most of life you may;
Life is short, and wears away.

"To Anacreon in Heaven" became popular in England, and with different drinking-song words, the tune also caught on in Ireland. Then it came to America, where, as Richard Hill has noted, it was widely adapted. One of the earliest of these adaptations was the Boston patriotic song "Adams and Liberty" by Thomas Paine in 1797. Others were "Jefferson and Liberty," "The Battle of the Wabash," and "When Death's Gloomy Angel Was Bending His Bow," which commemorated George Washington's death. Some of these were known to Key, so it is quite possible he had the tune in mind when he wrote his stirring verses.

The new version of the tune became popular immediately, but its acceptance by all Americans as their anthem was an uphill struggle. It was widely printed, in *The National Songster*, *The American Muse*, and the *Analectic Magazine*, though Key's name was often omitted, with a credit line reading simply, "A new song by a gentleman of Maryland." It was 1850 before it appeared in most songbooks for school use, but by 1861 "The Star-Spangled Banner" had become one of the top national songs.

Wars did as much to increase its popularity as anything. During the Civil War both sides claimed it. It was, in fact, played at Fort Sumter, where the first shot was fired, when the stars and stripes were lowered in surrender by the federal forces. Indignant at this act, Oliver Wendell Holmes penned a fifth stanza that appeared in songbooks published in the North.

Before becoming the official anthem, "The Star-Spangled Banner" was played at Manila Bay after Dewey defeated the Spanish there, and in Hawaii when it was annexed as a territory. The Navy Department finally adopted it in 1889 as the official tune for the ceremony of Colors. In 1904 Secretary of War Moody ordered it substituted for "Hail Columbia" by all armed forces.

The United States entrance into World War I at last inspired congressional action toward making "The Star-Spangled Banner" the national anthem. A resolution was introduced into the House of Representatives in 1913. Even so, it wasn't until six more were submitted by Maryland congressman Linthicum that the bill was passed.

Opposition had come from two fronts. The first was those people who preferred other songs, including "Hail Columbia," "Yankee Doodle," and "America the Beautiful." The second was those people who felt "The Star-Spangled Banner" was not suitable. Their arguments were that (1) it was hard for the average person to sing; (2) the peculiar meter made memorizing the words difficult; (3) it was a "borrowed" English tune; and (4) the national anthem shouldn't be coupled to a drinking song. There was even a national anthem writing contest sponsored by opponents to the bill in 1928. Forty-five hundred songs were submitted for the $3,000 prize, but no decision was ever reached.

Ultimately, the perseverance of Congressman Linthicum was rewarded. On March 3, 1931, an act of Congress made "The Star-Spangled Banner" the official national anthem of the United States.

It seems, however, that the opposition has never really given up, since periodically someone has tried to change our anthem ever since. The usual objection to "The Star-Spangled Banner" is that it is just too difficult for the average untrained voice to sing, covering a range of an octave and five tones. But other arguments have surfaced.

Westbrook Pegler, a nationally syndicated columnist of the 1950s and 1960s, sarcastically suggested substituting "The Maine Stein Song" with new lyrics. His argument was that if the American people want a barroom ditty for a national anthem, it should at least be a spirited one, not an eighteenth-century English dirge.

Particularly in the Vietnam era, antiwar factions pressured legislators to change the anthem because of its militaristic tone, with its "rocket's red glare," and "bombs bursting in air." Perhaps they forgot that it was the Americans who were attacked at Fort McHenry.

A syndicated columnist for the *Washington* [D.C.] *Star-News* added his vote to change "Key's off-key contribution" (April 1974), stating that, to his ear, "The Star-Spangled Banner" ranks behind only the Soviet Union's dirge-like anthem as world's worst, and perhaps Greece's, which has 158 verses to remember. On the other hand, a Roper Center for Public Opinion Research poll, sponsored by *U.S. News & World Report*–CNN in July 1986, found three of every four people (from 1,000 adults sampled) preferred to stick with "The Star-Spangled Banner" as the national anthem and not switch to "America the Beautiful."

What are the alternative suggestions? Usually the front runner has been "America the Beautiful," though ever since singer Kate Smith introduced Irving Berlin's "God Bless America" on Armistice Day of 1938, it too has had strong backing. Both *Parade* magazine and *The National Enquirer* have run unofficial polls on the question, "Should we change our national anthem?" *Parade* reported, from its August 1988 poll, that almost 400,000 readers responded, with 74,000 voting against any change, but 315,000 in favor of change. The change most endorsed was to "America the Beautiful," the choice also of Rep. Andrew Jacobs (D–IN), who had authored the accompanying article. The *Enquirer*'s poll of August 27, 1985, which reported Representative Jacobs' introduction of legislation to Congress that would replace the national anthem, reported 68 percent of respondents preferring "America the Beautiful" over "The Star-Spangled Banner," but never stated how many respondents there were.

The tune of "America the Beautiful" was written in 1882 by Samuel Augustus

Ward, but lyrics weren't penned until 11 years later by Katherine Lee Bates, a professor of English at Wellesley College in Massachusetts. Words and music were published together in 1895. Musical historian Sigmund Spaeth, in his authoritative book *A History of Popular Music in America*, described "America the Beautiful" as "a great and deservedly popular song, definitely superior in both words and music to 'The Star-Spangled Banner.'"

Many, however, argue against change. Steve John Manyak of Fredericksburg, Virginia, answered the *Enquirer* poll this way: "The Star-Spangled Banner has pride, can immediately be identified with the United States and fits with the identity of the flag. And, though many may not be able to sing along, the tune is very stirring, heartfelt and triumphal." An unidentified *Parade* respondent also pressed that last point: "Many *can* hit the high note, but, if they can't, so what? Not everyone is a mechanic. Not everyone can walk the high wire. And not everyone can sing!"

Even "Dear Abby" readers got in on the act eventually. One lady wrote that pollution, racial strife, and other social ills in America belie the noble words of "America the Beautiful." She ended by noting that "'The Star-Spangled Banner' may be more difficult to sing, but we should not consider changing it to 'America the Beautiful' until we clean up our act and live up to the words of the song."

Those who voted for "God Bless America" may have been thrilled with Kate Smith's rendition, but they should of course remember that it may not sound as good sung by just any old group of Americans.

The third most popular suggestion for switching would probably be Julia Ward Howe's "The Battle Hymn of the Republic" (one of Winston Churchill's favorite hymns, which he had sung at his funeral). The song was born during the Civil War, when the tune of "John Brown's Body" was coupled with Howe's poem ("Mine eyes have seen the glory of the Lord"). It doesn't have the stirring history of "The Star-Spangled Banner," but it has a simple tune and range of only one octave, so almost everyone can sing it.

The fourth choice might be "Columbia, the Gem of the Ocean" by Thomas A. Becket. *New York Times* writer Harold C. Schonberg suggests what he calls the "greatest piece of music ever written by an American," John Philip Sousa's "The Stars and Stripes Forever." Schonberg told the following tale in defense of his choice: When Eugene Ormandy and the Philadelphia Orchestra visited China in 1973, audiences in Beijing and Shanghai sat politely, but stonily, through programs that ranged from Beethoven through Copland. Not a flicker of enjoyment or understanding showed on their faces. The the orchestra played "The Stars and Stripes Forever" and, all of a sudden, faces broke into smiles, feet began tapping, and there was an electricity in the air. The story makes a good point.

Even Woody Guthrie's "This Land Is Your Land" has been suggested. It's a song he wrote as a Marxist response to "God Bless America."

In recent years, some rather unusual performances have somewhat debunked the claim that "The Star-Spangled Banner" is necessarily hard to sing. Rock groups and various singers have personally interpreted the anthem in non-traditional ways. One of the most moving renditions was Ethel Ennis's gospel version without backup music, presented at the end of the second Nixon inauguration on January 20, 1973.

The argument, of course, hasn't been one-sided against "The Star-Spangled Banner." Much has been written praising it. Butler University band director Bob Grechesky thinks all one has to do to be a convert is to listen to a really good rendition. He recommends a remarkable version written by Igor Stravinsky as a gesture of thanks to the United States for taking him in as a citizen. His arrangement is very elaborate, including both orchestra and chorus, with lots of unusual harmonics. Grechesky set Stravinsky's version up for a marching band and received rave notices.

Of course, Francis Scott Key did not compose the only poetic tribute to the United States flag. Among the earliest of praising writers was John Jay Daly. The poem he wrote in 1917 has appeared in 24 anthologies, been reprinted in newspapers and magazines across the country, and become, like Key's poem, a song. Titled "A Toast to the Flag," it was written to commemorate America's first Flag Day, a short time before Daly enlisted in the Army for World War I. After returning home he added the fourth verse and ultimately collaborated with Robert S. Taylor of Rileyville, Virginia, on copyrighting the poem as an unpublished song.

A Toast to the Flag*

Here's to the red of it —
There's not a thread of it,
No, nor a shred of it
In all the spread of it
   From foot to head,
But heroes bled for it,
Faced steel and lead for it,
Precious blood shed for it,
   Bathing it Red!

Here's to the white of it —
Thrilled by the sight of it,
Who knows the right of it
But feels the might of it
Through day and night?
Womanhood's care for it
Made manhood dare for it
Purity's prayer for it
   Keeps it so white!

*Courtesy of the author, John J. Daly.

Here's to the blue of it —
Beauteous view of it,
Heavenly hue of it,
Star-spangled dew of it
   Constant and true;
Diadems gleam for it,
States stand supreme for it,
Liberty's beam for it
   Brightens the blue!

Here's to the whole of it —
Stars, stripes and pole of it,
Body and soul of it,
O, and the roll of it,
   Sun shining through;
Hearts in accord for it,
Swear by the sword for it,
Thanking the Lord for it,
   Red White and Blue!

The famed stage entertainer George M. Cohan (1878–1942) wrote the words and music to another widely known patriotic song, "You're a Grand Old Flag." He wrote it in 1906 and introduced it himself in the musical *George Washington, Jr.* The words have been heard in subsequent productions such as the James Cagney movie *Yankee Doodle Dandy* and the stage version *George M.*, starring Joel Grey.

Other songs include "America" by Samuel Francis Smith, "The Flag of Our Union Forever" by George P. Morris, and "The Flag Song" by Harriet Prescott Spofford. Smith wrote "America" as a 24-year-old seminary student, and did it as a "serious parody" actually, putting words to the British anthem, "God Save the King." He titled it "My Country 'Tis of Thee."

Many other poems have become well known, at least in their time, without anyone ever thinking of putting them to music. Indeed, what is thought to be the first published reference to the flag came in poetic form, printed in the Boston newspaper *The Massachusetts Spy* on March 10, 1774:

A ray of bright glory now beams from afar,
Blest dawn of an empire to rise:

The American ensign now sparkles a star
which shall shortly flame wide through the skies.

Later poems were more detailed and elaborate, such as "The American Flag" by New Yorker Joseph Rodman Drake, written in 1819, just a year before his death:

THE AMERICAN FLAG

by Joseph Rodman Drake

I.

When Freedom from her mountain height,
  Unfurled her standard to the air,
She tore the azure robe of night,
  And set the stars of glory there.
She mingled with its gorgeous dyes
The milky baldric of the skies,
And striped its pure, celestial white
With streakings of the morning's light;
Then from her mansion in the sun
She called her eagle-bearer down,
And gave into his mighty hand
The symbol of her chosen land.

II.

Majestic monarch of the cloud!
  Who rear'st aloft thy eagle form
To hear the tempest trumpings loud,
And see the lightning lances driven,
  When stride the warriors of the storm,
And rolls the thunder-drum of Heaven!
Child of the Sun! to thee 'tis given
  To guard the banner of the free!
To hover in the sulphur smoke,
To ward away the battle stroke,
And bid its blendings shine afar,
Like rainbows on the cloud of war,
  The harbingers of victory.

III.

Flag of the brave! thy folds shall fly
The sign of hope and triumph high;
When speaks the trumpet's signal tone,
And the long line comes gleaming on,
Ere yet the life-blood, warm and wet,
Has dimmed the glistening bayonet,
Each soldier's eye shall brightly turn
To where thy sky-born glories burn;
And, as his springy steps advance,
Catch war and vengeance from the glance;
And when the cannon-mouthings loud
Heave in wild wreaths the battle shroud,
And gory sabers rise and fall,
Like shoots of flame on midnight's pall —
Then shall thy meteor glances glow,
  And cowering foes shall sink beneath

Each gallant arm that strikes below
That lovely messenger of death!

IV.

Flag of the seas! on Ocean's wave
Thy stars shall glitter o'er the brave;
When death, careering on the gale,
Sweeps darkly round the bellied sail,
And frighted waves rush wildly back,
Before the broadside's reeling rack,
Each dying wanderer of the sea
Shall look at once to Heaven and thee,
And smile to see thy splendors fly
In triumph o'er his closing eye.

V.

Flag of the free heart's hope and home!
  By angel's hands to valor given;
Thy stars have lit the welkin dome,
  And all thy hues were born in Heaven.
Forever float that standard sheet!
  Where breathes the foe but falls before us,
With Freedom's soil beneath our feet,
  And Freedom's banner streaming o'er us.

Other tributes include "Ye Sons of Columbia" by Robert Trent Paine, "The Stars and Stripes" by Lucretia G. Noble, and the following paean from 1862:

THE FLAG

by Geo. H. Boker

Spirits of patriots, hail in heaven again
  The flag for which ye fought and died,
Now that its field, washed clear of every stain,
  Floats out in honest pride!

Free blood flows through its scarlet veins once more,
  And brighter shine its silver bars;
A deeper blue God's ether never wore
  Amongst the golden stars.

See how our earthly constellation gleams;
  And backward, flash for flash, returns
Its heavenly sisters their immortal beams
  With light that fires and burns, —

That burns because a moving soul is there,
  A living force, a shaping will,
Whose law the fate-forecasting powers of air
  Acknowledge and fulfill.

At length the day, by prophets seen of old,
  Flames on the crimsoned battlefields;
Henceforth, O flag, no mortal bought and sold,
  Shall crouch beneath thy shade.

That shame has vanished in the darkened past,
  With all the wild chaotic wrongs
That held the struggling centuries shackled fast
  With fear's accursèd thongs.

Therefore, O patriot fathers, in your eyes
  I brandish thus our banner pure:
Watch o'er us, bless us, from your peaceful skies,
  And make the issue sure!

Some poems were known more because they were written by well-known persons. Julia Ward Howe, author of "Battle Hymn of the Republic," wrote a poem called simply "The Flag," not to be confused with another of the same name by Lucy Larcom. James Whitcomb Riley wrote one called "The Name of Old Glory" (1897). Henry Van Dyke wrote one titled "Who Follow the Flag" (longest of these with its seven long verses), and one-time chief justice Oliver Wendell Holmes wrote both "The Flower of Liberty" and "Union and Liberty," which starts with the wonderful line, "Flag of our heroes who left us their glory."

Patriotic poetry has continued over the years, though it has received less and less acclaim or attention.

Patriotic essays are likewise still making appearances in praise of the flag. One brief but moving piece by Marine master sergeant Percy Webb (1879–1945) was published in the first "Our Flag" booklet issued by the United States Marine Corps, which was first distributed at the Chicago World's Fair of 1933. The most recently published version — the reference to "fifty sovereign states" is of course an update from the original — reads as follows:

I am Old Glory

I am Old Glory: For more than nine score years I have been the banner of hope and freedom for generation after generation of Americans. Born amid the first flames of America's fight for freedom, I am the symbol of a country that has grown from a little group of thirteen colonies to a united nation of fifty sovereign states. Planted firmly on the high pinnacle of American Faith my gently fluttering folds have proved an inspiration to untold millions. Men have followed me into battle with unwavering courage. They have looked upon me as a symbol of national unity. They have prayed that they and their fellow citizens might continue to enjoy the life, liberty and pursuit of happiness, which have been granted to every American as the heritage of free men. So long as men love liberty more than life itself, so long as they treasure the priceless privileges bought with the blood of our forefathers; so long as the principles of truth, justice and charity for all remain deeply rooted in human hearts, I shall continue to be the enduring banner of the United States of America.

In a 1986 sermon television evangelist Robert Schuller spoke as the flag:

I Am the American Flag

I have lived long, traveled far, and I have something to say to my country today.

I have earned the right to speak. The price paid for my freedom of speech was paid by those buried in Flanders Field in France ... the outskirts of Manila in the Philippines ... and in many other places.

I fly proudly over their green graves at all of these places, praying that wars might end forever.

Yes, I've been torn, spit upon and defiled by some ... still I know of no other people who have been swifter to rescue beleaguered people the world over.

On our own shores, our people know freedom unsurpassed anywhere. There's freedom to each man, woman and child to choose his or her life's work.

Freedom to borrow and build, to buy and sell, to make an honest profit.

Freedom to worship or not to worship.

Freedom to speak, write, praise, question or criticize anyone, no matter how high his station or rank.

Freedom to try and succeed — and freedom to fail.

I see the harvest of my 50 states and I am proud. I see my best minds bringing forth drugs to destroy forever ancient plagues.

I see tools that handle any task — be it reaching the moon or penetrating the inside of a human heart.

Listen to the rustles of my stars and stripes as I cry out to every man and woman: Dream your dreams! Dare to believe! You can make it in America!

I am the flag of freedom. I live in the hearts of all men who yearn to laugh, to love, to pray, to play, to marry and have children. I say to my people: Be proud. Be humble. And be renewed.

Only two centuries ago my people were a motley group of foreigners. But somehow they managed to overcome prejudices, hostilities and differences to pull together. It was, I say, a miracle of God.

Hardly had they achieved nationhood when the land was torn by a ghastly Civil War — neighbor against neighbor, father against son.

But my country survived. Again war came, and depression and soup lines. Yet somehow a deep faith surged from the very depths of my country's soul — and America survived!

Then came another war, another and still another: four wars in just six decades of this century. Still America survived!

How? Why? What has kept this tough, young giant standing on her feet? Where did the courage come from? From where did the American endurance spring?

From her churches, her temples and her Bibles! The explanation for our strength can be found in the words of Jesus Christ, who said, "Whosoever hears the word of God and follows it, I will compare him unto a wise man, who built his house upon a rock.

"And the rain descended, the floods came, the winds blew, and beat upon that house; and it fell not; for it was founded upon a rock."

Yes, the high price of freedom is faith in God!

As I dream of the next 100 years, I see our unquenchable, indestructible, imperishable spirit of human freedom spreading to the uttermost parts of the world. We stand on the threshold of a new day, a new age.

Do you feel it?
Rise up and make your country great!*

Patriotic words are often stirring; so is patriotic music, at least when well performed. However, the music of the United States anthem, in addition to being hard for the untrained voice to sing, is difficult to play correctly. Partly for this reason, the Department of Defense has decreed that only official military bands — meaning those so designated by the authority in each service branch — may play the anthem at official functions. The reasoning is that the anthem, like the flag, should never be "desecrated" in any way. This would include accidental sour notes by amateur musicians or intentional off-key parodies by political dissidents. The actual and sensible reason, as stated in the Navy Public Affairs Manual, is that the orchestration for the anthem is precise, calling for a large number of instruments and professional skill in playing them. Not many amateur or even professional musical aggregations can conform to both instrumentation and skill.

A clear indication of the validity of this stand — which, of course, has no actual bearing on civilian play of the anthem, since the Department of Defense rules only the military — was the idea of having a lone guitarist play the anthem at the December 1972 professional football game between the Baltimore Colts and the Miami Dolphins. The anthem came across sounding weak and stumbling, and it was hard for fans to follow in their sing-along as well.

Also not bound by military regulations is informal, emergency playing, such as playing "The Star-Spangled Banner" during barroom brawls or street riots to get everyone to stop. It happens mostly in the movies, but such off-the-cuff miniconcerts have been authenticated in real-life dramas as well, several times in Madison Square Garden at boxing matches. However, it is impossible to determine whether the first movie version copied a real-life incident or real-life incident or real followed reel versions.

Deliberate misplaying of the anthem has not been the big problem flag desecration has. When it has occurred it has usually been incidental to a larger problem, such as happened near Bithlo, Florida, in March 1970. When a rock group known as Storm requested a permit to hold a rock festival on a dude ranch, county judges refused. The rock group proceeded anyway, and the opening number they played, apparently deliberately off-key, was "The Star-Spangled Banner," dedicated to "all the judges in Florida."

§171. Conduct during playing
During rendition of the national anthem when the flag is displayed, all present except those in uniform should stand at attention facing the flag with the right

---

hand over the heart. Men not in uniform should remove their headdress with their right hand and hold it at the left shoulder, the hand being over the heart. Persons in uniform should render the military salute at the first note of the anthem and retain this position until the last note. When the flag is not displayed, those present should face toward the music and act in the same manner they would if the flag were displayed there.

An obvious oversight here is that people in wheelchairs and some other disabled persons cannot stand for the anthem (or the Pledge of Allegiance, or the passing of the flag). Otherwise, the role for civilians is straightforward: Stand and place the right hand over the heart. Men wearing hats should remove them.

The various branches of the military have additional rules for their personnel. For example, military personnel in uniform — and this means entire uniform, including hat or cap — will salute during the anthem unless in a boat or vehicle. In a boat only the coxswain stands and salutes. Vehicles within sight or hearing pull over and stop, and persons riding sit at attention. Persons in charge of military vehicles, other than the driver, render the hand salute.

Originally service personnel were not allowed to wear civilian clothes, even when off duty. They were considered to be on duty (and thus on call) 24 hours per day. They were considered out of uniform if they were outdoors (except during athletic participation) or on duty indoors without hat or cap being worn.

With changing times, service personnel not in uniform now use the civilian salute; police and fire personnel often use the military salute; and servicewomen carry over the civilian women's role into military life and "forget" to uncover when indoors.

Indoors — for example, at a basketball game — military personnel in uniform but not on duty (which excepts ushers, military police, etc.) do not wear hats or caps. At such times they behave toward anthem and flag as civilians.

The next interesting part of armed forces regulations that differs from civilian is that service personnel in uniform do not salute the flag and sing "The Star-Spangled Banner" at the same time. Civilians do. This differentiation is not made in the Flag Code, but in the body of military regulations (PIO manual — Navy).

Another fine point of order, not generally considered, is that the civilian salute calls for the *hand* to cover the heart. If a male is wearing a hat, he removes it with his right hand usually and holds it *at shoulder level*, with his hand resting over the heart. Women civilians, by tradition, do not remove the headdress, but merely cover their hearts with their right hands.

Exceptions to the above procedures are practiced by some organizations. These have never been approved in the federal code, but they have grown from each organization's rules to become accepted practice.

Police personnel in uniform, for example, render the military salute

	INDOORS		OUTDOORS	
WHEN TO SALUTE	Civilian Attire	In Uniform	Civilian Attire	In Uniform
During playing of National Anthem	stand at attention	stand at attention; if under arms salute	salute (1) (2) (3) (4)	salute (1) (2) (4)
When Flag passes by in parade or review	stand at attention	stand at attention; if under arms salute	salute (3) (5)	salute (5)
During ceremony or hoisting or lowering Flag, or posting of colors	stand at attention (4)	stand at attention	salute (3) (4)	salute (4)
During recitation of Pledge of Allegiance	salute (3)	stand at attention	salute (3)	salute

(1) Flag, if visible, is faced and saluted; if not visible face toward source of music and salute; if music is recorded face front and salute.

(2) Salute is rendered at first note of music and held until last note.

(3) Proper form of salute when in civilian attire:
MEN – remove hats and hold at left shoulder with right hand, right hand over heart; without hats, place right hand, palm open, over heart.
WOMEN – place right hand, palm open, over heart.

(4) When in athletic clothing face flag or music, remove hats or caps and stand at attention; hand salute is not rendered.

(5) Salute is rendered when flag is 6 paces from viewer and held until it has passed 6 paces beyond.

NOTE: No salute is rendered indoors or outdoors during **playing or singing** of "America," or **singing** of the National Anthem ("The Star Spangled Banner").

without uncovering the head. This has, by practice, grown to include even private, commercial uniformed police forces patrolling condominium developments and handling security for industrial complexes. Their reasoning is that they are on duty and serving the public. However, they serve only a small segment of the people, not the country as a whole as do armed forces personnel. It would seem, under this thinking, that this practice is belittling the flag somewhat. When many exceptions are made, you no longer have a rule. Because the organization adopts the military code does not change the Flag Code for that organization. The federal code takes precedence always.

Already some fire departments have adopted the military code, and I have had one uniformed doorman at a large hotel in San Francisco tell me he also used the military code. He thought that anyone in uniform followed it, since the code states, "those in uniform," without elaboration. It's just another illustration of how badly the code needs rewriting.

Not many people outside the Shriners organization realize that their internal code requires the "uniformed" Shriner to also render the military salute, without removal of his fez. Given some of the gaudy, circus-atmosphere uniforms the Shriners affect, it becomes apparent that the federal code has been badly bent.

Other parts of this section need rewriting as badly. The code states that a person is to stand and face toward the music if no flag is displayed during the rendering of the anthem. No qualifications or exceptions are given. Yet a host of happenstances are left without solution.

Take, for instance, one Flag Day in the Houston Astrodome. As the crowd for the evening's baseball game settled into its seats, a squad of 13 men from a patriotic organization marched onto the field and formed a semicircle around home plate. Each carried a form of the American flag as it has progressed through history. Each of the 13 men stepped forward in turn and recited a short speech about the flag he carried and its significance. After each speech, the national anthem was played. The crowd came to its feet 13 times in the traditional observance of the song. It was helpless even to vent its frustration. How can you boo the national anthem?

Then there is the problem of home observance. What does an informal group in the parlor do upon hearing the national anthem played over the radio or on a late-night television sign-off? According to etiquette expert Amy Vanderbilt, "The hearing of the national anthem at home over radio or television does not require the rising of those present if they are gathered informally in a small group." This is logical, but it doesn't change the code. It is merely Ms. Vanderbilt's opinion.

Opposite: The Rotary Club provides this summary of flag-salute etiquette, including the provisions of the United States Flag Code, sections 171 and 177. (Courtesy of the Colorado Springs Rotary Club.)

Besides, what if they are gathered at a home for a formal ball? Especially at a costume ball, with many guests *in uniforms* of one sort or another from various periods in history? Do they come to attention, salute, or ignore the playing of the anthem because they are in a home in a more or less informal setting?

During World War II, when musical groups were hard to procure for social affairs, jukeboxes were often pressed into use. Since it was a patriotic time, the anthem was often included in the selections for opening activities. Was it correct for the assemblage, as the code states, to face the music at attention? Or would it be too incongruous for a group like this to come to attention and face the gaudy, flickering automated player, looking like savages paying homage to an idol? As the code reads, of course, the assemblage faces the music no matter if it's the Ritz Brothers playing the anthem on combs and tissue paper. The code obviously needs clarification and updating in this area also. When it was written, television was not such a part of our lives, with its own chapel area in nearly every home.

One issue the Flag Code leaves to personal preference is whether to sing along when the anthem is played. There is no legislation requiring people to sing. On the other hand, there has actually been one attempt to legislate *against* singing. In 1988, Sara Sprague, a high school senior in North Kingstown, Rhode Island, and a member of the school choir, began humming along when the anthem was played over the school's intercom. Katherine Janis, her teacher, reprimanded her. The next day Sara sang along with the anthem, and found herself in the principal's office and ultimately banished from school for three weeks. She said her humming and singing were a "spontaneous reaction to the music." "It's not a question of patriotism, it's a question of who's in charge," retorted Principal Paul Rennick.

The issue went public when Sara wrote a letter to a local newspaper in protest, and her mother, Jane Sprague, backed her. "It's hard for me to believe that a school supported by local, state and federal taxes won't let students sing the national anthem if they want to," she said.

SPORTS EVENTS AND THE ANTHEM

A "rhubarb," in sports parlance, is a big disagreement. And that's what exists concerning the anthem being played at sports contests. No federal or state regulations or laws govern the practice.

In 1916, so the story goes, President Woodrow Wilson stated that "The Star-Spangled Banner" was his favorite song, and it began to be played at sporting events. It made its major league debut at the opening game of the 1918 World Series. When the fans stood for the seventh inning stretch, the band played the anthem. No one seems to have asked why. However, the crowd stood at attention during the rendition and applauded wholeheartedly afterward. Players, including Babe Ruth, stood at attention, too, and a serviceman (there was a war on, remember) stood in center field saluting the flag. The anthem was repeated at the next two games, and when the series shifted to Boston, the anthem was played before each game. Since that time it has become the accepted thing to do at a ball game, any ball game. So, if anyone can be credited with this tradition, it would be Harry Frazee, the Broadway producer and owner of the Boston Red Sox (though he will probably be more remembered — and forever vilified in Boston — for selling the Babe to the Yankees).

The tradition continued through World War II as a patriotic gesture by the home front folks (and professional baseball officials perhaps self-conscious about continuing sports as usual during wartime) and has continued to the present, until now it seems to be an unbreakable tradition, however badly it needs breaking.

A prime example of the unexpected things that can happen was the national media story when the NBA's Denver Nuggets' star guard Mahmoud Abdul-Rauf, who adopted the Islamic faith in 1991, refused to stand for a pre-game playing of the anthem. He said he meant no disrespect to the flag, but his religious principles were more important than his job. He feels "The Star-Spangled Banner" is a symbol of tyranny and oppression, and contends the Koran forbids nationalistic ritualism. He thus violated a league rule that requires players, coaches and trainers to "stand and line up in a dignified posture" during the playing of the American and or Canadian anthems.

The NBA suspended him, without pay ($31,707 per game), and he received mailed death threats, so that extra security guards were hired to protect him, even after the situation was settled. The NBA lifted its suspension when he agreed to stand during the anthem, while also honoring his faith with silent prayer.

The question that needs asking is, "What is patriotic about a sports event (other than international competition, of course)?" And the follow-up question is, "How many people at a sports contest actually pay their respects to the flag and anthem during this traditional ceremony?" Look around next time. Mostly people are still looking for their seats, loading up on peanuts and beer, greeting their neighbors, or waiting in line at the john.

Eminent sportswriter Jim Murray stated his objections to the tradition thus:

> It [the anthem] has a range harder to cross than Texas and is just as windy and dull in stretches. It can be musically scaled successfully only by Yma Sumac, Tarzan of the Apes, a mountain goat or two and a cat with his tail caught in the door — none of whom can be counted on to open a World Series.
>
> It's lyrics have been muffed by Nat [King] Cole, Robert Goulet, Lauritz Melchoir and every schoolboy in memory. There are more people who know Einstein's theory than know the second and third verses. The fourth verse could be used for a sobriety test. I have seen eye charts that make better sense.

Part of the problem, however, may be that promoters, in the search for novelty and a way to grab the spectators' attention, have wandered too far afield in selecting their anthem purveyors. "Pat" Morita, the diminutive Asian-American actor from the *Karate Kid* movies, for example, sang it to start the PSN-TV fights (January 26, 1990). He really shouldn't have!

Another evening, in June 1991, Irish Jerry Quarry, the one-time heavy-weight boxing contender, sang a very quaveringly bad anthem before the Prime Sports Network's fight night audience, and still another evening fight fans were subjected to a jazz version of the anthem on solo violin. Then, before a pro bas-ketball game (1990) a werewolf sang the anthem (actually, of course, an actor in costume from the play *Curse of the Werewolf*).

Cal Cardieri, father of head basketball coach Ed Cardieri of the University of South Florida, played the anthem on his harmonica before a game against defending national champion Miami (March 1986). James Carter whistled the anthem before a World Boxing Association heavyweight championship fight between Michael Dokes and Jorge Dascola (February 1990). And who will ever be able to forget television comedienne Roseanne Barr's execrable rendition prior to a National League doubleheader between the San Diego Padres and Cincinnati Reds (August 27, 1990)? The home team Padres issued an apology to the public the next day, after more than 2,000 phone calls flooded the switch-board by midday.

Washington state Senator Al Bauer, in February 1986, introduced a bill into the state legislature that would have made it a crime to "jazz up" the national anthem. The bill died, and it seems that ever since, various musicians have been vying to put their special stamp — whether country, rock-and-roll, gospel, blues, jazz, or indescribable — on the anthem. But perhaps that is only bad when the rendition and performer is bad. The melody and rhythm of the anthem are not so sacred that a singer can't put his or her stylistic imprint on them. After all, a good many gospel singers have infused a higher level of energy into traditional hymns without any fear of reprisals from God, according to Keith Johnson of Clarkton, Washington.

Besides, changes might make the anthem work better. An Army morale officer and a Pennsylvania State University music professor combined forces to produce a streamlined arrangement in the key of A flat. It's "easily singable." Maybe this is the solution the rabble rousers are looking for.

As for the propriety of playing the national anthem before sporting events, the players' viewpoints should also be considered. One waggish professional footballer commented, "When was the last time they played the national anthem before *you* went to work?"

Fred Williamson, a former cornerback for the Kansas City Chiefs who became a successful movie actor, put the thoughts of many athletes into per-spective when he related his irritation at the pre-game ceremony. "We go out on the field all charged up, then some announcer says, 'Please stand for the national anthem.' Here I am, my heart beating in my head, and I have to turn everything off and stand quietly at attention. By the time it's over, I'm empty and I have to find some way of pumping myself up again."

Professional baseball players must go through this trauma 160 to 170 times per season. Willie Mays, in his 22-year career, probably stood for over 3,900 anthem playings, which would add up to about eight and a half days.

Mitch Webster, an outfielder who played in the major leagues for the Toronto Blue Jays and Montreal Expos before being traded to the Chicago Cubs, had a comment that brought up a further problem. "It'll be great not to have to listen to *two* national anthems," he said.

Both singers and fans may feel the same way. New York Yankee fans, before the first of three crucial Yankee–Blue Jays games, booed the Canadian national anthem. Then, before the third game, American singer Mary O'Dowd began the United States anthem, but forgot the words, returned to the dugout for a copy, and went back to the microphone to begin again. This time she forgot the tune. In fairness to Yankee fans, they booed her, too.

Even stranger things happen further afield. In Athens, 10,000 soccer fans, awaiting the start of an exhibition match between Greek and Chinese all-star teams, rose and stood in respectful silence for what they took to be the Chinese national anthem coming from the faulty loudspeakers. The Chinese team, observing all those standing Greeks, also came to polite attention, assuming the Greek anthem was being played. Then a lilting voice rose above the unfamiliar music, extolling the virtues of a brand of toothpaste.

Some players have discussed the problem among themselves. They wonder why they can't just stay off the field — remain in the clubhouse, for example — until after the anthem. Most agree that their sports careers would probably be ended the first time a reporter learned they were boycotting the anthem.

The buck has been passed back and forth in deciding who is responsible for the settling-in of this tradition. The promoters say the fans insist upon it; the fans say the promoters use it to cloak their cash registers in civic righteousness. Both have arguable points. But it was true that the reason listeners didn't hear the anthem on ABC-TV's Monday Night professional football sportscasts was that the network was selling that time instead to sponsors at $50,000 per half-minute. One November 1975 anthem-length spot allowed them two commercials and a National Football League promotional announcement. The promo was for an essay contest: "The NFL's Role in American history."

Philadelphia Phillies manager John Felske recalled that once, after a two-hour rain delay at Chicago's Comiskey Park, a game was begun without the anthem. A White Sox pitcher threw his first pitch. Then he had to stop, because fans in right field were singing anyway. The game was held up until they finished.

Strange things occur because of the playing of "The Star-Spangled

Banner." People who haven't had a patriotic thought all week suddenly become righteously indignant at someone disagreeing with the norm. At New York's Shea Stadium, for example, when a group of shaggy-haired young people refused to stand for the anthem as a protest against United States intervention in Vietnam, they were beaten up by neighboring spectators.

In Skokie, Illinois, Forrest Byram, then a 17-year-old high school football player, protested the Vietnam war by refusing to remove his helmet during the anthem. The coach fired him from the team. The school's principal ordered his reinstatement, and the entire coaching staff quit. Byram then quit the team voluntarily and joined the band. "Now," he said, "the anthem is just another piece of music...."

At West Virginia University, Philip Mack, a black cheerleader, showed his feelings about racism in the United States by standing with a clenched fist upraised in a black-power salute during the anthem. When he was told to cease, he quit the squad, and a female black cheerleader quit in sympathy.

The Eastern Michigan University mile relay team, composed of Eugene Thomas, Willie Sims, Stanley Vinson, and Michael Shepherd, was disqualified from the Knights of Columbus track meet in Uniondale, New York, in January 1973 for continuing warmup exercises during the anthem, so they wouldn't stiffen up. When the crowd began to jeer and show their displeasure, the athletes agitated them further by jogging around the track with clenched fists upraised in the black power salute. All the officials threatened to walk out if they weren't disqualified.

In an attempt to short-circuit other such racial demonstrations, Roy Wilkins, executive director of the NAACP, wrote a directive to member groups: "There is no national anthem for Negroes. There is only one National Anthem. It is for all Americans."

To the credit of promoters, they have tried eliminating the anthem from sporting events. In June 1972, under the reasoning that it was tradition only, and tradition, when exhausted, should be changed, the Kansas City Royals dropped the playing of the anthem from home baseball games except for Sundays, holidays, and "special occasions." The policy was changed after only two games because 200 indignant complaints poured in.

Likewise, the anthem was to be dropped from the February 16, 1973, Olympic Invitational Track Meet in New York's Madison Square Garden. The decision was based, according to meet director Jesse Abramson, "on the fact that if so many people are not really paying attention, why put the anthem on the spot?" Referring to the earlier problem with the Eastern Michigan foursome, he continued, "Obviously, another consideration was the avoidance of possible protest demonstrations." Madison Square Garden officials reversed Abramson's ruling, however. Then Thomas J. Cuit, majority leader of the New York city council, introduced a bill to make the playing of the anthem mandatory before every sporting event open to the public where admission is charged.

The Baltimore Orioles once stopped playing the anthem for a week (1954). Baltimore, of course, is where the anthem was born. The team's general manager at that time was Arthur Ehlers, a former American Legion commander and World War I veteran. He said, "The frequent repetition of the anthem at sports events tends to cheapen the song and lessen the thrill of response. I remember the old days of vaudeville when the management would bring out the flag to strengthen a weak act. I want the Banner played only on holidays and special occasions, such as Memorial Day."

Baltimorans were outraged. The city council passed a resolution that the song be played before every Baltimore home game. And it has been.

Controversy continues. The point which seems forgotten is that a person can be patriotic and still object to the playing of the anthem at insignificant events. Patriotism, like religion, is found in the heart, not in the adherence to rituals and symbols, especially made-up rituals that have nothing to do with the federal Flag Code.

The association of anthems with sports doesn't even have universal acceptance. In France "La Marseillaise" is never played at sporting events. "God Save the Queen" is played in Britain only after national and international soccer and rugby matches. Even in baseball fanatic Japan, only the Toei Tigers play the national anthem before home games.

The logical solution for American promoters — if they must continue the tradition — would be to start playing the anthem *after* games. This would have practical advantages. It might allow police time to protect players from overzealous fans, keep playing fields and goal standards from being demolished or vandalized, and cool riotous behavior of fans, which is becoming increasingly dangerous to everyone. But, of course, how long would it be before anthem post-play was being ignored just as much as it is now in pre-play? Police would be moving into position, players would be running for the locker room, fans would be racing to beat the traffic, etc.

But there are solutions. Promoters of athletic events should consider flying the stars and stripes as codified, up at sunrise (or 8 A.M., as in the military) to the highest point in the stadium. (Remember, it is contrary to the Flag Code to raise the national standard in the middle of the day, a point that seems to have been forgotten entirely in this controversy.) Then, instead of playing "The Star-Spangled Banner" to start the contest, render "America the Beautiful" or the official state song, or even a spirited rendition of "Take Me Out to the Ball Game," and raise the state flag, or even a special team franchise pennant, on the scoreboard or at some other vantage point, keeping it below the height at which the stars and stripes is displayed.

§172. Pledge of allegiance to flag; manner of delivery

The Pledge of Allegiance to the Flag, "I pledge allegiance to the Flag of the United States of America, and to the Republic for which it stands, one Nation under

God, indivisible, with liberty and justice for all.", should be rendered by standing at attention facing the flag with the right hand over the heart. When not in uniform men should remove their headdress with their right hand and hold it at the left shoulder, the hand being over the heart. Persons in uniform should remain silent, face the flag, and render the military salute.

Earlier generations sometimes learned in school or in scouting programs to begin the pledge with the right hand over the heart, then to extend the hand, palm upward toward the flag on the phrase "to the flag." This procedure was written into the very first version of the Flag Code (June 1942) but was removed from the code by amendment passed only six months later.

The code originally did not even mention facing the flag when rendering the pledge. This requirement was not added in writing until the amendments of 1976. Prior to that time, however, it was always simply understood, as demonstrated by a true story from a Newport Beach, California, civic club luncheon.

The president of the club rose for the traditional Pledge of Allegiance to find no flag. He apologized and announced the pledge would be given anyhow if everyone would just face the corner where the flag usually stood. This was followed by a local minister standing to give the invocation. With a smile, he said, "I am happy to report that God is where He is supposed to be today, so let us pray."

Another unusual pledging ceremony took place in Huntsville, Alabama. Someone neglected to set up the flag before a meeting of the Toastmasters club, so when the meeting was called to order, members thought the Pledge of Allegiance could not be carried out. But one member, rising to the occasion, rummaged in her purse and came up with a 29-cent postage stamp picturing the flag. They stuck it on the wall and directed the pledge to it.

For years a controversy brewed over whether the Pledge of Allegiance was authored by Francis Bellamy or James B. Upham, editor of *Youth's Companion Magazine,* for whom Bellamy worked. It first appeared in the September 8, 1892, issue.

Bellamy claimed authorship as early as 1930, the year before he died in Tampa, Florida. According to a speech he gave:

> It has been repeated by generations of new voices, not only in every public school in the nation, but by organizations of men and women who have used this familiar formula to express their patriotic sentiment, until at last it has been called by some enthusiasts the National Creed. ... I have the happiness of realizing that I once, in my young manhood, contributed to my Country an easily remembered symbol of patriotism which has become historic and has been in many millions of individuals a spur to their love of Country and Flag.

Nevertheless, the state of Massachusetts has long given credit to James Baily Upham (of Malden, Massachusetts) as author. With credit going to

Bellamy in an *American Legion Magazine* article and an article in *The Christ-ian Science Monitor*— in October and November 1955, respectively — the then-editor of the *Malden Evening News* was "provoked" into seeking "the truth of the matter." After three months of research, he presented a five-part series in the paper, written by Archie B. Birtwell, a member of the editorial staff. The findings convinced this editor that Upham was the author.

In the late nineteenth century Upham resided in Boston, where he was an editor and partner of the firm that published *Youth's Companion*. In 1888, according to Birtwell, Upham conceived a plan to place the flag in front of every schoolhouse. This project resulted in hundreds of flags being distributed to schools across the country, at cost.

Upham died in 1905, long before the pledge achieved any great fame. But an article in *Youth's Companion*, dated December 20, 1917, stated that "Mr. Upham had already written a form of the Pledge very much like that which is now so well known, and with the help of other members of the firm and of members of the editorial staff the present and final form was written."

A leaflet later issued by the *Companion* for library files read, "Various patriotic men with whom Mr. Upham talked over the Pledge ... have been mentioned as the authors, but there is no evidence to show that they did more than discuss and approve the rough draft prepared by Mr. Upham, and after-wards condensed and perfected by him and his associates of the Companion force."

These statements, plus personal knowledge of Mr. Upham's work on the pledge, were the basis for Upham descendants' belief that their forebear was the author of the pledge. Seeking a resolution of the controversy after the Bellamy articles, the Uphams wrote to various members of the *Companion* staff who had worked at the magazine office when the pledge was first written, asking what they understood about the authorship.

Most staff members concurred that Upham had been the true author, and they issued sworn affidavits to that effect. Charles M. Thompson, who had been the editor at the time the pledge was written, stated, "Mr. Upham wrote it; it was handed to each of the editors and partners in turn for comment, criticism and suggestion.... Among those to whom it was submitted, I was one."

The affidavit of Ira Rich Kent, former *Companion* editor, stated, "After consultation with many who were members of the Companion staff at that time, I am convinced ... the idea and the original draft of the Flag Pledge came from Mr. James B. Upham. Mr. Upham submitted his wording very naturally to his associates, and ... it is possible, indeed probable, that some minor pol-ishing was contributed by other members of the Companion group.... All those who have knowledge of the matter insist emphatically that it is highly erroneous to describe anyone except Mr. James B. Upham as the 'author' of the Pledge."

Herbert S. Sylvester, another staff member, wrote, "I credit it to Mr. James B. Upham.... I can recall his reading it and explaining it to me, and his enthusiasm concerning it as combined with the flag-on-every-schoolhouse campaign."

However, one former staff member of 1892, Harold Roberts, stated that he had been a close associate of Bellamy's and that Bellamy was the author. He said he recalled how Bellamy had been good-naturedly kidded about having written the pledge by those with whom he came into contact. He further stated that everyone in the office understood that the pledge had been written by Bellamy.

Tom F. Hancock, a Brooksville, Florida, attorney who was present at an interview between Mrs. Bertha Upham Proctor and Francis Bellamy in Tampa in 1929, wrote in 1936 about that interview. Bellamy admitted "that he had none of the original notes, or even proofs of the Pledge; and further, that the only proofs he could produce were those that came into existence after the death of Mr. Upham." Hancock also made personal observations. "From the result of the interview I became thoroughly convinced that Mr. Bellamy was not the author of the 'Pledge to the Flag.' His conduct was that of a gentleman throughout during the interview, but somewhat theatrical, and I formed the distinct impression that he was a lover of publicity and not opposed to seeking it when the occasion was presented."

Another argument for Upham, put forth by Birtwell in his series, was the article prepared for a 1917 issue of the *Companion* by staff member Seth Mendell, crediting Upham. Furthermore, a letter to Bellamy from the Perry Mason Company's *Youth's Companion*, dated August 1, 1923, read:

> Dear Sir: Your third letter in regard to the Companion Pledge of Allegiance does nothing to change our convictions. We repeat that Mr. Mendell's account of the origin of the Pledge was prepared with deliberate care soon after the event and that Mr. Mendell was a man beyond most men, exact and scrupulous in statement. We add that your intimation that Mr. Mendell was actuated by any "malignity" towards you to make a "dishonest" report of the facts is preposterous. Against the careful statement of this honorable man, you bring only your own unsupported and interested assertions. We believe Mr. Mendell's account implicitly.
>
> In the circumstances we see no need for any personal interview between you and Mr. Kelsey, or between you and any other officer of the Perry Mason Company.

The controversy, of course, continued. And Bellamy seems to have been the winner. In 1939, a committee of historians who examined the records declared Bellamy to be the true author.

Bellamy was a Baptist minister turned journalist. According to his version of the story, he was asked to compose a pledge of allegiance to arouse patriotic zeal in school children especially for Columbus Day, October 1892, which was the commemoration of the four hundredth anniversary of the discovery of America. He took only two hours to compose the pledge before it was publicly recited for the first time on October 12, 1892, by 4,000 Boston high school students. The original text read: "I pledge allegiance to my flag and to the Republic for which it stands, one Nation indivisible, with liberty and justice for all."

In 1923, at the first National Flag Conference held in Washington, D.C., the words "my flag" were changed to "the flag of the United States." The next year the words "of America" were added after "United States."

This version of the Pledge of Allegiance was given official sanction in 1942, when Congress incorporated it into the Flag Code. The phrase "under God" was added by a congressional act of 1954, mainly as the result of an intense campaign led by the American Legion in collaboration with the Hearst newspaper chain and the late Luke E. Hart, leader of the Catholic Knights of Columbus fraternal order.

That modification was the last, though other suggestions for changes to the pledge have been made from time to time. For example, Charles N. McEathron, in a letter to the editor of the Santa Ana, California, *Register*, suggested adding the word "responsibilities" to the final line so it would read: "One Nation under God, indivisible, with liberty, justice and *responsibilities* for all." "Real freedom," he said, "is impossible unless there is responsibility, too."

Nothing came of his idea, even though it was reprinted in the July 1972 *Reader's Digest* and thus widely read. But the idea has merit.

Lorain (Roman) Catholic High School of Lorain, Ohio, changed the Pledge of Allegiance to read, "with liberty and justice for the born and unborn" as part of United States Catholic schools' "Respect for Life" week in October 1990. Reporters trying to interview students about the change were asked to leave the school grounds, but not before junior Angela Martinez stated, "It's like changing the Constitution," and senior Robert Garcia complained, "I feel the 'born and unborn' shouldn't be added. The Pledge is a pledge to your country.... The Pledge deals with patriotism."

Authorship and wording are not the only controversies surrounding the pledge. Ever since its official recognition in 1942, citizens have argued strenuously over whether recitation of the pledge should be mandatory in any situation, especially in the schools. There has never been a federal law requiring recitation, but at one time it was incorporated into the laws of many states. In recent years, some states have removed those laws as court decisions have leaned against them.

The issue is far from being laid to rest. For example, in 1976 the Philadelphia Board of Education voted to begin the school day with the Pledge of Allegiance and a moment of silent prayer. Those of the 260,000 students who did not wish to participate did not have to. The resolution was introduced by an outspoken board member named Felice Stack, who said she was shocked to learn that prayer and the Pledge were not part of classroom activity throughout the school system.

In 1978 Ruth Wyatt, a student at Wiley H. Bates Junior High School in

Annapolis, Maryland, was told she had to have a note from her parents to approve her decision not to stand and recite the Pledge. Her parents and the American Civil Liberties Union objected, forcing an announcement that "any child can be excused from reciting the Pledge." However, no other students joined her boycott, and her stand prompted considerable adverse student attention for her personally, as well as a number of hate letters in the local newspaper.

A year earlier, 16-year-old Debbie Lipp of Mountain Lakes, New Jersey, campaigned with an American Civil Liberties Union lawyer for the same privilege, to sit and not participate in the school's morning pledge. This confrontation went to court, and United States District Judge H. Curtis Meanor ruled unconstitutional New Jersey's law requiring students to stand during the pledge to the flag.

Debbie's reason was that she believed the phrase "with liberty and justice for all" was a lie. The judge asked, "Is there any reason to doubt she believes 'with liberty and justice for all' isn't so? Many other persons don't believe it. I know, I've sentenced a lot of them."

Judge Meanor based his decision on two federal appeals court cases, one going back to 1943 (*West Virginia Board of Education vs. Barnette*) that ruled a person does not have to participate in the Pledge of Allegiance.

Government bodies have shown confusion, ambivalence, or neglect toward pledge recitation even within their own walls. In the state of Louisiana, it wasn't until July 4, 1970, that state representative P.J. Mills of Shreveport noticed that the Pledge of Allegiance hadn't been part of the house opening procedure. He suggested making the pledge a daily opening ceremony. Other house members promptly agreed and made the pledge.

It is interesting that unlike the national anthem, the Pledge has had no real competition over the years. Other "salutes" to the flag have been written, of course. One of the most notable was the classic Flag Day address by Franklin Knight Lane, Secretary of the Interior, in 1914. He talked as he imagined the flag itself would speak:

> I am not the flag; not at all. I am but its shadow. I am whatever you make me, nothing more, I am your belief in yourself, your dream of what a People may become. I live a changing life, a life of moods and passions, of heartbreaks and tired muscles.
>
> Sometimes I am strong with pride, when men do an honest work. Sometimes I droop, for then purpose has gone from me. Sometimes I am loud, garish, and full of that ego that blasts judgment. But always, I am all that you hope to be, and have the courage to try for.
>
> I am song and fear, struggle and panic, and ennobling hope. I am the day's work of the weakest man, and the largest dream of the most daring. I am the clutch of an idea, and the reasoned purpose of resolution. I am no more than what you believe me to be and I am all that you believe I can be. I am what you make me, nothing more.

I swing before your eyes as a bright gleam of color, a symbol of yourself, the pictured suggestion of that big thing which makes this nation. My stars and my stripes are your dream and your labors. They are bright with cheer, brilliant with courage, firm with faith, because you have made them so out of your hearts. For you are the makers of the flag and it is well that you glory in the making.

If this speech had been shorter and simpler it might have become the Pledge of Allegiance.

Just how familiar is the pledge today? It would be an interesting experiment to send out a letter with the words of the Pledge of Allegiance written on it (without the title), along with a short statement reading, "This is to be presented as a petition to Congress. Sign and return if you agree with it." How many citizens would even recognize it?

There is a precedent for the idea, of course, with humorous results (if the macabre overtones can be ignored). For example, at an American Army base in West Germany 252 United States soldiers were read the following sentence: "We hold these truths to be self-evident, that all men are created equal, that they are endowed by their creator with certain inalienable rights, that among these are life, liberty, and the pursuit of happiness."

They were not told this sentence was straight out of the American Declaration of Independence. They were told only to sign the statement if they agreed with it. Seventy-three percent refused to sign.

In a similar experiment a Berkshire County High School student government association (Pittsfield, Massachusetts) circulated a petition they said they intended to submit to Congress. The "petition" was actually the first amendment to the United States Constitution, which guarantees all citizens freedom of religion, speech, press, peaceable assembly, and the right "to petition the government for a redress of grievances."

Of 1,154 persons polled, only 4 percent recognized the first amendment; 42 percent agreed with the statement; 35 percent disagreed; and 23 percent refused to commit themselves one way or the other.

Some of the comments of adults to the student pollsters: "People like you make me sick"; "I'll ask my husband"; "I'd punch you in the mouth but you're a girl"; "I never sign anything"; "I work for the federal government so I can't comment"; "No, the Constitution is all right the way it is"; and "Children should be seen, not heard."

It is evident that few Americans know enough about their national documents and insignias. Furthermore, some, especially worthy of popular usage, lie, hardly remembered, in reference sources, like the *World Atlas*. Among these are the "Civic Creed," "The American's Creed," and the national motto.

The "Civic Creed" has no official status whatsoever. Maybe it should. Read it and decide for yourself.

Civic Creed

God hath made of one blood all nations of men, and we are His children, brethren and sisters all. We are citizens of these United States of America and we believe the flag stands for self-sacrifice for the good of the people. We want, therefore, to be true citizens of our great country and will show our love for her by our works. Our Country does not ask us to die for her welfare only — she asks us to live for her, and so to live and so to act that her government may be pure, her officers honest, and every corner of her territory a place fit to grow the best men and women, who shall rule over her.

"The American's Creed" also has no official status, though it was written by a clerk of the United States House of Representatives, William Tyler Page. It has persevered since 1917, mostly through annual reprinting in such references as the *World Almanac and Book of Facts*, which newspapermen browse through when searching for an inspiration or a two-inch filler item on page 10.

The American's Creed

I believe in the United States of America as a government of the people, by the people, for the people; whose just powers are derived from the consent of the governed; a democracy in a republic; a sovereign Nation of many sovereign States; a perfect Union, one and inseparable; established upon those principles of freedom, equality, justice and humanity, for which American patriots sacrificed their lives and fortunes. I, therefore, believe it is my duty to my country to love it; to support its Constitution; to obey its laws; to respect its Flag, and to defend it against all enemies.

The national motto *is* official, having been so designated by Congress in 1956. Its designation is codified as section 1868 of the same chapter of the United States Code that contains flag law: Title 36, Chapter 10, "Patriotic Customs." Unlike the creeds above, it is seen almost every day by every American. It is one of those things that has become so common it now escapes the sight altogether.

The motto—"In God We Trust"—originated during the Civil War as an inscription for United States coins, though it was used earlier in slightly different form by Key when he wrote "The Star-Spangled Banner." The creation of a motto is credited to the Reverend M.R. Watkinson of Ridleyville, Pennsylvania. On November 13, 1861, when Union troops' morale had been seriously shaken by defeats in the field, the Reverend Watkinson wrote secretary of the treasury Salmon P. Chase, "From my heart I have felt our national shame in disowning God as not the least of our present national disasters." He went on then to suggest "recognition of the Almighty God in some form on our coins."

Secretary Chase ordered designs prepared and ramrodded legislation which authorized use of this slogan. It appeared first on some United States coins in 1864, disappeared, then reappeared on various coins until 1955, when Congress ordered it placed on all paper money and coins.

5

The Origin of
the Stars and Stripes

The origin of the stars and stripes has been tangled in claims and in counter-claims through United States history, though scholars have pretty well accepted one over all others.

BETSY ROSS AND OTHER MYTHS

Though the "Betsy" Ross home in Philadelphia — 239 Arch Street — is still pointed out to tourists as the birthplace of the national ensign, as commissioned by a committee of George Washington, Robert Morris, and George Ross, this claim has been refuted by modern historians. Elizabeth "Betsy" (Griscom) Ross and her descendants — she lived to age 84 and was three times married — were upholsterers turned flag-makers until 1858, but she did not originate the design or color scheme for the Star-Spangled Banner. Records show she did make and receive pay for some ship's flags for Pennsylvania's navy, and it may have been that the order for these was mistaken for the request for an ensign.

According to some of her descendants, Betsy Ross did claim to have originated the United States flag. A paper read to the Pennsylvania Historical Society on March 14, 1870, by William J. Canby, Betsy's grandson, claimed that the trio of Washington, Morris, and Ross came to Betsy Ross in June 1776, showed her a design and asked her to make it. She did, and the flag was taken to the state house and adopted by Congress as the flag of the United States. Canby said the paper had been dictated to him in 1857 by his aunt, Betsy's daughter, who said her mother had told the story many times. Yet actual records contradict the paper's account.

Unfortunately, this popular misconception was perpetuated by the United States Post Office when it issued a 1952 stamp commemorating the twentieth

This painting of Betsy Ross supposedly making the first United States flag was painted by Frank McKernan.

anniversary of the birth of Betsy Ross. The stamp pictured the three committeemen seated in her parlor being shown the original version (though only 11 stripes can be counted) of the stars and stripes by Betsy herself.

One of the largest flag-making companies in the United States also had a hand in keeping the myth alive. Annin Company of New Jersey has, from time to time, presented a "Betsy Ross Award" to individuals who have furthered the cause of patriotism by some deed or contribution.

In January 1975, women prisoners at the Maryland Correctional Institution for Women (at Jessup) proposed making replicas of "Betsy Ross's stars and stripes" for use by state agencies and nonprofit organizations in Bicentennial celebrations. They were turning out 200 per week as their contribution to both the Bicentennial and the myth of Betsy Ross, when a "more historically Maryland" flag was switched into production — the "Cowpens" flag, also 13-starred.

Another flag-making story, wholly imaginary, describes how some girls of Portsmouth, New Hampshire, made a stars and stripes from ballroom dresses (which were no longer needed with a war on) for John Paul Jones in July 1777. That flag was supposed to have gone down with Jones's ship, the *Bon Homme Richard*.

Jones does have a genuine association with one version of the stars and stripes, however. He hoisted "the American Stars" for his victory in the Irish Sea over HMS *Drake* on April 24, 1778, the first known baptism of fire for Old Glory. On February 14 he had obtained the first international recognition for the stars and stripes when the French fleet returned his salute from the *Ranger* off Quiberon Bay.

Some experts still admit to the possibility that Francis Hopkinson, a New

The Betsy Ross House in Philadelphia is called "The Birthplace of Old Glory." Legend holds that in this little Colonial dwelling Betsy Ross, seamstress and patriot, stitched the first American flag. (Photo courtesy of the Philadelphia Conventions and Visitors Bureau.)

Jersey judge and signer of the Declaration of Independence who served two years as chairman of the Navy Board, might have had something to do with the design of the flag. He was a noted draftsman as well as an acknowledged expert on heraldry, and there is a letter on file from him to the admiralty board suggesting payment for his work "designing sundry seals and devices, also the Flag of the United States" (billed at £9 for the flag, one of the great all-time bargains, ranking alongside the purchase of Manhattan).

His request was denied when Congress resolved (August 31, 1781) "that the report relative to the fancy work of F. Hopkinson ought not to be acted upon." Members seem not to have been convinced he had been the sole designer of all the things he claimed, including some issues of paper money.

SAMUEL CHESTER REID

The accepted story of the birth of the stars and stripes is also the story of Captain Samuel Chester Reid. He was the man with a history as proud as the flag he became responsible for. It was one of the greatest matchups of all time. Yet Captain Reid, in all other ways, was an incongruous choice for the job of flag designer for a country. He was very young, a "down east" sea captain, and had absolutely no artistic talent or training.

Before Reid was called in, Congress had actually already approved a flag for the Union. On June 14, 1777 (which present-day Flag Day commemorates), a resolution offered by the Marine Committee of the Second Continental Congress at Philadelphia was adopted: "that the flag of the United States be thirteen stripes, alternate red and white; that the union be thirteen stars, white in a blue field, representing a new constellation." Note that nothing is said about having those thirteen stars in a circular pattern, or any other special pattern.

Who suggested that design, who made the first flag, and where it was first flown is not known. Another unproven story that lingers on, though, is that it was taken from a new coat of arms of the Washington family. That remains just a story.

When two new states were admitted to the Union in 1795, two new stars and stripes were added to the flag. It was this 15-starred-and-striped version that was made by Mary Pickersgill in Baltimore's Flag House and flew over Fort McHenry to become Francis Scott Key's inspiration for the national anthem.

By 1816, with more new states already accepted and still others seeking to join the Union, it had become evident that the flag would become overbalanced and unwieldy if the practice of adding both a star and a stripe for each additional state was continued. It was then that Congress turned to its returned hero, Captain Sam Reid — who had staged one of the most heroic defenses of the flag's honor in United States history — and placed the flag's future in his hands.

The story of Reid's action has been well documented. It was retold by James Poling in a popular national Sunday newspaper supplement several years back, under the title "He Designed Our Flag." According to Poling, toward the end of the War of 1812, Reid sailed a privateer called the *General Armstrong* into Fayal, Portuguese Azores, a neutral port. While he was taking on fresh water, into the port sailed three British ships under the command of Commodore Robert Lloyd. In violation of the laws of neutrality, Lloyd ordered Reid to surrender. Fully aware of the odds against him — the British force of 2,000 men and 130 guns left the Americans' 90 men and 7 guns pathetically outnumbered — Reid nevertheless refused.

When the first British party boarded the *General Armstrong*, they were met with hand-to-hand combat so fierce that they withdrew to regroup. At midnight they attacked the privateer again, this time with 560 men in armed boats.

Legend has it that Reid fought a two-handed battle, brandishing a sword with one hand and firing his pistol with the other. He himself killed the commander of the British force, Lieutenant Matterforce, then led his men in the attack that drove the British over the side after only 40

Captain Samuel Chester Reid, designer of the United States Flag.

The 13-star Reid flag flies daily over the Evans Farm Inn of McLean, Virginia, to maintain its colonial decor. It is located on a one-time plantation, with two slave cabins still on view. (Photo by Bob Loeffelbein.)

minutes of fighting. One hundred and twenty British sailors died and another 130 were wounded, while Reid's crew suffered two fatalities and seven other injuries.

The British did not give up immediately. The next day they attacked with the full force of the brig *Carnation*. Within ten minutes, that ship was so badly damaged that it withdrew from the fighting. However, when the remaining two ships (the 74-gun *Plantagenet* and *Rota*) moved toward him, Reid decided that the danger to his men was too great. Keeping them covered with artillery fire, he moved most of his crew to shore, then sank his own ship and went ashore with the remaining crew members.

When Commodore Lloyd notified Reid that he and his men would be taken captive, the Americans took defensive positions in an abandoned convent. The British force never came. The next day, in an unprecedented move, a group of British officers met with Reid at the British consulate to honor him with cheers and toasts.

When the war ended, Reid returned home and was showered with honors, among them the request from Congress to produce a workable lasting design for the national banner. He and his wife made up a model, returning the original 13 stripes for the original 13 states, with a blue field to which a new star could be added for each new state. Congress approved the design, and President James Monroe signed the act making this flag official as of April 4, 1818. Days later, with full ceremony, Mrs. Reid, accompanied by her husband, handed the flag she had made to the president and he had it hoisted over the Capitol for the first time. The date: April 13, 1818.

It is a sad commentary that within a relatively few years both Captain Reid and his part in our flag history had been forgotten. With evident bitterness his great grandson once wrote an enquirer, "Capt. Sam C. Reid has been forgotten by the United States of America, for which he did so much, for he lies in an unmarked grave in Green-Wood Cemetery, Brooklyn."

This grandson, Sam C. Reid IV, served aboard the U.S.S. *Reid* during the New Guinea campaign of World War II. This was the third destroyer named for the original Sam Reid, and it was sunk in the December 1944 invasion of Leyte.

A happier ending was imminent, however. Rep. Francis E. Dorn (Brooklyn, New York) tendered a bill to Congress to provide a fitting memorial for Reid's gravesite. The Associated Granite Craftsman's Guild offered to erect the monument. Today the monument stands proudly at the grave, graced with the American flag.

HERALDRY AND THE AMERICAN COLONIES

Heraldry, the practice of devising, blazoning, and granting armorial insignia and of tracing and recording genealogies, seems to be as old as the human race, and the carrying of banners has been the habit of nations since nearly the beginning of civilization.

To illustrate, Sir John Marshall, head of the archaeological service of the Indian government some years ago, discovered two abandoned cities in northern India, at Mohenjo-Daro and Harappa, believed to have been thriving around 3500 B.C. and in close contact with the earliest civilization of Babylonia. One of the historical items he found was a seal, evidently used to stamp official documents. It pictured a procession of seven men carrying square, rigid, boardlike standards held aloft on poles, something like modern-day flags.

We don't know who

Rep. Francis E. Dorn (Brooklyn, New York) drafted a bill to Congress to provide a memorial for Captain Sam Reid's gravesite, here in the Green-Wood Cemetery, Fifth Avenue at 25th Street, Brooklyn, New York (Lot 13108, Sec. 172). (Photo courtesy of Green-Wood Cemetery.)

first used flags. But, for centuries, bits of colored cloth tied to sticks have been carried before kings, explorers, and men of destiny leading men through crusades, into battles, and on to new worlds. They have been utilized both for identification and a means of communication.

They were probably first used in the Orient. It is believed a white flag was carried before a Chinese emperor as early as 1122 B.C. and that flags were carried into those early battles on chariots of sorts and on elephants. In both ancient China and India, flags often pictured birds, tigers, and dragons on fields of green and scarlet.

In the Western world, the first flags weren't flags, but carved figurines attached to poles. These were called "standards" and were common throughout the ancient Mideast. An Assyrian monument from 671 B.C. shows a soldier carrying his unit's standard into battle. Many other monuments, tombs, and pottery remnants show such standards being carried before ancient Egyptian pharaohs, both in military units on land and aboard ships at sea.

Standards spread from the Mideast to Crete and into the Aegean. Greek city-states used them topped with their cities' symbols. Roman ones had effigies of animals, generals, and gods topping them.

Toward the end of the Roman Empire, standards were replaced by the *vexillum*, a square banner attached to a bar that was, in turn, fastened cross-wise to a carrying pole. This was used into the Middle Ages, being especially popular in Christian Europe because of its crosslike shape. (In France, early in the twelfth century, the vexillum was changed to an *oriflamme*, a banner split at one end to form flame-shaped flying edges.)

It was in the Middle Ages that the flag idea was really born. During that period a group of independent city-states grew up in Italy. Since they had no king or other ruler, the idea evolved for a flag to symbolize the entity itself. One of these city-states was Genoa, which had its own flag by A.D. 958.

The beginning of the Crusades also spurred the development of flags to aid in distinguishing one group from another. As knights from every part of Christendom assembled for the Holy Wars, closed helmets came into fashion, and some mark became necessary to distinguish allies. The cross was a logical choice, and soldiers of various armies began to wear different colored ones and differently designed ones on their outer garments. When these wars ended and warriors returned home, they wore their crosses with pride. And in many cases the crusader's cross became a part of early national flags. By the end of the Third Crusade, flags were used throughout Europe.

American history, from its earliest recorded times, has some unusual heraldry incorporated. The Vikings, sometime claimants to the title of "discoverers" of America, flew a banner bearing a black raven on a white flag. When Columbus sailed to the American shores in 1492, his three small ships flew the Spanish flag displaying two crowned and rearing red lions on white fields diametrically opposed to two yellow castles on red fields. And it is amazing how many other countries' flags flew at one time or another over sections of the Americas, or even over just that part that became the United States. In fact, only one state — Idaho — has never had a foreign flag flown over it.

In contrast, the state of California has seen 11 flags other than official United States ones, including: (1) the Spanish Empire flag, raised by Juan Rodriguez Cabrillo, the discoverer of California, at San Diego in 1542; (2) the flag of England, raised by Sir Francis Drake and his buccaneers, who claimed the land for England in 1576; (3) the Spanish national ensign hoisted in 1785 when Father Serra began colonizing San Diego for Spain; (4) the flag of Russia, flown at Fort Ross, the Russian fur trading colony in northern California, in 1812; (5) the Russian-American Fur Company "house" flag, also flown at Fort Ross in 1812; (6) the Buenos Aires Flag, used unlawfully by a band of renegades who attempted to seize California in 1818; (7) the Mexican Empire flag, raised

Flags that have flown over California, left to right, *top row*: Spanish Empire flag, flag of England, Spanish national ensign, flag of Russia; *middle row*: Russian-American Fur Company flag, Buenos Aires flag, Mexican Empire flag, Mexican Republic flag; *bottom row*: Fremont flag, first bear flag (1846), American flag (1846), redesigned bear flag (1911). (Illustrations courtesy of the San Diego Gas and Electric Company.)

at Monterey in 1822 after a successful revolt against Spanish rulers; (8) the Mexican Republic flag, adopted by Mexico with the establishment of a Mexican republic in 1823; (9) the Fremont flag, carried by Captain John Fremont on his California expeditions between 1844 and 1846; (10) the first bear flag, raised by American settlers who proclaimed California an independent republic in 1846; and (11) the redesigned bear flag in 1911, California's official state flag.

It was natural for early colonists to have their own flags. Most colonial behavior and culture followed homeland heritages. The Dutch brought their own striped flags when they settled New Amsterdam (New York). The British flag, under which the English colonization of America was effected, remained the flag of the colonists for over 100 years, giving it special significance in the evolution of the United States national banner. Separation from the mother country was gradual, so it was really by degrees that the union flag of Great Britain was discarded.

Before the adoption of the official American flag, colonial and regimental flags were created in infinite variety. Many designs were symbolic of the hopes of the colonists and their struggles with the wilderness of the new land. A national patriotism did not really exist yet. Affection was given the home colony, which was all most people could see at the time. Their lives were bound up only in the colonies.

Because many early colonial activities were tied in with some special trees, trees were a popular motif on colonial flags. Other designs showed heavens, anchors, and rattlesnakes, singly or in combination with appropriate slogans also imprinted.

The changeover from the British to American flag is commemorated each May 15 in Williamsburg, Virginia. Here, from the original Capitol building, the British Great Union flag, which flew over England at the time of the American Revolution and for years before the revolution in the American colonies, is flown daily. It is done with special permission for the historical effect. Each May 15 it is taken down and replaced by the Grand Union flag of the colonies, to commemorate the legislators' vote of 1776 to adopt the Virginia Resolution for Independence.

One of the special trees was a fine old elm in Boston's Hanover Square, known as the Liberty Tree because the Sons of Liberty met under it. A huge oak in Charleston, South Carolina, was another, because beneath its branches the Declaration of Independence was first read to the people of that city. Another South Carolina flag (1776) bore a crescent and a (locally grown) palmetto tree. But the most famous of all was the Massachusetts Pine Tree.

When the colony of Massachusetts first established a mint, in 1652, the general court ordered all money printed there to bear the picture of a tree on one side. Thus the famed "pinetree" shillings were born.

Later the same tree showed up on a flag used by the Massachusetts State Navy. This green pine tree was centered under the inscription "An Appeal to Heaven" on a white background, and ultimately became familiar on the high seas as the ensign of cruisers commissioned by General Washington.

Two all-black units fought in the Continental Army. Very little is known of one, a Massachusetts company called "The Bucks of America," but at the end of the war John Hancock presented the unit with a silk banner (bearing both his and George Washington's initials) as "a tribute to their courage and devotion." This flag showed a powerful buck deer at the base of a pine tree.

Still later, as the rattlesnake theme had a period of increasing prestige, a coiled serpent was added at the base of Massachusetts' pine tree. This rattlesnake symbol appears again and again in early American flags. Benjamin Franklin, in a way, deserves the credit for conceiving the snake design; it was he who remarked that since England insisted upon exporting its criminals to the colonies, the colonies should return the favor by sending back all their rattlesnakes.

A warning slogan, "Don't Tread on Me," almost always accompanied American usage of the snake emblem. A flag of this type was the standard of the South Carolina State Navy, another version was the emblem of the Culpepper Minute Men of Virginia, and still another variation — a rattler superimposed upon a yellow field — was the Gadsden flag, first hoisted by Lieutenant

The Bucks of America flag, presented by John Hancock to an all-black unit of the Continental Army as "a tribute to their courage and devotion."

John Paul Jones' flagship *Alfred* in Philadelphia on December 3, 1775. It was later adopted by Commodore Esek Hopkins, commander in chief of the Continental Navy.

The rattlesnake flag later disappeared and wasn't seen aboard a United States Navy ship for nearly 200 years. The year 1975, however, was the two hundredth anniversary of the Navy, and the rattlesnake flag was reinstated for the occasion. It was hoisted on October 13 and flew on Navy ships around the world through December. The resurrection idea came from a Chicago attorney named Frederic O. Floberg. He sent his idea to Rear Admiral William Thompson, then Navy Chief of Information, who had it approved through the channels of command.

The "Don't Tread on Me" flag had another rebirth in July 1984. Fifty thousand gay rights marchers adopted it as their emblem at that year's presidential nominating convention.

Reasons varied for the popularity of the rattlesnake design. Its deadly bite was probably foremost in the minds of users, though one writer of the time noted that the snake's eyes were brighter than those of any other animal; that its lack of eyelids might be taken as a symbol of eternal vigilance; and that its traits of never beginning an attack, especially without warning, nor, once engaged, ever surrendering, made it at once an emblem of magnanimity and of true courage. Which all sounded fine, but showed the writer really didn't know much about rattlesnakes.

The Moultrie flag was the first distinctive American flag flown in the

The snake on this rattlesnake flag of America's Continental Navy had 13 rattles, symbolic, some say, of the 13 rebellious colonies. Note the non-apostrophied "Dont," which is historically correct. (U.S. Navy photo.)

South. It flew over the fort on Sullivan's Island, in the channel leading to Charleston, South Carolina, when the British fleet attacked on June 28, 1776. British ships opened fire about 10:30 A.M. and continued a bombardment for 10 hours. At one time during this bombardment a British shot dropped the Carolina flag into the mud, and both British and Americans thought the fort had surrendered. But daring sergeant William Jasper crawled out a gunport, fastened the flag onto a cannon ramrod, and ignored shells whistling by on all sides to climb to the top of the fort and mount the flag again.

The garrison of 375 regulars and a few militia, under command of Colonel William Moultrie, made such a spirited defense that the British were forced to withdraw a few hours later under cover of darkness. The South didn't see another Redcoat for two years. The victory also marked the first defeat of a British naval force for a period of several years.

The design of the Moultrie flag — blue field with a white crescent in the upper left corner — was suggested by the blue uniforms of the garrison and their silver crescent cap ornaments, which were inscribed, "Liberty or Death."

The Rhode Island regiment had a distinctive flag also, showing a blue

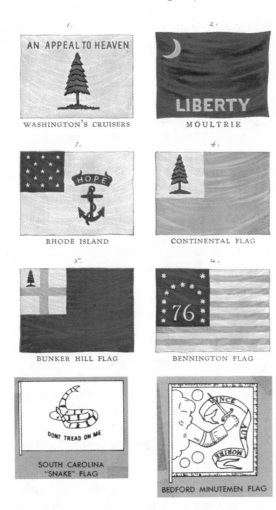

fouled anchor on a white background under the word "Hope," with a blue canton showing 13 white stars. This canton is believed by many historians to have suggested that part of the original stars and stripes design, along with Washington's stripes, to Captain Sam Reid's wife.

Noteworthy among New England flags was that carried by American colonials against British regulars at the Battle of Bunker Hill June 17, 1775. It was one of the first to use the pine tree symbol, though the tree was only an incidental design on the all-blue flag with its white canton quartered by a red cross.

A banner carried by Vermont forces at the Battle of Bennington (August 16, 1777) where militiamen smashed a raiding column from General Burgoyne's army and made inevitable his surrender at Saratoga, was strikingly similar, with its red and white stripes and its white stars in a blue canton, to the ultimately selected stars and stripes. Some claims have been made for the Bennington flag as the true forerunner of today's national banner, but nothing has been

Flags of the Revolution. (1) Famed pine tree flag used by the Massachusetts State Navy. (2) First distinctive American flag to fly in the South, in South Carolina. (3) Many people think this flag suggested the starred field for the original stars and stripes to Captain Sam Reid. Today's Rhode Island state flag is similar, but without the blue field; the anchor and legend are in the center, with the stars surrounding them in a circle. (4, 5) Two of the first flags to use the pine tree emblem. (6) This flag may have suggested the circle arrangement of stars on the original stars and stripes. (7) Officially known as the first United States Navy "Jack." (8) The legend of the Minutemen of Bedford was "Conquer or Die."

found in recorded history to verify such a claim. It remains more plausible that the design was a composite.

The Hanover Associates of Pennsylvania flew a red flag with a rifleman in hunting costume in the center above the words "Liberty or Death." New York's flag bore a beaver to celebrate her fur trade. New Hampshire's banner centered a chain of 13 links and the motto, "We Are One." The only "flag to April's breeze unfurl'd" at Lexington and Concord was brought by the Minutemen of Bedford, and showed a silver arm and sword on a red background, with the words "Vince Aut Morire" (conquer or die). The Philadelphia Light Horse troop which escorted General Washington to Cambridge, Massachusetts, in June 1775 had a flag which centered a knot tied with 13 cords, and at the peak had a union of 13 blue and silver stripes.

Most of these sectional banners disappeared, naturally, after the adoption of the stars and stripes, though many of the designs can still be noted incorporated into today's state flags, such as those of South Carolina's crescent and palmetto tree and Rhode Island's fouled anchor and 13 stars.

THE CONTINENTAL COLORS

The immediate predecessor to the flag of the American colonists was the one George Washington raised January 1, 1776, atop a 76-foot staff on Prospect Hill at Somerville, Massachusetts, outside Boston. It consisted of 13 alternating red and white stripes (representing the 13 colonies) with the British Union Jack composing its canton, or top left corner, signifying union with the mother country. It was called the Grand Union flag, sometimes referred to as the Continental Colors. It had actually been flown previously as the ensign of colonial ships in the Delaware River on December 3, 1775, after Commodore Esek Hopkins assumed command on the flagship *Alfred*.

The Union Jack, which comprised the canton, has a distinguished history of its own. It was a scale model of Great Britain's empirical ensign, which had been formed from England and Scotland joining together.

For centuries the flag of England had been the red cross of St. George (shaped like a plus sign) on a white field, while the flag of Scotland had been the white cross of St. Andrew (shaped like an X) on a blue field. When James VI of Scotland took the English crown on the death of Elizabeth I in 1606, the two countries and their two flags were consolidated, with England's St. George design superimposed onto the Scottish St. Andrew design. The maritime Union Jack resulted, but it wasn't adopted as the flag of Great Britain for a hundred years. Then it was changed again in 1801 when the Irish Republic, symbolized by the red diagonal cross (another X) of St. Patrick, was added to the British empire.

This interests historians because it made Washington's flag, which was

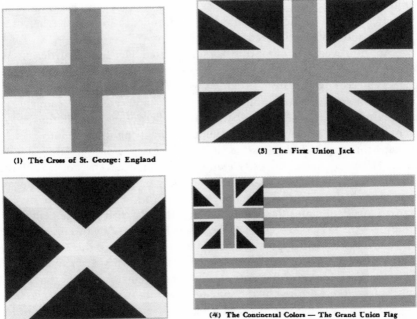

(1) The Cross of St. George: England

(3) The First Union Jack

(2) The Cross of St. Andrew: Scotland

(4) The Continental Colors — The Grand Union Flag

Steps in the evolution of the Grand Union flag, flown by General George Washington before the first starred flag was adopted.

officially adopted by Congress in 1777, only some 70 years younger than that of the mother country. And, with Britain's 1801 change, the Grand Union flag actually became older than that of mother England!

Washington raised the Grand Union on the day the colonies were declared in rebellion by the king of England. Thus the new flag became the banner of the Continental Army. The 13 stripes showed the colonies firmly united in a stand to fight for their human rights, yet the Union Jack remained, a plea for reconciliation, showing the colonists' reluctance to defy and break entirely from the mother country.

The Grand Union flag served the Continental Army well. It was carried by American Marines and Bluejackets with an expeditionary force to the Bahamas, West Indies, in March 1776. It was also flying over the Battery at New York City when the British arrived that summer. Some form of it was flown by Benedict Arnold on his flagship *Royal Savage* at the battle of Valcour Island on October 11–12. And on November 16, 1776, the *Andrea Doria*, the American ship-of-war flying the Great Union flag, saluted the Dutch fort on the island of St. Eustatius in the West Indies. It received, after due deliberation, a return nine-gun salute, making this incident the first international recognition of a

United States flag. (The return salute came only after Captain Israel Robinson presented a copy of the Declaration of Independence to the governor of St. Eustatius and that worthy read it carefully.)

An improved version of this flag was hoisted over Fort Schuyler on August 3, 1777, when the British attacked there. According to legend, overnight a flag was pieced together from a soldier's white shirt, red stripes from the flannel petticoat of another's wife, and the blue from a captured British camlet cloak (belonging to Captain Abraham Swartwout, who presented a bill for the garment). Since the account of this action tells of cutting the blue into "strips," perhaps this flag had blue instead of white stripes, as did the later Guilford Court House stars and stripes. We don't know for sure. The story is still disputed. In fact, contrasting records exist showing this whole incident happened at an entirely different fort, Fort Stanwix, New York. One retelling of the Fort Stanwix incident states that the pieced-together flag had a "blue field, background for the 13 stars representing the original colonies." By this time the Continental Congress had approved a design with 13 stars, so if this report is true, it indicates that the flag constructed at the fort was the first stars and stripes to fly in the face of an armed enemy. Nothing now remains of the original fort; only blue markers erected by the state of New York mark the site of the siege. But the city of Rome, New York, which grew up around the fort, has not forgotten the siege. It inaugurated an annual Fort Stanwix day on August 3, 1955. The celebration included a parade, display of a replica of the original flag, and a pageant depicting the historical event. The Pledge of Allegiance concluded the patriotic program.

Other flags under which the colonists fought included that of the third Maryland Regiment at Cowpens, South Carolina, on January 17, 1781. In that battle the Americans, backs to a river, routed an elite corps of the British army. Their flag was nearly the same as the original 13 stripes — 13 stars, except it had 12 stars in a circle surrounding the thirteenth (for Maryland) on the blue canton.

Perhaps the most unusual flag was that of the North Carolina militia at the battle of Guilford Court House on March 15, 1781, in which the Carolinians decimated Lord Cornwallis's army, forcing him to begin a retreat that eventually led to his surrender at Yorktown. Their flag had the colors shifted around — blue and red alternating stripes, and a white canton with 13 blue eight-pointed stars on it.

Once the Declaration of Independence was signed there was no need for other banners, so many of them faded away into history. The Grand Union flag, of course, was the first to go. Its continued use, with its British Jack canton, made no sense in view of the escalated war, so it disappeared less than six months after it had been born, and a new symbol took over the favorite's spot. Stars, symbolizing the formation of a new constellation (union), came into popular usage. The flag at last became the Star-Spangled Banner that would evolve into the present-day symbol of the United States.

The Guilford Court House flag, from the collection of the North Carolina Museum of History, Division of Archives and History, Department of Cultural Resources, in Raleigh, North Carolina. It was presented to a Masonic Lodge in 1854 by Edward Bullock, then aged 81, who had received it from his father, Micajah. According to family legend, he had been about eight years old when his father brought home the flag from Guilford. However, there is some debate as to whether this flag actually flew over the battle at Guilford Court House, which took place in 1781. Some scholars suggest that it is likely a later design, possibly from the 1790–1812 era. Their conclusions are largely based on the probability that the flag originally had as many as 16 stripes. Stripe fragments found on the original staff support the existence of at least 15, and possibly 16. However, there is no evidence of 15 stars, except the rather awkward arrangement of the canton. (Photo courtesy of the North Carolina Museum of History.)

THE EVOLUTION OF THE STARS AND STRIPES

No one will ever know the direct line of evolution taken by the American national banner, but certain clues have emerged.

The colors of red, white, and blue are no mystery. They were the colors used most frequently in flags everywhere at this time in history. The fabric-making and dyeing technologies were in their infancies. And there were, of course, a lot fewer nations then, so fewer color schemes were needed.

The idea of using stripes to designate the number of states can easily be traced back to the first Dutch colonists of New Amsterdam, who brought their homeland flag with them. It had consisted of seven red and white alternating

It was here in the old Capitol Williamsburg, Virginia, that George Washington and Thomas Jefferson listened to the fiery oratory of Patrick Henry and where the United States Constitution and Bill of Rights were hammered out ... and where the old Grand Union flag is still flown, by special dispensation. (Photo by Bob Loeffelbein.)

stripes, to symbolize their seven united provinces, freed from Spain. This idea kept recurring right up to the day Washington hoisted the Grand Union flag. The Grand Union was probably suggested, at least partly, by the banner of the Philadelphia Light Horse Regiment — 13 blue and silver stripes — carried when a troop escorted George Washington to Cambridge as the newly united colonials confronted Boston's British garrison. Captain Abraham Markoe had presented the original of this flag to his troop in 1775, and they carried it at Trenton, Princeton, Brandywine, and Germantown. It is preserved in the Philadelphia Armory.

The British East India Company, which was very active in opening American frontiers and which later lost some of its tea in Boston Harbor, used the Grand (or Great) Union flag, though it wasn't yet called that, and it varied the stripes from 5 to 15. This may be where Washington got the idea for his Grand Union flag.

The idea of a blue field canton was first used by the Rhode Island Regiment's "Hope" flag.

The idea of placing 13 stars in a circle, so no one star (state) should be given precedence or preference, may have been suggested by the semi-circle arrangement on the 1776 Bennington flag. The later turn to staggered rows of stars may have been inspired by the Rhode Island "Hope" flag or by the naval ensign of 1777.

Although the 1777 resolution establishing a United States flag called for 13 stars on a blue union, the arrangement of the stars was not specified. The wording was: "That the flag of the thirteen United States be thirteen stripes, alternate red and white; that the union be thirteen stars, white in a blue field, representing a new constellation." Consequently, the pattern of the stars varied widely. In fact, any one person would be hard-put to imagine all the possible ways in which 13 stars could be arranged. Historian Grace Cooper, curator of textiles at the Smithsonian Museum of History and Technology, provides a historical overview in her book *Thirteen-Star Flags* (Washington, D.C.: Smithsonian Museum of History and Technology, 1973). A summary of her findings is presented on pages 156 to 157.

Thirteen-star flags were the official banner only from 1777 to 1795. But they were made into the twentieth century, meaning they were made over a longer period than any other version of the stars and stripes. They were used in small vessels, like submarines and torpedo boats, through the year 1912 and probably longer. Many Navy contractors probably kept supplying them, with individual captains using them, for some time. In fact, on October 29, 1912, executive order #1637 by President William Howard Taft okayed the 13-star ensigns to identify small boats belonging to the government. The practice was supposedly stopped by Franklin D. Roosevelt during his tenure as secretary of the Navy in 1916.

As early as 1778, commissioners Ben Franklin and John Adams had been having their problems describing the American flag to various European governments. One record shows one or the other of them describing it simply as consisting of "13 stripes, alternately red, white and blue." He didn't even try to explain the "new constellation." It is possible neither of them had yet seen the new banner.

Correspondence shows that George Washington made many requests to the board of war about supplying standards and "colours" for his army. He finally received the requested flag in March 1783 — when the fighting was over. History doesn't record what that flag looked like, though some historians think it must have resembled the standard known to have been carried by one infantry regiment of 1790: a blue banner with a spread-winged eagle. The eagle held arrows in one talon and the shield of the United States in the other. Behind the eagle, as background, was a sunburst, topped with 13 gold stars underscored with the motto "E Pluribus Unum." This design must have been the inspiration for the Great Seal of the United States, for a good many postage stamp decorations, and for imprint designs on both United States coins and currency.

After the union admitted Vermont (March 4, 1791) and Kentucky (June 1, 1792), Congress changed the flag. In keeping with the idea of honoring every state with a stripe and a star, the flag established by act of Congress on January 13,

SUMMARY OF 13-STARRED FLAGS

The idea of using 13 stars to represent the 13 states in the Union was prevalent in the eighteenth century, but there were no guidelines for how they were to be arranged. So here are 18 ways they were actually shown. Note, too, that the stars themselves were inconsistent, varying from 4 points to 8, and that blue stripes occasionally slipped into the red-and-white pattern. (Source: *Thirteen-Star Flags* by Grace Cooper [Washington, D.C.: Smithsonian Museum of History and Technology, 1973.])

Star Arrangements		Stripe Arrangements	Earliest Date Used
* * * * * * * * * * * * *	8 pointed	red, white alternate	1779
	6 pointed	red, white alternate	1782
	5 pointed	red, white alternate	1783
	6 pointed	red, white, blue alternate	1793
* * * * * * * * * * * * *	8 pointed	red, white, blue alternate	1779
	4 pointed	red, white alternate	1796
	7 pointed	blue, red, white in mixed combination	
* * * * * * * * * * * * *	Square of 4, one in center, 6 pointed	red, white alternate	1780s
* * * * * * * * * * * * *	6 pointed	red, white alternate	1781
* * * * * * * * * * * * *	5 pointed	red, white alternate	1781
* * * * * * * * * * * *	5 pointed	red, white alternate	1781
* * * * * * * * * * *	7 pointed	red, white alternate	1781
* * * * * * * * * * * * *	5 pointed	red, white alternate	1782

(circle of stars)	?? 6 pointed	red, white alternate red, white, blue alternate	1792 179?
(3 × 4 grid of stars)	??, but had an eagle at the bottom	red, white alternate	1784
(vertical column of stars)	4 pointed	red, white, with alternating blue and white fields	1796
(two columns of stars)	4 pointed	red, white alternate	1796
(X-shaped arrangement of stars)	4 pointed	red, white alternate	1796
(cluster of stars)	4 pointed	red, white alternate	1796
Circle of 12, one in middle of flag proper	8 pointed	red, white alternate, but where the blue field usually is	1812
One large star in middle of blue flag	5 pointed	none	1861

The flag that waved defiance over Fort McHenry in 1814, inspiring Francis Scott Key to write "The Star-Spangled Banner," is this one, now on display in the Museum of History and Technology at the Smithsonian Institution. At that time the flag had 15, instead of 13, stripes.

1794, had 15 of each. That's how the flag remained for 14 years and three wars: through the suppression of French privateers (1798–1800), against the Tripoli pirates (1801–1805), and in the War of 1812 against Great Britain (1812–1815).

When this flag was hoisted over the Tripolitan stronghold in Derne on April 27, 1805, by Lieutenant O'Bannon of the Marine Corps and Midshipman Mann of the Navy, it became the first American flag to be hoisted over a fortress of the Old World. This is the source of the reference to "the shores of Tripoli" in the "Marine's Hymn." (The "halls of Montezuma," mentioned in the same line, refer to the expedition under General Quitman to Mexico City, where the stars and stripes were hoisted on September 14, 1847.)

It was this 15-starred-and-striped flag that flew over Fort McHenry on September 13, 1814, when Francis Scott Key wrote his initial version of "The Star-Spangled Banner." It was also the United States' banner in the Battle of Lake Erie, and was flown by General Jackson at New Orleans.

The most unusual 15-stripe flag to turn up was at the historical Myers House, the oldest house in Norfolk, Virginia, in 1969. Donated by a local patron, it was considered quite a find, until some tourist noticed that the stripes ran eight white and seven red, the opposite of what they should be. No one ever got to the bottom of this historical put-on, but the flag was suddenly banished, never to be seen again.

The Union grew rapidly, and Congress and flag-makers were apparently hard-pressed to keep up. For example, no 16-star flags are known to exist. The 16-star flag was never officially adopted, even though there were 16 states in the Union from June 1, 1796, to March 1, 1803. Such a flag appears on a ship painting dated 1802, which is displayed at the Abby Aldrich Rockefeller Folk Art

Collection in Williamsburg, Virginia, with 15 stars arranged in a rectangular shape and the sixteenth in the middle. If the artist, M.F. Corne, actually painted what he saw — and there are serious doubts — the flag would have been a local one, since it was always a principle of federal flag designers never to give any one star (state) precedence over another, as this design would seem to do.

Seventeen-starred-and-striped flags were furnished by the United States government to its factions, though no law was passed approving them, either. None of these still exist.

No accounts have been discovered of 18- or 19-star flags. One 20-star flag remains intact, though the law for it lasted only one year.

Some foresighted members of government soon recognized that adding a stripe for every state was simply not going to work. One congressman remarked that if the practice continued, the tallest pine tree in the state of Maine would be an insufficient flagpole. Among those who sought to address the problem was New York City representative Peter H. Wendover (1768–1834), who had been a delegate to his state's constitutional convention in 1796. Wendover made it nearly his life's work to have Congress establish a workable and standardized national flag. He wrote hundreds of letters to influential people, pointing out that flags then flying in the city of Washington bore variously 9 to 18 stripes. According to the *Dictionary of American Biography* (American Council of Learned Societies, 1943), it was Wendover who consulted Captain Sam Reid regarding flag design. Reid suggested returning to 13 stripes and keeping that number fixed while the blue field added a star for each new state.

And so was born the congressional resolution passed on April 4, 1818, which declared:

> That from and after the fourth day of July next, the Flag of the United States be thirteen horizontal stripes, alternate red and white: that the Union be twenty stars, white in a blue field.
>
> That on the admission of every new state into the Union, one star be added to the Union of the Flag; and that such addition shall take effect on the fourth of July next succeeding such admission.

A further proposal by Sam Reid did not make it into this resolution. He suggested that the union's stars be arranged in parallel rows on military flags, while for nonmilitary purposes (such as flags flown on merchant ships) the stars could be gathered together to form one large star. Congress not only ignored this suggestion but actually failed, once again, to include in its resolution any instructions for arranging the stars. As new states joined the Union, the stars continued to be arranged in various designs according to the flag-maker's fancy.

Unusual numbers of stars (states) led to unusual "new constellations." Two unusual versions of the 34-star flag were flown, for example:

```
* * * * * * *                          * * * * * * * *
* * * * * * *                          * * * * * * * * *
* * *     * * *         and            * * * * * * * * *
* * * * * * *                          * * * * * * * *
* * * * * * *
```

The 35-star flag had five rows of seven stars each and the 36-star flag had six rows of six each, but then came problems again with the 37-star flag. It too came out in dual versions:

```
* * * * * *                            * * * * * * * *
* * * * * *                             * * * * * * *
* * * * * *                            * * * * * * *
* * * * * *            and              * * * * * * *
* * * * * *                            * * * * * * *
* * * * * *                             * * * * * * *
```

On October 29, 1912, President William Howard Taft issued an executive order providing that the stars on the flag, which by then numbered 48, be arranged in "six horizontal rows of eight stars each." And so it remained for nearly 47 years.

Thirty-four-star flag, in Fort McKinley Museum (glass-enclosed).

THE "SECOND FRONT" IN AMERICA

When 11 southern states seceded from the Union in 1860 and 1861 to form the Confederate States of America, they produced — just as the colonies had earlier — a variety of individual state and regimental banners, as well as several Confederacy flags.

On March 5, 1861, the provisional Southern Congress selected a standard, the stars and bars, which was so close to the United States flag in colors and general arrangement as to cause confusion between forces at the Battle of Bull Run. The stars and bars retained the blue field section with a circle of stars — using only seven at first, eleven later — and the alternating red and white stripes, but settling for only those "bars" of red-white-red.

The *Richmond Dispatch* of December 7, 1861, contained an article advocating a change in the design of the Southern flag:

> The adoption of our present flag was a natural, but most pernicious blunder. As the old flag itself was not the author of our wrongs, we tore off a piece of the dear old rag and set it up as a standard. We took it for granted a flag was a divisible thing, and proceeded to set off our proportion. So we took, at a rough calculation, our share of the stars and our fractions of the stripes, and put them together, and called them the "Confederate flag." Even as Aaron of old put the gold into the fire, and then came out this calf, so certain stars and stripes went into committee, and then came out this flag. All this was honest and fair to a fault. We were clearly entitled to from seven to eleven stars, and three or four of the stripes.
>
> There is but one feature essential to a flag, and that is distinctness. Beauty, appropriateness, good taste, all are desirable; but the only thing indispensable is distinctness, — wide, plain, unmistakable distinction from other flags. Unfortunately, this indispensable thing is just the thing which the Confederate flag lacks; and failing in this, it is a lamentable and total failure, absolute and irredeemable.
>
> We knew the flag we had to fight; yet, instead of getting as far from it, we were guilty of the huge mistake of getting as near to it as possible. We sought similarity, adopting a principle diametrically wrong. We made a flag as nearly like theirs as could, only under favorable circumstances, be distinguished from it. Under unfavorable circumstances (such as constantly occur in practice), the two flags are indistinguishable.
>
> There is no case in history in which broad distinction in the symbols of the combatants was more necessary than it has been in the present war. Our enemies are of the same race with ourselves, of the same color, and even shade of complexion; they speak the same language, wear like clothing, and are of like form and stature.

After Bull Run the more distinctive Confederate battle flag was produced. It was a square red flag with a blue diagonal cross, with 13 white stars spaced inside the cross. The stars represented the 11 seceding states plus Kentucky and Missouri, which stayed with the Union but had many sympathizing citizens fighting on the South's side. The design, again, may have been dredged from United States history. It was similar to the flag of Russia that had flown over Fort Ross, California, in 1812.

This was the flag known affectionately as the "Southern Cross." A poem titled "The Southern Cross" was written by St. George Tucker of Virginia in commemoration.

A third, flag, popularly known as the second Confederate flag, was ordered by the Confederate Congress on May 1, 1863. This flag used the battle flag design as the canton on a plain white rectangular banner. After February 4, 1864, a red band was added along the flying edges for easier visibility.

Two of the three have remained on the scene. The Mississippi state flag retains the battle flag canton of the third Confederate banner design, but on a flag with three large stripes of blue, white, and red. The Georgia flag incorporates the Southern cross on its main body, adding a blue banner inscribed with the state seal next to the staff edge.

The Union evidently did not consider defeat by the rebels a possibility, for no stars were subtracted from the national flag. Indeed, stars continued to be added during the Civil War, including a thirty-fourth star for the state of West Virginia. A preserved 35-star flag is on display in the Philadelphia Maritime Museum.

With all these flags in American history, it is interesting to note that there is one spot of Americana where the American flag is not and has not ever been flown. It is a United States naval station, too, which confounds the issue. This station is at Rota, Spain. It is an American complex on a Spanish base, and therefore only the Spanish flag flies there.

The Stars—State by State

The United States flag incorporates the history of a nation, including its expansion and territorial development. This history has made the flag a dynamic, living entity. No other national standard has been "constructed" in exactly the same way, historical piece by historical piece. That which perhaps comes closest is the motherland banner of Great Britain, with its Scottish and Irish overlay additions.

It is often thought that each star in our flag's constellation represents a particular state in the order of admission to the Union, but there is no confirmation of this. In fact, even before the arrangement of stars was standardized, Congress and federal flag designers took pains to avoid giving any one star precedence over another. We can only contemplate the dates on which the various states joined the Union:

1. Delaware	Dec. 7, 1787	5. Connecticut	Jan. 9, 1788
2. Pennsylvania	Dec. 12, 1787	6. Massachusetts	Feb. 6, 1788
3. New Jersey	Dec. 18, 1787	7. Maryland	April 28, 1788
4. Georgia	Jan. 2, 1788	8. S. Carolina	May 23, 1788

9.	New Hampshire	June 21, 1788	30.	Wisconsin	May 29, 1848
10.	Virginia	June 25, 1788	31.	California	Sept. 9, 1850
11.	New York	July 26, 1788	32.	Minnesota	May 11, 1858
12.	N. Carolina	Nov. 21, 1789	33.	Oregon	Feb. 14, 1859
13.	Rhode Island	May 29, 1790	34.	Kansas	Jan. 29, 1861
14.	Vermont	March 4, 1791	35.	West Virginia	June 20, 1863
15.	Kentucky	June 1, 1792	36.	Nevada	Oct. 31, 1864
16.	Tennessee	June 1, 1796	37.	Nebraska	March 1, 1867
17.	Ohio	March 1, 1803	38.	Colorado	Aug. 1, 1876
18.	Louisiana	April 8, 1812	39.	N. Dakota	Nov. 2, 1889
19.	Indiana	Dec. 11, 1816	40.	S. Dakota	Nov. 2, 1889
20.	Mississippi	Dec. 10, 1917	41.	Montana	Nov, 8, 1889
21.	Illinois	Dec. 3, 1818	42.	Washington	Nov. 11, 1889
22.	Alabama	Dec. 14, 1819	43.	Idaho	July 3, 1890
23.	Maine	March 15, 1820	44.	Wyoming	July 10, 1890
24.	Missouri	Aug. 20, 1821	45.	Utah	Jan. 4, 1896
25.	Arkansas	June 15, 1836	46.	Oklahoma	Nov. 16, 1907
26.	Michigan	June 15, 1836	47.	New Mexico	Jan. 6, 1912
27.	Florida	March 23, 1845	48.	Arizona	Feb. 14, 1912
28.	Texas	Dec. 29, 1845	49.	Alaska	Jan. 3, 1959
29.	Iowa	Dec. 28, 1846	50.	Hawaii	Aug. 21, 1959

Something a lot of people don't know is that Senator Herbert H. Lehman (D–NY) submitted a bill to Congress that would have added a forty-ninth star before Alaska and Hawaii were even being considered for statehood. His star would have broken tradition entirely, because it wasn't meant to honor a state at all. He wanted to add a gold star to the constellation to honor all armed forces personnel who had died in the service of their country.

This idea was not incorporated, so it wasn't until the admission of Alaska to statehood on January 3, 1959, that the flag received its forty-ninth star. President Eisenhower announced the new design to be seven staggered rows of seven stars each, to take effect July 4, 1959. Weeks later, on August 21, 1959, the flag was given a fiftieth star for Hawaii. The new, and present, design consisted of nine rows of stars (five rows of six and four rows of five). The 50-star flag was approved for flying July 4, 1960.

Naturally, the addition of two new stars presented a challenge to the flag-making companies. Annin and Company of New Jersey, the company that makes more flags than any other, had a backlog of 48-star flags they didn't know what to do with, and orders for new flags they couldn't fill until the new design was decided. At the time no one was sure whether one or both of the territories were to be given statehood. C.D. Beard, a company vice-president, said, "Either way we'll have a big job to do. There are probably half a billion flags in the U.S. And all of them will have to be replaced."

The General Services Administration, which supplies flags for federal buildings throughout the country, was using about 51,000 per year at that time. Average life of a flag is three to eight months. At least one replacement for each flying flag is kept on hand. Most of these are 9'9" × 5'2" in size, though smaller 6'8" × 3'6" ones are often flown in inclement weather because they don't whip themselves to shreds so fast against a pole. Even so, the wet-weather flags are destroyed as soon as they get dirty or wear out. Fair-weather flags are dry cleaned at least twice during their lifetime. All this presents an idea of the cost of a flag changeover just for federal facelifting. (A letter to the General Services Association elicited a printout of United States flag consumption by the federal government in 1991: 158,435 flags of various sizes, at a cost of about $3,556,188.55. This includes no flags or banners other than the stars and stripes.)

Before the flag change was approved, a design had to be established. The president had a lot of help in creating the 49- and 50-star designs — probably more help than he wanted. Everyone was designing star constellations, if the number of designs printed in the country's newspapers was any indication. It was the first time the United States — or any large country, in fact — had had the mass communication media to contend with in "helping" select a national flag. The newspapers, radio, and television were saturated with the novelty of it for weeks.

One classic example came courtesy of Postmaster Joe Kelly, who owned the small post office building at Harper's Ferry, Iowa. He jumped the gun, painting the 50-star design he guessed would be accepted all the way across the upper part of the building before the design was finalized. As it turned out, he guessed wrong.

Delegate Joseph R. Farrington of Hawaii, one of the two states most concerned with the changeover, was pictured by the Associated Press with a design he favored: stars in staggered horizontal alternating lines of six and five. The advantage of the design was that space was left in the blue field next to the staff for the possible future addition of another complete row of stars.

Naturally the flag factories were in on the action. A Vernon, New Jersey, company produced a sample showing the two extra stars added into the top stripe, forming a sort of panhandle on the right side. This, of course, would have shortened the top red stripe, offering an uneven flag field. Hardly anyone took it seriously, for there were other ways to solve it more artistically.

Concerned citizens like Marge C. Seyforth of Verdugo City, California, wrote letters to editors of national newspaper supplements like *The American Weekly* (May 6, 1950) with their designs. Ms. Seyforth revised the blue field by adding a triangular section with two new stars in it, pointing out that current 48-star flags could be salvaged, at a huge monetary savings both to the government and to flag-makers caught with unmoveable inventories.

Four other suggested possibilities, each with its own supporting claque, came from the heraldic branch of the Army Quartermaster Corps. They included "USA" spelled in stars and two stars-in-a-circle formations.

One of the many persons offering designs for the new flag-to-be was a descendant of Betsy Ross. Mrs. Roy Gaston Booker of New York traces her ancestry from Betsy Ross's third marriage, to John Claypool. Her arrangement showed five horizontal rows of 10 stars each, retaining the 13 stripes.

Alex Raymond, then president of the National Cartoonists' Society (and creator of cartoon strip "Rip Kirby"), attacked the problem more logically. He wrote a series of articles on new flag designs and syndicated it across the country (King Features, 1950), culminating the series with a reader questionnaire on which design each preferred. One of the designs included was Mrs. Booker's — the winner.

The flag design ideas proferred by Raymond were adapted from earlier American flags and banners. His reason for getting into the imbroglio was that "most of our most popular Americans owe their origins to cartoonists. Uncle Sam, Columbia and Santa Claus sprang from the pens of artists of the press. The classic 'Spirit of '76' had first publication as a newspaper cartoon design. Cartoonists and other artists were influential in effecting acceptance of the Stars and Stripes as the national flag. Therefore it is appropriate for newspaper cartoonists to express views regarding the redesigning of the flag when two new stars must be added."

The problem, stated in Mr. Raymond's words, was:

> The change must be more than merely a matter of adding two new stars to the field. The 48 stars of the present flag are arranged in six equal rows of eight each. Placing 50 stars in even rows means that there must be five horizontal rows of 10 stars each, or two rows of 25 stars each, or 10 horizontal rows of five stars each.
>
> If the former of these three arrangements of 50 stars is chosen, the blue field must be made wider. That is, unless the size of the stars is reduced. If the latter of the three arrangements mentioned above is selected, the field must be made deeper.
>
> Since the appearance of the flag must be altered, consideration should be given to further changes advocated by artists who feel that the design could be improved.

It is true that the national banner evolved more or less by chance and not always in accord with the fundamentals of good design. It is also true that the flag has often been changed. In fact, the longest period it has gone unchanged is 42½ years, the period just prior to the addition of Alaska and Hawaii. For Raymond to redesign it, then, was certainly not violating tradition, so long as the colors and components were retained.

The first "artistically acceptable" design Raymond submitted to his readers was an arrangement of the 50 stars in five vertical columns on a blue field extending the entire depth of the flag, next to the staff side. "To an artist's eye," Raymond said, "it has better balance than a flag with a field in one corner. ... It provides adequate space for rearrangement of stars if further states need be added." The design was suggested by the Bennington flag of 1776, on which the blue field was considerably enlarged from the usual corner-filling canton, as well as by the state flags of Texas, Georgia, Iowa, and North Carolina, all of which have vertical blue fields running full depth.

Some of Raymond's designs and the historical banners that suggested them. *Top left:* This design was suggested by the original Bennington flag of 1776. *Top right:* This design was suggested by the Cowpens flag of 1781, which was flown by the Third Maryland Regiment. *Bottom:* This design was suggested by the Grand Union flag of 1776 and the Battle flag of the Confederacy together.

Raymond's second design utilized better balance also, but by extending the blue field completely across the top of the flag, cutting the number of stripes to seven.

Design number three involved a symmetrical placement of the 50 stars in three concentric circles. The precedents, of course, were the Third Maryland Regiment's flag of 1781, which showed "Maryland's star" surrounding by the other 12 in the Union, and the original stars and stripes with its circle of 13 stars.

As late as the Civil War, thanks to the vague Congressional design edict, flags were still being used that had as many as 30 stars arranged circularly.

Advantages of the circular design were twofold. It was more elastic, since circles could absorb new additions much more easily than rows, and without the necessity of continuing design changes. The circle design also returned to the idea that all states were equal, which was the original reason for the circle of 13.

Design number four was suggested by the Grand Union flag of 1776 and the battle flag of the Confederacy. It consisted of a diagonal blue bar with two rows of stars. The idea brought a lot of history to bear in one design, symbolizing a Union split and reunited, while also reflecting the first official flag flown by George Washington for the united colonies and showing as well the tie to mother country England.

Detractors of this design suggested it was perhaps too reminiscent of the Confederate flag, leaving the viewer wondering which side had actually won the Civil War. They said it "glorified the rebellion" and, in so doing, shamed the country all over again by, in affect, advocating slavery. It also harkened back to a flag design that could have provoked anger in that Cold War era: the flag of Russia that flew over the Russian fur trading colony in Northern California in 1812. That flag, too, had featured a diagonal cross design, though it contained no stars.

The number five design roamed farthest afield from the norm. It was a blue-bordered banner with the stars superimposed upon the border. It showed balance and symmetry right enough, and new stars could be added easily if

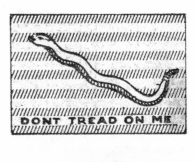

Top: One of Alex Raymond's more radical ideas for a new United States flag design was this star-spangled blue border one (left) borrowed partly from the old "Don't Tread on Me" flag from revolutionary days (right). *Bottom:* Another of Raymond's designs borrowed elements from the "Lone Star" Texas state flag.

Arthur E. DuBois, former Department of Defense director of heraldic affairs, showed some of the unsolicited ideas for 49- and 50-star flags that were sent in by the public. (Source: *American Weekly* magazine.)

necessary. But it was a radical departure, and Raymond's readers didn't cotton to it at all. Raymond stated that the historical forerunners were the rattlesnake ensign used by Lt. John Paul Jones as the first Navy Jack in 1776, and the so-called "American Stripes" raised over Detroit and posts in the Northwest Territory after the revolution by General Anthony Wayne's troops. Neither, however, would seem to be suggestive in any way, since neither entailed blue fields or star constellations of any kind in its design.

Design number six for readers to vote on featured a blue outline of a five-pointed star, with 50 white stars spaced along the blue outline, all superimposed on a field of 13 stripes. Balance, symmetry, and elasticity were again the key advantages listed. The disadvantage, again, was the radical departure from the existing stars and stripes. According to Raymond, the "Lone Star" Texas flag suggested the idea.

The final design, ultimately voted the consensus favorite across the country, was Mrs. Booker's design featuring a canton of five evenly spaced rows of 10 stars each. It followed the lead of President Howard Taft in 1912 when he decreed the 48 stars be arranged in six rows of eight stars each. Taft's design had been suggested by the joint Army and Navy flag board, of which Admiral George Dewey was a senior member. Nevertheless, the five-rows-of-ten design was not the one ultimately chosen for the 50-star flag.

Discussion of designs dragged on for over three years while politicians argued the merit of granting statehood to Hawaii or Alaska or both. Meanwhile, Arthur E. DuBois, then director of heraldic affairs for the Department of

Defense, quietly gathered more and more design ideas, some of which he shared with the public in a 1953 article in *The American Weekly* magazine).

DuBois thought it completely fitting that the flag of the leader of the free world should itself be free (to be changed). He was pleased that the flag's design had always shown that the individual states did not lose their identity to that of the national "state." "The Heraldic Division of the DOD is merely a research, design and development agency for the armed forces and the executive branch of the government," he made clear. "The people, through the Congress and the President, actually design the flag. No government agency or bureau in the federal government is responsible."

Some of the unsolicited designs received from the "people" — teachers, housewives, veterans, school children — by the heraldic affairs division included placing the stars in a wheel design, spacing them in equally sized triangular blue fields at each corner of the flag, and more than 150 others.

By this time three new bills had been introduced into the House of Representatives, all concerning flag changes. One would have set up a joint congressional committee to consider all suggestions and make a recommendation to Congress. One was readying a new star pattern in a square of seven rows of seven stars. And one would have directed the quartermaster general of the Army, under which the heraldic division works, to design any new flag which should become necessary.

As early as 1818, however, there had been precedent for flag changes being approved by executive decree. President James Monroe had asserted this right and ordered the stars arranged in four rows of five each. Unfortunately he didn't state whether he meant four horizontal rows of five or five horizontal rows of four, so both versions were flown by various governmental agencies.

Partly responsible for the foot-dragging decisions concerning Alaska and Hawaii were laws that weren't known to the citizenry in general. By an obscure regulation the flag cannot be changed except on the anniversary of American independence, July 4. Under the statehood bill for Hawaii, that state was not scheduled to become part of the Union until after its November 1954 elections. If Alaska was to be voted statehood before July 4, 1954, then there would be only one flag change necessitated, both stars being added at the same time. A 50-star stars and stripes could become official on July 4, 1955. And so it came to pass, right? Wrong. Alaska and Hawaii both jointed the Union in 1959, and the 50-star flag was raised for the first time officially at 12:01 A.M. on July 4, 1960, at Fort McHenry National Monument in Baltimore, where the anthem had also been inspired. This was in accordance with Executive Order 10834 by President Eisenhower. The stars were arranged in five rows of six, and four rows of five.

Other designs are still discussed from time to time, for future eventualities. Both Puerto Rico and Guam have been discussed as future states at one time and another. Fifty-two stars will, if that eventuality ever arises, be hard to design, so vexillologist Whitney Smith, director of the Flag Research Center,

Vexillologist Whitney Smith proposed a complete break with tradition, should the country increase to 52, or more, states. His design is pictured above.

has already come up with a possible solution. He retains the symbolism of 13, but through the use of one star targeted inside 13 stylized blue, white, and red stripes, which also make up star outlines (even though only part of each is actually seen on the flag).

FLAG SIZES

Other than in the military, there never has been any official size stipulated for the American flag. Thus they have ranged from 3¾ × 4½-inch miniatures designed for Pentagon desk top display up to what was reputed to be the world's largest flag, a 210 × 411 foot marvel that was rolled out on the lawn of the Washington Monument on June 14, 1980. That flag weighs seven tons and took 25 workers, two forklifts, and a crane just to unload it from its truck. There *are* officially established proportions for a flag, however, credited by different encyclopedias to presidents Taft (1912) and Wilson (1916). The now official ratio of width to length, 1 to 1.9, was set by President Eisenhower in 1959. This keeps a flag in proportion, no matter what size it is made.

A number of sizes have been designated for government agencies and armed forces that have differed slightly from that ratio, but the building manager of the Pentagon, after probing records, could only find two flag sizes that had ever been used there: the "standard" flag, 12 × 17 feet, for fair weather use, and the foul weather flag, 8 × 12 feet.

The size flag to be flown is determined by the size of the available flagpole. The rule-of-thumb correct size, aesthetically as well as to handle rough winds, is approximately one-fourth the height of the pole. The pole at the Officer's Candidate School, Newport, Rhode Island, Naval Station, which was the second largest in the world when constructed, takes six to eight people just to get the flag up on it during special ceremonies. If flag and pole were not kept in proportion, ceremonies of this type would get literally out of hand.

HERALDIC HASSLE WITH STATE FLAGS

Outside the Smithsonian's Museum of History and Technology in Washington, D.C., 54 flags flutter daily, weather permitting. They include the stars and stripes, the Smithsonian Institution's emblem flag, the flags of the District of Columbia and Puerto Rico, and the 49 state flags and one state pennion (Ohio) of the United States. Looking at them, it is brought home suddenly that few Americans could recognize more than one or two, and even if more people could tell them apart at close range, they couldn't do it while the flags were hanging on a pole because, heraldically speaking, they are both undistinguished and indistinguishable from each other. The science of flags has sadly declined. Strictly speaking, many of the state flags aren't flags at all, only misused state seals. Only a few, such as Maryland, Colorado, Hawaii, or New Mexico— can be easily recognized. And easy recognition is the purpose of a flag (though now the feeling is that the design should also incorporate a historical basis).

In heraldry, which is the basis for vexillology, the design of a flag either played on the surname of the family to use the flag, or represented some family situation, peculiarity, or special deed. Colors were distinct, arranged in stark contrasts, with easily noted figures. Fringe is not regarded as an integral part of a flag, but is intended only for beautification, so its use does not constitute an addition to the design. If all these points were well planned a flag had eye appeal and maximum visibility, and was also immediately recognizable.

Among the state flags a prime example of good design is Maryland's banner. It is an armorial banner, the shield of the Calvert family, who were the Colony's proprietors. It consists of quarters, the Calvert family represented in first and fourth and the Crossland family, to which Lord Baltimore's mother belonged, in second and third. The Calvert fields are divided into six vertical sections, alternating gold and black, with a diagonal stripe superimposed, which is divided into six countercolored sections. The Crossland fields are themselves quartered white and red with "cross botonnées" (one of heraldry's score of cross types), which are, in turn quartered and countercolored in red and white. The resulting banner blazes with color and can quickly be picked out of any score of flags.

On the other hand, look at the state flags of Kansas, Kentucky, Minnesota, Montana, Nebraska, New Hampshire, and Virginia. All are seals, with small printed messages, on blue fields. Their own citizens would be hard-put to pick

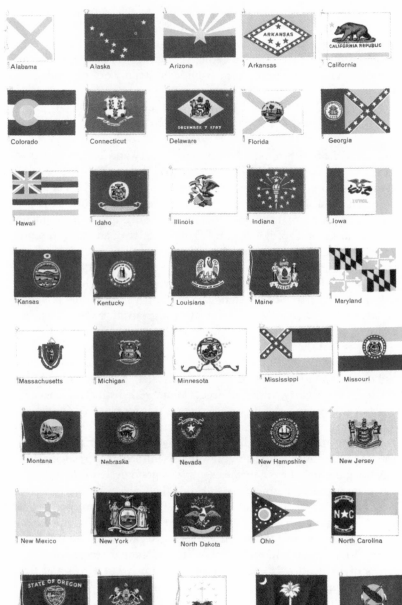

Alabama   Alaska   Arizona   Arkansas   California

Colorado   Connecticut   Delaware   Florida   Georgia

Hawaii   Idaho   Illinois   Indiana   Iowa

Kansas   Kentucky   Louisiana   Maine   Maryland

Massachusetts   Michigan   Minnesota   Mississippi   Missouri

Montana   Nebraska   Nevada   New Hampshire   New Jersey

New Mexico   New York   North Dakota   Ohio   North Carolina

Oregon   Pennsylvania   Rhode Island   South Carolina   Oklahoma

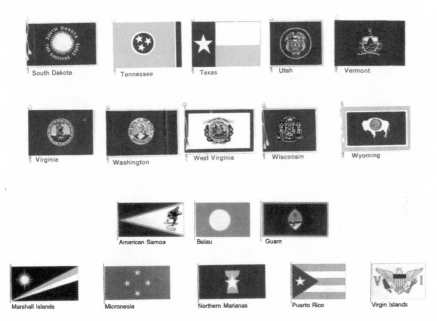

them out of a display. Those states really ought to do something about individualizing their banners. Perhaps they should consider contests for flag renderings. It would renew residents' interest in their state flags, and possibly result in some improved designs.

Opposite and above: United States state and territory flags.

6

Loving the Flag:
Tributes of All Stripe

The stars and stripes is seen in many ways by many people.

First, it is seen as a flag, a symmetrical piece of cloth with designs inherent. England's College of Arms, which records the pedigrees and registers of the coats of arms of the worlds' families, would describe it as "goulds with six barrulets argent on a canton azure with 50 mullets." (The coat of arms of the United States of America is not recorded at the College of Arms, though the American flag does show up in the records, having been entered in connection with a ceremony at the college shortly after World War II.)

A second way the flag is seen is in the meaning behind its parts. The star is a symbol of the heavens and the divine goal to which man has aspired from time immemorial. The stripe is symbolic of the rays of light emanating from the sun, our warming element in life itself.

Both star and stripe symbols have long been represented on the standards identifying nations, from the banners of the astral worshippers of ancient Egypt and Babylon to the 12-starred flag of the Spanish conquistadors that Cortez brought to the New World. They spread to the seventeenth century striped standard of Holland, and to the West India Company, and to the present patterns on the standards of many nations of Europe, Asia, and the Americas.

It may be interesting to note that most of these standards were, until very recent times, personal ruler's flags. The idea of each nation having its separate flag is new. The first "flag of the people" was probably the red cross of St. George, adopted by the British people. But the flag that was flown from forts and ships of war was the English *ruler's* flag. The national flag of Italy dates only from 1848; of Japan, from 1859; of Germany, from 1871; and of China, from 1872. In light of this, the United States national standard is a senior world citizen.

After the infant American republic had successfully defied an empire and the stars and stripes began to take on the characteristics of a symbol of sovereignty, the brilliant nationalist Henry Ward Beecher remarked on the third way the flag is seen: "A thoughtful mind, when it sees a nation's flag, sees not the flag, but the nation itself."

Beecher continued:

> Whatever may be its symbols, its insignia, he reads chiefly in the flag, the government, the principles, the truths, the history that belong to the nation that sets it forth. The American flag has been a symbol of Liberty and men rejoiced in it.
>
> The stars upon it were like the bright morning stars of God, and the stripes upon it were beams of morning light. As at early dawn the stars shine forth even while it grows light, and then as the sun advances that light breaks into banks and streaming lines of color, the glowing red and intense white striving together, and ribbing the horizon with bars effulgent, so, on the American flag, stars and beams of many-colored light shine out together....

Just as the cross symbolizes Christianity, so the United States flag symbolizes a country. It is a visible history. And, as Charles Sumner (1811–1874) wrote, "He must be cold, indeed, who can look upon its folds rippling in the breeze without pride of country."

When the new starred flag was first flown by the Continental Army, George Washington is reported to have said: "We take the stars from heaven, the red from our mother country, separating it by white stripes, thus showing that we have separated from her. And the white stripes shall go down to posterity representing liberty."

The colors have even been ascribed specific virtues. Various essays and poems, however, can't seem to agree on the meanings of the red, the white, and the blue. But that may be poetic license. For example, consider the following three pieces, all printed in *Our Flag in Verse and Prose* (New York: Dodd, Mead, 1936; Robert Haven Schauffler, ed.).

Old Glory
By A.S. Gumbart, D.D.

There are some lessons suggested to us by the colors of the flag. The white is the symbol of purity. It stands for the ideal virtue which should be exercised under certain circumstances and conditions. In a statesman it would stand for a pure and incorrupt citizenship; in a judge it would stand for integrity; in a business man it would stand for honesty; in view of sickness it would stand for humility, and in relation to the poor it stands for charity. In fact, it stands for everything that is godly.

The red stands for love. This color receives its symbolism from the blood, and reminds us that every true patriot should be willing to die for the love of country; to shed his blood if necessary in the hour of the Nation's peril. But more particularly does the red symbolize that divine love which should dwell in every breast and be the ruling passion in every soul.

The stars upon the azure are symbols of light and heavenly protection. They teach us that every state should be a symbol of light, of righteousness, of truth.

They remind us, also, that Heaven is above us, underneath, and around us, and that in the darkest hour of the Nation's peril God's eye is upon us.

All hail, Old Glory, flag of the brave and the free! All hail, thou glorious banner, God bless thee and help thee!

Our Flag
By Elsie M. Whiting

The stripes were to be red and white, and the stars white upon a blue sky. This was our first flag. And now shall I tell you what our flag means? When you see it waving in the air, it says to you: "This is a free land." The colors tell us something, too. The red says, "Be brave;" the white says, "Be pure;" the blue says, "Be true."

Our Colors
By Laura E. Richards

Red! 'tis the hue of battle,
The pledge of victory;
In sunset light, in northern night,
It flashes brave and free.
"Then paint with red thy banner,"
Quoth Freedom to the Land,
"And when thy sons go forth to war,
This sign be in their hand!"

White! 'tis the sign of purity,
Of everlasting truth;
The snowy robe of childhood,
The stainless mail of youth.
Then paint with blue thy banner,
And pure as northern snow
May these thy stately children
In truth and honor go.

Blue! 'tis the tint of heaven,
The morning's gold-shot arch,
The burning deeps of noontide,
The stars' unending march.
Then paint with blue thy banner,
And bid thy children raise
At daybreak, noon and eventide
Their hymn of love and praise.

Valor and truth and righteousness,
In threefold strength to-day
Raise high the flag triumphant,
The banner glad and gay.
"And keep thou well thy colors,"
Quoth Freedom to the Land,
"And 'gainst a world of evil
Thy sons and thou shalt stand."

In his 1917 Flag Day address, Woodrow Wilson offered these thoughts:

This flag which we honor and serve is the emblem of our unity, our power, our thought and purpose as a nation. It has no other character than that which we give it from generation to generation. The choices are ours. It floats in majestic silence above the hosts that execute those choices, whether in peace or in war. And yet, though silent, it speaks to us of the past, of the men and women who went before us, and of the records they wrote upon it.

We celebrate the day of its birth; and from its birth until now it has witnessed a great history, has floated on high the symbol of great events, of a great plan of life worked out by a great people....

It was mentioned earlier that Flag Day is now often celebrated for an entire week in many communities. Back about 1953 the Junior Bar Conference of the American Bar Association went a step further and sponsored the idea of Americanism Month, to be observed between Thanksgiving and Christmas. Though Governor Langlie of Washington State urged people to adopt the plan, and others also talked up its merits, it never really got off the planning board.

Two reasons probably account for the failure. The first is that people are just too busy during the Thanksgiving-to-Christmas season to add other things, regardless of merit. Also it is a bit difficult to combine the "babe in the manger" theme with "the spirit of '76." The Junior Bar men would have been better advised to observe their month prior to Thanksgiving, using Thanksgiving Day as a natural culmination. Or they could have planned it for June, kicking it off on Flag Day and carrying through the Fourth of July.

The second reason for failure is that a month is both too long and too short a time for a concerted program to run. There are already so many other special commemorative days that a month-long period would overlap anywhere it was placed on the year's calendar. That makes it too long. And at any rate, patriotism should be a year-round observation, so a month is also too short. As Adlai Stevenson once noted, "Patriotism is not a short frenzied outburst of emotion but the tranquil and steady dedication of a lifetime."

Months and even years have proved too short to defuse the flag-related confrontations with which the United States has been faced for many years. Differences of opinion make not only horseraces and families of 12, but confrontations between those with differing beliefs regarding what the flag stands for.

A classic case was that of Navy veteran and football player Bill Pierson at San Diego State University. A group protesting the Vietnam war wanted to take down the stars and stripes from the campus flagpole. Pierson didn't want them to. "I was born under that flag. I fought for that flag, and I'm going to college today because of what it represents. No one is going to desecrate it as long as I can defend and protect it," he said. And he stood by the flagpole for three hours in defiance of the protesters, none of whom chose to challenge him. Pierson stands 6 feet, 3 inches, weighs 250 pounds, and had already been drafted by professional football's New York Jets.

His stand made headlines across the country, but the school — despite the provisions of the flag code — half-masted the flag the following day, capitulating to the demands of the small group of dissidents. Nevertheless, Pierson remarked, "There are a lot of us who are fed up with the silly business of an administration letting a small group of radicals push around more than 20,000 students."

Patriots have been fighting the same battle as Pierson for a long time, as demonstrated by the following story:

> At an auction sale in Charleston, S.C., just before the breaking out of the war, an auctioneer, after knocking down odd lots of dry goods and remnants, picked up an American flag and cast it down with the contemptuous remark that he would not ask a bid for that useless rag.
>
> This was too much for one of the bystanders, a rough-looking man, and he called out:
>
> "I bid ten dollars!"
>
> At the word he elbowed his way through the crowd, took the flag and bore it off.

This is a story from *Personal Recollections of the Rebellion*, a book of the Civil War period. Another, more poignant story, is related by F.C. Hicks in his book, *Flag of the United States* (Washington, D.C.: privately printed, 1926).

> In the year 1863 the sixteenth Regiment of Connecticut volunteers, after three days' hard fighting, was forced to surrender with the rest of the command. Just before the enemy swarmed over the breastworks that they had defended for so long, the colonel of the regiment shouted to his men to save the colors — not to let the flag fall into the hands of the enemy. In an instant the battle flags were stripped from their poles and cut and torn into small fragments. Every piece was carefully hidden in the best way possible.
>
> The regiment, some five hundred strong, was sent to a prison camp where most of the men remained until the close of the war. Each piece of the colors was sacredly preserved. When a soldier died his piece was entrusted to a comrade. At the end of the war the weary prisoners returned to their homes, each bringing his bit of star or stripe with him. All these torn fragments were patched together and the regimental colors, nearly complete, are now preserved in the State House at Hartford.
>
> No devotion could be more simple, more resolute, more absolute, than this. And their love of the flag was not shown alone by their willingness to die for it on the field of action. They lived for it through long years of imprisonment, and brought it back whole to the State that gave it into their hands to honor and defend.

Pierson's stand at San Diego State did bring into focus just how lax our laws concerning the flag have become. As early as 1800 a man in New Orleans was convicted (by a military commission) and hanged for tearing down a United States flag that flew over the mint. Now vigilantes take it upon themselves to protect the flag when they feel the law has failed their cause.

For a few months after Pierson faced down his group of campus radicals such anti-war demonstration groups suffered almost daily run-ins in the larger cities with vigilante groups of construction workers, dubbed "hard hats" by the press because members wore their construction work helmets into frays like a uniform. One of the biggest brouhahas took place in front of the New York Stock Exchange on Wall Street, where the hard hats carried American flags right into the noontime peace demonstration, disrupting the meeting completely. Some 70 persons were injured in the melee. The hard hats then stormed city hall, forcing officials there to raise the American flag to full-staff, from half-staff where it had been placed in mourning for four students killed at Kent State University in a student riot.

Confrontations between hard hats and dissident groups became so bloody on occasion that it was questioned whether the cause was really worse than the cure. Too many innocent bystanders, and policemen merely trying to keep the peace, were getting hurt by just being caught in the middle.

Others making a stand against the dissidents found different, more peaceful, ways to make their point. For example, 30 seniors at Owensboro Catholic High School in Kentucky completed (in May 1969) a 180-mile, 22-hour jog, carrying an American flag that had been flown over both the United States Capitol and the Kentucky state capitol. Relays of six runners — the others rested and slept in following cars — left the state capitol at Frankfort, jogged throughout a night of chilling rain, and entered Owensboro at the head of a 100-car entourage of students and older citizens. The journey ended at the campus, where the student government president ran the flag up the staff while the crowd sang the national anthem and recited the Pledge of Allegiance.

The members of Mrs. Irene Priore's third grade class at Cleveland Hill Primary School in suburban Cheektowago, New York, undertook a campaign about that same time to show allegiance to the flag. They had become disturbed at what they considered disrespect toward the flag by demonstrators. The incident that triggered the project, though, was reading about two students in New York City who had refused to pledge allegiance to the flag. The class members began writing individual letters to get others to join them in holding a special "Pledge of Allegiance to Our Flag Day," scheduled for April 30, 1970, at 1:30 P.M.

"The American flag is the symbol of a country that keeps me free," was the way eight-year-old Don Whited wrote his feelings. Nine-year-old Alan Brzoskowski stated, "It's a symbol of God's protection." Others were in similar vein, but all in the children's own words.

Answers came back from President Nixon, members of his cabinet, senators, congressmen, governors, and officials of several national associations, and a flag that had been flown over the White House was sent them for use in their April 30 schoolwide program of patriotic songs and recitations.

Alvin Malinow of Los Angeles was another citizen with a self-styled flag project. He donated flags to scores of Boy Scout units, veteran, and community

Cub Scout Pack 82c of Los Angeles (November 1967) had an opportunity to "see" the United States flag for the first time in their lives when they received a special flag made by the Braille Institute of America. Its stars and stripes were raised so the cubs, all blind, could feel the flag's parts with their fingers. Cub Scouts shown (left to right) are Johnny Gelferman, Arturo Espinosa, Joe Marchese, and Richard Oehm. The volunteers shown are not identified. (Photo courtesy of the Braille Institute of America.)

service groups, including a specially made flag for Troop 82, a group of blind scouts. That flag was made at the Braille Institute and had raised stars and double ridges along the hems of the striping so the members could "see" the design through their developed senses of touch.

WAS THERE REALLY AN UNCLE SAM?

One famous flag-waver is himself a symbol of the United States. "Uncle Sam," the man in the morning suit, has been an American icon for many years. He first came to prominence on recruiting posters in the War of 1812, but he didn't always wear the now-familiar red and white striped pants and top hat. At one time, he was even clean-shaven. In the 1820s, New England cartoonists gave Uncle Sam a black hat and swallowtail coat, with solid red trousers. His beard appeared only after President Lincoln grew one, and the beard was black, not white. His physique, too, began to change in the Lincoln era, from short and somewhat portly to the tall and thin of today. By 1870, the Uncle Sam portrayed in the cartoons of Thomas Nast was approaching the style and

James Montgomery Flagg, creator of the "Uncle Sam" image used on the World War I recruiting poster shown. Legend has it that Flagg used himself as the model.

character of the present-day figure. Today's best-known version, however — the craggy-faced uncle pointing an accusing "I Want You!" finger — was the early twentieth century creation of artist James Montgomery Flagg, who used himself as the model.

Commissioned by the state of New York, Flagg's painting first appeared on the July 1916 cover of *Leslie's Illustrated Weekly* newspaper. The War Department had been looking for a suitable recruiting poster design to spur enlistments, and in 1917 Flagg gave his permission to use his painting. The words "I want you!" were added, and four million posters were printed.

So effective was this poster that it was revived during World War II. Another revival came in 1962, again occasioned by the Army, and this time a second legend seems to have grown which assigns a history to "the real Uncle Sam."

Uncle Sam, according to this legend, was an affectionate nickname given to Samuel Wilson of Troy, New York (1766–1854). He was, depending upon which story one believes, either a government inspector or merely a public-spirited meat packer supplying the Army during the War of 1812. He stamped supply casks with the initials E.A., for contractor Elbert Anderson, and U.S., designating United States government property. One story goes on to say soldiers at a nearby camp, who knew Samuel Wilson, translated the U.S. imprint to "Uncle Sam," and the nickname caught on. Another version states that on October 2, 1812, a fellow workman with Wilson facetiously remarked to the governor of New York, visiting the E. and S. Wilson Meat Company, that the U.S. initials on the barrels of meat ready for shipment stood for "our Uncle Sam Wilson, who inspects the meat for the United States." The joke was retold after, and, as many plant workers later joined the Army, they further spread this story. By 1813 newspapers were even referring to the men of the United States Army as "Uncle Sam's men."

Within five months, this second legend continues, the first image of Uncle Sam was printed in a broadside published in Albany, New York. In 1813 a visiting French journalist wrote home that "Americans are waking up to the fact that their Uncle Sam is a mighty fine gentleman." In 1825 federal employees in Washington, D.C., often jested with visitors, saying "We work for Uncle Sam." The character was firmly established.

Harvard historian Crane Brinton says, "The figure now is no more than a symbol, the kind of symbol it would probably take a revolution or dictator to change."

Although some foreign cartoonists depict him in an unfavorable light, to Americans he represents the best traits of the American way of life. He clearly has a sense of humor and doesn't look at all like the organization man.

Today, the figure of Uncle Sam is so recognizable that only a few stars and stripes can call it to mind, as was the case with an embossed envelope stamp designed for the U.S. Postal Service by artist George Mercer. Using only a star-spangled top hat with a matching shield below, Mercer successfully captured the Uncle Sam image with a minimum number of lines. Meanwhile, for the 1984 Olympic Games in Los Angeles, Walt Disney studios dressed up an eagle figure in an Uncle Sam–like costume, combining the national bird with a national icon to create a serviceable Games mascot of sorts.

Embossed envelope developed by the United States Postal Service suggests Uncle Sam with a few well-placed stars and stripes.

UNIQUE HOMEMADE FLAGS

When an image attains widespread popularity, people often seek to recreate that image in unique ways, to capture a little attention and express their individuality. As the Bicentennial anniversary of the United States drew near in the middle 1970s, many Americans focused such efforts on their national flag. By October 1975, such large department stores as Woodward & Lothrop in the greater Washington, D.C., area were offering "in the best American tradition" a kit and instructions for sewing one's own 3 × 5 foot flag, à la Betsy Ross.

Talented needlesmiths like Mrs. Rosalie Insley of Hollywood, Maryland, a retired teacher; Margaret Duffy of Scotland Beach, Maryland, wife of a tavern owner; and Margaret Sheppard of Mollusk, Virginia, a retired nurse, crocheted flags. Mrs. Sheppard said it took her a month and 60,000 stitches to finish her 50-star, 4 × 6 foot flag. Both the other ladies had crocheted *two* flags — a 50-star and either a Bennington or a "Betsy Ross" 13-star one.

Leslie M. Fisher, at age 89, knitted a flag for the Bicentennial. Her minister, she stated, "thought it was so great he draped it over himself when he was in the pulpit for his July fourth sermon." That was in South Bend, Ind.

And Monnie Cook of Pocahontas, Arkansas, made a quilt designed after the flag, 96 × 104 inches in size. She began work on it in March 1990 and finished it a month later as a gift for her son, George, who, with his twin sister, Georgia, was born on George Washington's birthday. There was only one problem. "With the way I arranged the stars in rows of five and six," Cook later admitted, I just ran out of room to sew on the fiftieth star. But I'm going to make another one, and I'll make sure to get 50 stars on it."

One woman contacted the Norfolk Flag & Emblem Company and asked for "just the field of stars." She wanted several to use as curtains in her home. The company president turned down the order.

That wasn't the end of ingenuity in the Bicentennial year, either. Michael Armendariz of Chicago went in for a haircut and got a one-of-a-kind with seven stars fore and aft on the crown of his head, flanked by 13 stripes. And, when city officials of Union City, California, ordered fire fighters there to remove flag decals from their helmets and trucks, Captain Mike Brown protested by also getting a flag-simile haircut. His covered the back of his head,

One of the newer gravesite memorials for veterans of American-fought wars is this simulated floral Star-Spangled Banner. The small staffed flag was added as a VFW project, a common Memorial Day addition in many cities across the nation.

showing a full flag of 13 stripes, but with no stars in the star-field because the scale was too small for the barber to fashion them.

The female side, not to be left out, was represented by a model on whom New York artists Julius Vitali and Terry Niedzialek spent four hours to create a waving-flag hairdo, using Tenax, clay, and water-based paints. It sort of waved off to one side of her head, and it took her 30 minutes to later wash out .

In 1991 a "fingernail artist" named Alex Cordia working at Paradise Nails in Reseda, California, demonstrated her patriotic flair by painstakingly gluing 400 tiny rhinestones into the shape of an American flag onto a three-inch-long fingernail on her left hand ring finger. The process took four hours. On the nail of the right hand ring fingernail she arranged red, white, and blue spangles to read "World Peace." That was for her brother who had served in Vietnam and her boyfriend who had died there. Her nail designs went over so well that the shop started advertising them, along with Victory Vs and other patriotic designs, to customers.

Patriotic fervor extended into some other unusual crafts. A writer named Richard Wolters said he planned to fly an American flag made into a kite (from the Kite Airplane Company) off the Matterhorn ... if he made it up on his second try. The first attempt had been "weathered out."

Sylvan Furniture Company of Lewiston, Idaho, combined business with patriotism by stocking antique-facsimile hope chests with a colonial flag design from the 1870s emblazoned on their fronts. This design, according to the Smithsonian Institution, is probably taken from a pasture gate on the old Darling Farm in upstate New York, which was placed in the Museum of American Folk Art in New York as a gift of Herbert W. Hemphill, Jr.

From flags on gates the next logical step might be flags on house fronts. As part of a promotional gimmick, a new painting company in Norwich, Connecticut, offered to paint (at no charge) the American flag on the front of the home of the first caller at their office. Mr. and Mrs. John Ballaro took them up on the deal, and their house soon sported the stars and stripes across its entire front, over windows, doorways and all.

They at least knew what was happening. But imagine the surprise of the Beasleys of DeKalb, Illinois, who returned from vacation to find their son, John, had done a similar Bicentennial paint job on their house! The only difference was that his flag featured a 13-star pattern.

This idea never actually seems to die. Around the Fourth of July each year someone always seems to make the news columns by painting the flag on another house, or going to other extremes with patriotic motifs. For Independence Day 1994, it was Dana Walk of Lewiston, Idaho. And for patriotic decoration, visit Bristol, Rhode Island, any year. That citizenry bands together for a parade, where people try to outdo each other, singly or in groups by dressing in flag fashions. They also vie for "most patriotically decorated" homes.

During the United States Bicentennial, a furniture company in Lewiston, Idaho, sold reproductions of an 1870s hope chest featuring a flag design on front. The design, according to the Smithsonian Institution, is taken from a farm gate in upstate New York that now resides in New York's Museum of American Folk Art.

Then there was Edward H. Torbeck, 70, a retired barber in Altamont, Illinois, who used patriotic themes in his hobby of growing "happy flowers" (so called because he treated them all to a belt of beer twice monthly). Some of his living floral designs — the St. Louis Cardinals' insignia, a clock, and a St. Louis Bicentennial design — won rave notices. On one corner of his lawn, in 1970, he created an American flag with loving plants, along with the accompanying message, "God Bless America."

A short time later T.P. Products of Ontario, Canada, blossomed forth offering mail-order "Living Flags." These consisted of pre-seeded matting of specially developed red, white, and blue flower seeds, all with the same rate of growth, that would bloom into a 3 × 5-foot American flag display.

Mr. and Mrs. Joyce Flerchinger of Clarkston, Washington, put their patriotism in lights. They developed a wire mesh signboard at their riverfront home that they decorate differently for every holiday with strings of lights forming pictures. The flag, with 600 lights in it, is for July 4, of course. Joyce's other designs include a champagne bottle pouring into a goblet for New Year's, a dove for Easter, wedding bells for June, and so on.

Another unique living design of the stars and stripes took even more planning than the flower gardens. It involved 10,000 sailors, some dressed in white uniforms and some in blue, standing at salute in a formation at Ross Field,

Wisconsin, which became a part of the Great Lakes Naval Training Station in 1911. The formation, performed in 1917, covered 7½ acres, with the staff and ball 800 feet in length. To get the correct proportion for the aerial photograph, the length of the top of the flag was four times the length of the bottom.

The following year the Army placed 30,000 soldiers in the shape of a star-spangled shield, while at Camp Dodge, near Des Moines, Iowa, another group designed a human Statue of Liberty using 18,000 soldiers. The men forming the flame of the torch were a quarter mile away from those forming the base of the statue.

Top: Dana Walk of Lewiston, Idaho, painted this flag on her house for July 4, 1994. "The house needed painting," she said, "and this seemed like a fun thing to do." (Photo by Bob Loeffelbein.) *Bottom:* The home of Candi and Dave Lawrence in Bristol, Rhode Island, where townsfolk deck their houses in patriotic dress for Independence Day. (Photo courtesy of Kathy Brownell.)

Top: A unique Star-Spangled Banner is this floral display tailored by maintenance personnel at Rocky Reach Dam near Wenatchee, Washington, on the Columbia River. (Photo courtesy of Chelan County Power Company, Wenatchee, Washington.) *Bottom:* Mr. and Mrs. Joyce Flerchinger of Clarkston, Washington, erected this signboard at their riverfront home as an unusual hobby. They post different designs in colored lights for each holiday. This 600-light American flag is for July 4th. (Photo by Bob Loeffelbein.)

In 1917, 10,000 sailors of the United States Navy stood at salute to form this human flag. The formation covered 7½ acres.

In January 1919, the Marine Corps, not to be left out, put 9,100 Marines into a human Marine Corps logo (a world globe pierced by an anchor, all clutched in the talons of an eagle) at Parris Island, South Carolina.

The two companies really rating a prize for novelty flag display were Hilltop Supermarkets, Inc., of East Brunswick, New Jersey, and the Tupperware

This 90 × 150 foot flag is made entirely of red, white, and blue Tupperware bowls. Over 70,000 20-ounce bowls were used. (Photo courtesy of Tupperware Home Parties.)

Company. For the supermarket display, in cooperation with the Coca-Cola Company, 20 men worked 20 hours to build a huge American flag entirely of soda cans. The finished flag replica was 60 feet long and 20 feet tall, and in the center was a 16-foot replica of the Statue of Liberty. The market's Ted Jordan counted 6,400 cases of soda cans used, including red Coca-Cola Classics, white Diet Cokes, and blue Dr. Peppers. "It also really increased sales of soda," he added. As for the Tupperware Company, they constructed a spectacular 90 × 50 foot flag made entirely of 70,000 red, white, and blue 20-ounce Tupperware bowls.

But 1,200 people — including nearly every child in the school district in Itasca, Illinois — took on (and failed at) an even more spectacular task. Under organizer Phil Valenti, they blew up 300,000 red, white, and blue balloons, tied them to a string grid, and made ready to release them in the shape of a giant flag. Then 20 m.p.h. winds came up, unearthed the holding stakes, and blew away whole sections.

Flag replicas have even been called into service for recreation. One playground leader made up two variations of the old pin-the-tail-on-the-donkey game. The first game consisted of a map of the United States mounted on a cork

This Living Flag costume, seen here in the Macy's Thanksgiving Day parade, was the brainstorm of Andrew St. Ours, a mail carrier in Bristol, Rhode Island, in 1989. Various friends have, at various times, made up the six-person display, but here they include (left to right) Andrew, as the flagpole with an eagle hat, Gary Whynot, Chuck Staton, Carol Botchko, Carolyn Mott Jaques, and Marilyn Mott St. Ours, Andrew's wife. (Photo by Kathy Brownell.)

bulletin board. Each participant, in turn, was blindfolded, given a miniature flag mounted on a pin (made in crafts period by the children), twirled around, and told to pin the flag on Washington, D.C.

The second game, planned for Armistice Day, consisted of a large flag replica on a cork bulletin board, with its blue field devoid of stars. Participants were divided into teams, with each member given a star on a pin. The winning team was that which placed all its stars most nearly correctly on the flag, while blindfolded.

You can even bake a sort of flag, if you like:

Flag Cake

Hull and divide 2 pints fresh strawberries.
Thaw 1 (10–12 oz.) frozen pound cake and cut into 10 slices.
Divide 1⅓ cups of blueberries.
Thaw 1 (12-oz.) tub of whipped topping.

Slice 1 cup of the strawberries and set them aside. Halve the remaining strawberries and set them aside also.

Line the bottom of an 8 × 12-inch baking dish with the cake slices.

Top them with 1 cup of the sliced strawberries and 1 cup of the blueberries. Top
these with all the whipped topping.

Place the strawberry halves and remaining ⅓ cup of blueberries on top of the
whipped topping in an American flag design.

Refrigerate until ready to serve. Can serve 15.

Parade magazine and Eastman Kodak Company held a "Let Freedom Ring"
photography contest in 1991 which brought out some winning photos featuring the American flag design. Teresa Turko of Garland, Texas, won with a
photo at a Dallas cemetery on Memorial Day showing flags flying over veterans' graves; that photograph is featured on this book's cover. And Kathy
Brownell of Bristol, Rhode Island, was another winner with a picture of what
she calls "our Living Flag" outfits. These outfits were first unveiled at a July
Fourth parade in Bristol, but have since been entered in countless parades,
taken part in many homecomings for Operation Desert Storm servicemen and
women, and greeted President George Bush on his arrival at Green State Air-
port, where the AP News Service snapped photos that were printed widely,
even in Russia's *Pravda* newspaper.

Another picture of the Living Flag outfits taken during the Macy's Thanks-
giving Day parade, was reprinted and sent to many soldiers stationed in the
Gulf. On the back of each print the costume originators, Andrew and Marilyn
St. Ours, put this quote from Franklin K. Lane:

> I am not the flag; not at all. I am but its shadow. I am whatever you make me,
> nothing more. I am your belief in yourself, your dream of what a people may
> become…. I am no more than you believe me to be and I am all you believe I can
> be. I am whatever you make me, nothing more.

7

Other Flag Laws:
Crime and Punishment

The homemade flags in the last chapter are all good examples of how strongly the question of intent figures into every argument about use and misuse of the flag. If the flag code were strictly enforced, wouldn't those who wore, pinned, and grew the flag be guilty of violations? Yet none of these examples seems to raise anyone's hackles much. On the other hand, some uses of, or depictions of, the flag have had to be considered under the laws of the time — all because of their intent.

Take, for example, the case of Stephen Radich. In 1967 Radich, a Manhattan art dealer, had displayed flag-draped structures in a manner casting contempt on the flag, according to the charge. He was arrested for violating a New York state law against debasing the flag, and his case went through state and federal courts and all the way to the Supreme Court.

Radich denied any intent to dishonor the flag, even with one sculpture that used a flag to depict a male sex organ attached to a cross. The message, he testified, was that religion and patriotism were being used to justify the Vietnam War, which he and the artist deemed a war of national aggression.

The American Civil Liberties Union contended that Radich was being punished, not for sullying the flag, but for expressing unpopular beliefs. They asked why New York authorities didn't punish pro-war users of the flag, like those using "Honor the Flag" bumper stickers, if they were really interested in punishing unlawful use of the flag?

In March 1971 the Supreme Court denied Radich's request for a rehearing of his conviction by a lower court. A divided Court affirmed the lower court's decision, upholding New York's flag desecration law in spite of appeals for freedom to use the national banner in "protest art."

Such court decisions never deterred the outspoken Abbie Hoffman, perhaps the most flamboyant and notorious of the "Chicago Seven," who spent a

193

good part of his life before television cameras and law courts advocating freedom to break the law if the individual disagrees with it. He carried a flag-replica handkerchief around with him as a stage prop so he could whip it out and blow his nose on it. A warrant was finally issued charging that he "unlawfully, wilfully and publicly defaced, defiled and cast contempt upon the Flag of the United States by blowing his nose on said flag."

The Supreme Court had allowed voice dissent as lawful, but that body had also held that individuals must still be responsible for their actions under the law.

The language under which Hoffman was charged is not found in the federal Flag Code. In fact, the Flag Code contains no language at all regarding criminality or prosecution, and several court decisions have held that its provisions are merely declaratory or advisory (State of Del. ex rel. *Trader vs. Hodsdon*, District Court of Delaware, 1967; *Lapolla vs. Dullaghan*, Supreme Court of Westchester County, New York, 1970; and *Holmes vs. Wallace*, District Court of Alabama, 1976). However, the Flag Code is not the only body of regulations concerning the flag of the United States. For example:

(1) An Act of Congress approved 8 February 1916 provided certain penalties for the desecration, mutilation, or improper use of the flag within the District of Columbia.

(2) A warning against desecration of the American flag by aliens was issued by the Department of Justice, which sent the following notice to Federal attorneys and marshals: "Any alien enemy tearing down, mutilating, abusing or desecrating the United States Flag in any way will be regarded as a danger to the public peace or safety within the meaning of Regulation 12 of the Proclamation of the President issued 6 April 1917, and will be subject to summary arrest and punishment."

(3) An Act of Congress approved 16 May 1918 provided, when the United States is at war, for the dismissal from the service of any employee or official of the United States Government who criticizes in an abusive or violent manner the Flag of the United States.

(4) By Act of Congress, 5 July 1968, Title 18, Chapter 33, of the United States Code was amended by adding the following provision: "Whoever knowingly casts contempt upon the Flag of the United States by publicly mutilating, defacing, defiling, burning, or trampling upon it shall be fined not more than $1,000 or imprisoned for not more than one year, or both."

Most states have preferred to take the matter of flag desecration into their own hands and have long had on the books their own laws establishing the who, what, where, how and don'ts of stars and stripes display. Such legislation is consistent with the opinion of the Supreme Court of the United States of America as rendered in 1907 by Justice John Marshall Harlan, which noted that every state should enact adequate laws for the protection of the flag (*Halter vs. the State of Nebraska*, March 4, 1907).

Reasonable guidelines for state laws might include the following provisions:

1. That June 14, Flag Day, be set apart by proclamation of the governor recommending that Flag Day be observed by people generally by the display of the flag of the United States of America and in such other ways as will be in harmony with the general character of the day.

2. That the Flag of the United States of America be displayed on the main administration building of every public institution.

3. That the Flag of the United States of America, with staff or flagpole, be provided for every schoolhouse and that the Flag be displayed during school days either from a flagstaff or, in inclement weather, within the school building.

4. That the Flag be displayed in every polling place.

5. That printing or lettering of any kind on the Flag be prohibited.

6. That the use of the Flag for advertising purposes in any manner be prohibited.

7. That the use of the Flag as a receptacle for receiving, holding, carrying or delivering anything be prohibited.

8. That fitting penalty, fine and imprisonment, be provided for public mutilation, abuse or desecration of the Flag.

Notice that once again no attempt was made to tie down what is meant by "flag," so there remains confusion whether these laws pertain to only the current national emblem or all former ones as well.

It is up to each state, of course, how much or how little of the federal Flag Code they will adopt. This is the reason the laws, and their penalties, differ from state to state. Some, like Virginia's Uniform Flag Act, are explicit and strict. Others, like Nevada's act, are less well defined and more lax in prosecution. In Texas desecrating the flag can bring up to 25 years imprisonment; in Indiana, it is more likely to bring a $5 or $10 fine.

Even laws which are strict and supposedly specific are open to different interpretations, however, and this makes a court system a necessity in flag desecration cases. It is simply not possible for a written law to encompass every circumstance that might arise concerning the United States flag. The question of "intent" to desecrate or defile enters into this problem of loophole-proof lawmaking, too. Intent must be evidenced and shown. Mere mindreading is out.

A case in point would be the wearing of a flag patch on the seat of the pants. Intent here is obvious. And ignorance of the law is held as no excuse. Wearing a flag patch on a jacket, however, might be okay, depending upon how the person was dressed otherwise, what he or she was doing or saying, and how he or she was acting. Contributory factors must be considered in "intent" cases. All these factors must be judged by a policeman at the time of arrest.

This step in the judicial process is by far the most important in stopping flag defilement, because if the arrest isn't made the process doesn't get started. "Much more justice is dispensed in the streets than in the courts in such cases," stated Audre Evans, attorney for the Commonwealth of Virginia, who credited policemen with "ability and common sense" in their treatment of such cases, which often involve young people simply following fads.

Testing laws often results in more useful legislation. As various circumstances are probed, the laws can be rewritten to fit the situations better. Interpretation of common law and law by precedent become less a factor. The Virginia Uniform Flag Law is a fairly all-encompassing example of good, useful legislation. For example:

ARTICLE 2.

18.1-423. Definition of a flag, standard, etc.— The words flag, standard, color, ensign or shield, as used in this article, shall include any flag, standard, color, ensign or shield, or copy, picture or representation thereof, made of any substance or represented or produced thereon, and of any size, evidently purporting to be such flag, standard, color, ensign or shield of the United States, or of this State, or a copy, picture or representation thereof. (Code 1950, 18-354; 1960, c.358.)

18.1-424. Exhibition or display.— No person shall, in any manner, for exhibition or display:

(1) Place or cause to be placed any word, figure, mark, picture, design, drawing or advertisement of any nature upon any flag, standard, color, ensign or shield of the United States or of this State, or authorized by any law of the United States or of this State.

(2) Expose to public view any such flag, standard, color, ensign, or shield upon which shall have been printed, painted or otherwise produced, or to which shall have been attached, appended, affixed or annexed, or such word, figure, mark, picture, design, drawing or advertisement; or

(3) Expose to public view for sale, manufacture or otherwise, or sell, give or have in possession for sale, for gift or for use for any purpose, any substance, being an article of merchandise, or receptacle, or thing for holding or carrying merchandise, upon or to which shall have been produced or attached any such flag, standard, color, ensign or shield, in order to advertise, call attention to, decorate, mark or distinguish such article or substance. (Code 1950, 18-355.)

18.1-425. Mutilating, defacing, etc.— No person shall publicly burn with contempt, mutilate, deface, defile, trample upon, or by word or act cast contempt upon any such flag, standard, color, ensign or shield. (Code 1950, 18-356; 1960, c.358.)

18.1-426. To what article applies.— This article shall not apply to any act permitted by the statutes of the United States or by the laws of this State, or by the United States armed forces regulations, nor shall it apply to any printed or written document or production, stationery, ornament, picture or jewelry whereon shall be depicted such flag, standard, color, ensign or shield, with no design or words thereon and disconnected with any advertisement. (Code 1950, 18-357; c.358.)

Such flag codes have now been incorporated into most state bodies of law. At least one city, Madison Heights, Michigan, has also adopted a flag code into its local laws. This Detroit suburb outlawed contemptuous acts against the American *or* Michigan state flags in a May 5, 1970, passage. The city commissioner said the measure became necessary because federal laws against flag desecration were not being enforced. The ordinance provides for a maximum sentence of 90 days in jail and a $500 fine.

Virginia's legislation clearly defines what constitutes an American flag, stating that no one may defile "any flag ... or copy [of any kind] ... evidently purporting to be such flag ... of the United States...." This, then, includes former national banners and any close approximations used to give the impression of the United States flag. Many legal arguments about flag desecration have involved such approximations.

For example: Do local, state, and federal flag laws apply to *all* American flags, past as well as present? Or is the current flag the only one that cannot be defiled? Do laws apply only to exact representations, so that an arresting officer must peer at a patch on the seat of some juvenile's jeans and count the stars and stripes and note their exact arrangement? If the component parts of the stars and stripes have been rearranged, such as the stars arranged in a peace sign, does a derogatory meaning result? Is that proof of intent to desecrate?

The federal Flag Code doesn't get this specific. Title 18, Section 700, of the United States Code of Law, does, at least in defining desecration and the flag itself. It reads: "Whoever knowingly mutilates, defaces, physically defiles, burns, maintains on the floor or ground, or tramples upon any flag of the United States shall be fined under this title or imprisoned for not more than one year, or both." Note that it says "any flag." It goes on to define "flag of the United States" as "any flag of the United States, or any part thereof, made of any substance, of any size, in a form that is commonly displayed."

One test case in Virginia receiving a lot of publicity involved the display by a commercial concern at the resort city of Virginia Beach in 1970. Ron Herrick, 24-year-old owner of a hard-rock emporium of strobe and sound melange called the Magical Mystery Tour Coliseum, was arrested for exhibiting at his place of business a "disfigured" American flag, one with the stars — 26 of them — arranged on the blue field in the then-popular "peace" symbol — variously called a "crucifixion cross" or "the footprint of the American chicken," depending on who is defining it.

Herrick insisted his flag wasn't an American flag. "It's a message, a wish, a hope," he told reporters. "Its message is peace. It's a peaceful way of saying we don't want to be in this war."

The citizen who made the complaint against him and the arresting officer viewed it differently. "Think of all the guys who died so we could walk the streets in peace," the officer said. "Can you imagine [Herrick's] flag flying over Arlington National Cemetery?"

In the end Herrick was fined $250 and sentenced to six months in jail by a police court judge. He appealed, and a corporation court with a five-person jury lowered his sentence to 30 days, setting the precedent by which future flag defilement cases would be governed in Norfolk and the state of Virginia. The state penalty, however, since 1968 has "a maximum fine of $1,000, a year in jail, or both," updated from $100 fine and a maximum of 30 days in jail.

A concerned citizen of Norfolk, Virginia, John Wells, an unsuccessful candidate for city council, followed up the Herrick case with a demonstration of his own, to find out how far afield the new precedent would be explored by police. He made a stand on the Public Safety Building steps, with a flag very similar to the one Herrick was arrested for flying, different only in the number of stars making up the "inverted Y inside the circle" design. A plainclothes policeman in the crowd he drew, however, heard him mention his "Liberian" flag and, believing it, did nothing except have a police photographer take a picture of Wells and his flag. The Liberian flag actually has 11 red and white stripes and one large five-pointed white star in the blue field. Perhaps Wells didn't know that, and obviously the U.S. Flag and Signal Company of Virginia Beach didn't know it either, for in Wells' pocket, as a hedge against trouble, was a receipt from that company for $7.25 for one Liberian flag.

This resurrects a question that was raised at the time of Herrick's trial: Shouldn't the flag-maker be held just as responsible as the flag-waver? The Norfolk Flag and Emblem Corporation, who made Herrick's flag, either didn't know or didn't care about state and federal flag laws. Yet it seems obvious that a flag manufacturer, above all, should be familiar with such laws and, if necessary, warn a prospective customer about possible consequences if they order flags that are in violation.

If laws were enforced at the source of trouble, in the flag-maker shops, problems would be minimized. Instead of police fighting the street battle item by item, the relatively few sources could be regulated and inspected quite easily.

Flag rental companies would have to be made part of such regulation. Some of them, like Copeland's in Alexandria, Virginia, do tremendous business with Washington, D.C., embassies and party givers. And any United Nations member-country flag, complete with nine-foot pole, can be rented from the United Nations Association in Washington. Or bought, if one prefers.

The problem isn't that the laws to force flag-makers and novelty producers to conform aren't available. They are. The problem lies in enforcement, systematic enforcement, by police and courts already overloaded with more immediate problems, crimes against persons. Enforcement is undertaken only when the public outcry becomes so loud it cannot be ignored, such as that raised in the 1960s and 1970s against wearing clothing made from an American flag. The Flag Code states that a person cannot wear clothing made from an American flag, and the fact of this law's existence has been established in many courts now.

Abbie Hoffman was convicted in the court of general sessions for defiling the American flag after he wore a shirt patterned after the flag at a 1968 House Un-American Activities Committee hearing. In 1969 an 18-year-old student at Virginia Commonwealth University was sentenced to one year in jail for making a vest out of a stolen American flag. A Norfolk State College student was placed on probation in 1970 for defiling the American flag at a campus peace rally. In Brevard County, Florida, a high school student was convicted for wearing the American flag as a sleeveless shirt at school. Sentence imposed by the judge was a 10-day term of raising the American flag at 7 A.M. in front of Titusville City Hall. When the young man failed to wake up on time for his first day as flag raiser, the judge issued a bench warrant for his arrest to impose the suspended sentence of a $100 fine and 20 days in jail.

Judges making such decisions have no easy time. Just where they draw the line that separates defilement, as defined by written law, from misplaced patriotism, as judged by unwritten law, must be carefully studied. If the letter of the present law were enforced, even the cartoon character Uncle Sam, which represents the United States to most of the world (and also decorates armed forces recruiting posters), would be illegally garbed, with his star-spangled vest, red and white striped pants and striped top hat with its white-starred blue band. Even the American ground squirrel, sometimes referred to as the "federation squirrel," might have to shed his fur coat, since it has 13 (usually) brown and white stripes on its body, with light spots showing through, which look not unlike stars from a distance.

Decals and novelties using a stars and stripes motif seem to be judged somewhat differently under the law from flag-like clothing articles. The reason is probably that bric-a-brac items are usually considered removed from the dissident scene. They are sold and bought under a different context. Their reason for being or "intent" is not usually political in nature, if you will.

Whatever the reason, the star-spangled novelty business is in a continuing boom. Whether some of the novelties are in conflict with the laws hasn't been fully determined, in spite of some pretty specific wording. Each case, it seems, is decided on its own merits. The confusion is unfortunate, since when you have the exceptions thus making the law, you no longer really have a law.

Title 4, section 3, of the United States Code (enacted into law July 30, 1947, and amended July 5, 1968) presents a specific legislation covering use of the flag for advertising purposes. Unfortunately it includes the phrase "within the District of Columbia," meaning it is in force only in that area:

> Any person who, within the District of Columbia, in any manner, for exhibition or display, shall place or cause to be placed any word, figure, mark, picture, design, drawing, or any advertisement of any nature upon any flag, standard, colors, or ensign of the United States of America; or shall expose or cause to be exposed to public view any such flag, standard, colors, or ensign upon which shall have been printed, painted, or otherwise placed, or to which shall be attached, appended, affixed, or annexed any word, figure, mark, picture, design, or draw-

ing, or any advertisement of any nature; or who, within the District of Columbia, shall manufacture, sell, expose for sale, or to public view, or give away or have in possession for sale, or to be given away or for use for any purpose, any article or substance being an article of merchandise, or a receptacle for merchandise or article or thing for carrying or transporting merchandise, upon which shall have been printed, painted, attached, or otherwise placed a representation of any such flag, standard, colors, or ensign, to advertise, call attention to, decorate, mark, or distinguish the article or substance on which so placed shall be deemed guilty of a misdemeanor and shall be punished by a fine not exceeding $100 or by imprisonment for not more than thirty days, or both, in the discretion of the court. The words "flag, standard, colors, or ensign," as used herein, shall include any flag, standard, colors, ensign, or any picture or representation of either, or of any part or parts of either, made of any substance or represented on any substance, of any size evidently purporting to be either of said flag, standard, colors, or ensign of the United States of America or a picture or a representation of either, upon which shall be shown the colors, the stars and stripes, in any number either thereof, or of any part or parts of either, by which the average person seeing the same without deliberation may believe the same to represent the flag, colors, standard, or ensign of the United States of America.

The rise of flag usage around the 1970s can be traced back to two incidents, with somewhat opposing appeals and viewpoints. About 1969 *Reader's Digest* sent out thousands of flag decals for car and home windows. About a year later Gulf Oil Company began giving similar decals away with the purchase of gasoline. About this same time some Navy bases gave similar decals to all registered car owners on those bases. What had started as a public relations gimmick had blossomed into a national rage and a flood of visual patriotism all over the country. Most people who displayed these flag emblems were those who felt the American presence in Vietnam was justified. They were often the same citizens who sported "America — Love It or Leave It" bumper stickers.

Then came a movie, *Easy Rider,* mediocre as a movie but with a strong appeal to dissenting youth of the country. In the movie the disaffected biker Peter Fonda wears a stars and stripes motif on his helmet and an American flag stitched to the back of his leather jacket; the gas tank of his cycle is also painted like the flag. Overnight the flag became the rage of the college crowd, too, but as a symbol of dissent.

The use of the flag motif in dissent was not universal among young United States citizens, of course. Many, like William Doyle, of Tucson, Arizona, were proud of the flag and the country it stands for. Doyle was inducted into the Air Force. When he received leave and transfer orders from Langley Air Force Base to Thailand, he painted up a 1955 Ford with the back half in red and white stripes and star-spangled the hood portion preparatory to driving home on leave, through Virginia, West Virginia, Tennessee, Arkansas, Oklahoma, Texas, New Mexico, and Arizona, before driving back to Fairchild Air Force Base in Washington and shipping out. In his words, "I wanted to arouse people's curiosity so they'd ask, 'Why did you paint your car like that?' then I could answer, 'I'm on my way to Thailand to defend this country, to stop people from trying to overthrow it.'" Doyle said he believed the Indo-China war to be "a political thing, meant to undermine this country, especially the youth here."

With the tightening of laws and policing of those laws, intentional flag misuse waned. By mid–1972, in fact, flag dealers discovered their sales escalating. The Norfolk Flag and Emblem Corporation doubled sales within three months before Armistice Day 1971. "I sell them as fast as I get them done," stated the company president happily. "Many of the buyers have never owned a flag before, and sales are spread quite evenly among all age groups."

One story of a new owner came out of Inglewood, California, in 1967. A high school girl and her mother there went to ten stores looking for an American flag to give to a girl classmate from Indonesia, just sworn in as an American citizen, before finding one in neighboring Westchester.

By 1975, however, as the Bicentennial Commission readied the populace for the two-hundredth anniversary of the United States, flags were much easier to find; in fact, flag companies geared to triple output. By June 1975, Dettra Company, one of the largest flag producers, was telling retailers they would have a wait of eight to ten weeks for delivery. The flag business was flying high.

"Flag making, like everything else, is automated today," Frank Hicks, national sales manager for Dettra, stated then, "but even machines have limits." Daniel G. Conners, advertising manager for Annin & Company, the largest flag-makers, reported both the Bennington and "Betsy Ross" styles selling at the rate of about 1,000 per week (by mid–1975), where 1,000 hadn't been sold the whole previous year.

Flag-makers agreed that the Bennington — with its 13 stars (seven-pointed) and big "76" in the canton — was outselling all others, except the regulation 50-star ensign, for the Bicentennial. That was because it was said to be the first stars and stripes to be flown in battle by land forces, carried by the Vermont militia during the battle of Bennington, August 16, 1777. The original flag is preserved in the museum of North Bennington, Vermont.

This "first flew in battle" title, as in the case with many reports of that era, has another claimant. A plaque marks the site at Fort Stanwix (Rome, New York) and states that "the stars and stripes first flew in battle" here in the summer of 1777. Research has shown this was more likely a Grand Union flag though.

Another research has the flag first flying July 9, 1777, over Fort Anne, New York, where a British officer recorded in his journal, "The 9th took their [U.S.] colours.... They were very handsome, a flag of the United States, 13 stripes alternate red and white in a blue field representing a new constellation."

The New Spirit of '76 Foundation, a private organization with headquarters in Washington, had been pushing the Bennington flag for years and claimed credit for a large part of its success. Dwight Fuller Spear, founder, said 16 governors signed a declaration circulated by the foundation stating it would be appropriate to fly this as the Bicentennial flag.

The flag of the American Revolution Bicentennial Association (ARBA), which President Gerald Ford, in a Flag Day proclamation, urged government installations and ships at sea to fly along with the American flag, naturally became a big seller as well. It was designed by Chermayoff and Geisman Associates of New York, who were selected through a design competition. It was a double-star effect, using red, white, and blue in the center on a white background. Circling the inner decoration was black lettering: "American Revolution Bicentennial 1776–1976." Critics, however, likened it to the Ballantine beer symbol.

It's difficult to judge the size of the flag industry today, partly because very few companies sell only flags. Dettra is one of the few manufacturers in the United States that produces flags exclusively, though not all are patriotic banners. The company also produces 80 percent of the hole flags for golf courses in the United States, for example.

Theodore Christensen is president and part-time salesman of the Copeland Company of Alexandria, Virginia, founded 1862 and listing embassies and government agencies in Washington as prime customers. Christensen explained the reason most companies are not exclusively flag sellers: "People used to tell us, 'You're promoting patriotism for a profit.'" So the company got into the flagpole business, soft-pedaling the flags, and started production of banners and pennants for sporting events as well. "The flag business is not big nationwide," he added. "The top four firms have 85 percent of all the business, which amounts to a relatively modest $40–50 million annually. They are the ones that get the big orders, like 90,000 casket flags for the Veteran's Administration."

Those big four included, at the time, the Annin Company of Verona, New Jersey, founded in 1847 and then producing about a million flags a year; the Dettra Company of Oaks, Pennsylvania (1901); the Collegeville (Pennsylvania) Flag Company; and the Valley Forge (Pennsylvania) Flag Company. Others have come and gone since. By 1990, for instance, the Colonial Flag Company of Ohio was producing 3,000 flags per day. "Business is the best ever," the manager said.

BURNING THE BUNTING

The burning of the United States flag as a gesture of protest has never ceased to inflame both public opinion and private emotion.

By the mid–1980s a public hullabaloo had once again arisen over the issue of flag burning, beginning with a case that smoldered six years before flaming into a Congress versus President George Bush argument of law-versus–Constitutional amendment to control future flag burners.

The case that brought this confrontation to the fore was a protest rally at the 1984 Republican National Convention in Dallas, Texas, which culminated with Gregory (Joey) Johnson of New York City, a member of the Revolutionary Communist Youth Brigade, burning an American flag. He was charged with violating a Texas state law against flag desecration and destruction and sentenced to a year in prison and a $2,000 fine. A sharply divided Supreme Court decided 5–4 that burning the American flag as a form of political protest was protected by the Constitution's free-speech guarantee and that Texas authorities had violated Johnson's rights (*Texas vs. Johnson*, 1989).

Writing for the majority, Justice William Brennan stated:

> If there is a bedrock principle underlying the First Amendment, it is that the government may not prohibit the expression of an idea simply because society finds the idea itself offensive or disagreeable…. We do not consecrate the flag by punishing its desecration, for in doing so we dilute the freedom that this cherished emblem represents.

In a separate dissent, Justice John Paul Stevens stated:

> Sanctioning the public desecration of the flag will tarnish its value — both for those who cherish the ideas for which it waves and for those who desire to don the robes of martyrdom by burning it.

A Korean War veteran who had scooped up the fragments of the flag after Johnson's 1984 burning remarked: "I still do not know what they were protesting. If they were interested in exercising their freedom of speech, they should jolly well be able to talk and identify what it is that they were protesting."

Senate Majority Leader George Mitchell (D–ME), in discussing the Johnson case, said: "We are being asked to believe that the flag which neither Hitler nor Stalin could defeat is now threatened by a single misguided person who most Americans never heard of and don't care about."

An American Bar Association committee, which included former Nixon and Carter administration officials, agreed. Through Randolph Thrower, formerly Nixon's Internal Revenue Service commissioner, they stated: "All through human history tyrannies have tried to enforce obedience by prohibiting disrespect for the symbols of their power. The American flag commands respect and love because of our country's adherence to its values and its promise of freedom, not because of fiat and criminal law."

Like Texas, most states have laws against flag desecration. Some list rather severe penalties, and some people, like Tennessee state senator Shelby Rhinehart, have tried to make them still more harsh. He sponsored a January 1990 bill — approved by a state house committee — that would have made the penalty for beating a person who burns the United States flag a $1 fine. (Assault normally carries a sentence of 11 months, 29 days and a fine up to $2,500 in Tennessee.)

"For many widows or parents of loved ones who were killed in wars, all they have left is the flag," Rhinehart told the House Judiciary Committee. "If they want to beat the heck out of someone who burns the flag, so be it."

On the national scene, 12 weeks after the 1989 Supreme Court ruling, the United States House of Representatives voted 380 to 38 for a new federal statute to focus solely on the act of flag burning, rather than on the political message of the flag burners:

HR 2978

§1. **Short Title.**

This act may be cited as the "Flag Protection Act of 1989."

§2. **Criminal Penalties with Respect to the Physical Integrity of the United States Flag.**

(a) **in general**— Subsection (a) of section 700, title 18, United States Code is amended to read as follows:

"(a)(1) Whoever knowingly mutilates, defaces, burns or tramples upon any flag of the United States shall be fined under this title or imprisoned for not more than one year, or both.

"(2) This subsection does not prohibit any conduct consisting of the disposal of a flag when it has become worn or soiled."

(b) **definitions**— Section 700(b) of title 18, United States Code is amended to read as follows:

"(b) The term 'flag of the United States' means any flag of the United States, made of any substance, in a form that is commonly displayed."

General reaction to the Supreme Court decision focused more on emotional appeals than rational analyses of the issue at hand: Which should be protected, the flag of the United States or the principles of individual liberty, responsibility, and self-government upon which the United States was founded and which the flag is supposed to symbolize?

If the latter is chosen, toleration for such acts as flag burning is the price that must be paid for living in a free society. It does seem, however, looked at logically, that anyone burning the flag is actually protesting his right to those freedoms it symbolizes!

The reason the individuals burn the flag also would seem to be personal aggrandizement as much as anything else. The action is like spouting vulgar words, which used to be good for shock value before they became so common. There is little shock value left in such words, but their widespread acceptance has cheapened United States society. And so it is with burning the stars and stripes.

It is the press's job to report the news, and news is defined as anything that interests readers. Unfortunately, news feeds on itself. If an item of news gets attention, reporters are sent to search harder for follow-up information. In this way, reporters and editors actually tend to control or bias the news, by selecting what they cover, or even occasionally manufacturing news, with personal involvement.

For example, the flag-burning news grabbed a lot of reader attention. Thereafter, every group of dissenters anywhere in the country was sure of press coverage for whatever they did, as long as it involved a flag in flames. Here, for example, is part of an Associated Press report out of Seattle on October 29, 1989, by Jim Klahn:

> As an unruly crowd of street people chanted "Burn, baby, burn," members of a radical Vietnam veterans group torched a pile of American flags early Saturday, minutes after the federal anti-flag desecration law went into effect.
>
> "We will not stand for this law to be passed," said Brian Chambers of Seattle, an Army veteran who served near Pleiku, Vietnam, in 1970–71. "We're burning the flag to say we will not stand by to see forced patriotism. Abridgement of the First Amendment right [of free speech] is the first infringement."...
>
> The Seattle group of hundreds, including street people, neo–Nazi skinheads, gays and counter-culture types of every stripe, cheered wildly and profanely as two small piles of flags were set afire.
>
> They also sang the national anthem as a flag was hauled down from a pole outside the U.S. Post Office where the demonstration was staged, soaked with lighter fluid, and burned as it was raised back into the night sky.

No uniformed police were seen in the vicinity, according to the report. When contacted, police dispatcher said, "The FBI is handling that. We are not handling it." But Hal Kulgren, a police spokesman, had stated prior to the demonstration that arrests would be made if a law was broken.

Perhaps the Seattle police were aware that the just-passed Flag Protection Act had little time to live. A subsection of the act had requested that the Supreme Court give speedy consideration to its constitutionality, and the Court responded with its 1990 decision in *United States vs. Eichman* and *United States vs. Haggerty*. In a 5–4 decision, the Court affirmed the judgment of the two district courts that had dismissed charges against the flag-burning defendants, holding that the Flag Burning Act could not be upheld under the First Amendment.

And so the argument goes on. But that is good. Controversy is healthy. It shows that the American society is a thinking, changing one, not a stagnating one.

No matter how much one faction of the citizenry would like to see those who won't embrace the stars and stripes wind up in only stripes, the rights of all must be protected. All viewpoints must be considered. We cannot lose sight of the fact, however, that laws are created, rightly or wrongly, for the benefit of the most people. However, viewpoints change over time, and changed viewpoints often mean changed laws. Through it all, though, the United States Constitution upholds the true democratic freedom for all people.

Woodrow Wilson stated it better than most of us can, in his 1917 Flag Day address:

Woe be to the man or group of men that seeks to stand in our way in this day of high resolution when every principle we hold dearest is to be vindicated and made secure for the salvation of the nation. We are ready to plead at the bar of history, and our flag shall wear a new luster. Once more we shall make good with our lives and fortunes the great faith to which we were born, and a new glory shall shine in the face of our people.

Appendix:
The United States Flag Code

The following are the sections of the United States Code that pertain to the flag. The first section, from Title 36, contains what is usually referred to as the Flag Code itself. The second excerpt, from Title 18, includes legislation on flag burning that was passed in 1989. Finally, an excerpt from Title 4 addresses the use of the flag for advertising purposes, as well as mutilation of the flag.

Title 36, Patriotic Societies and Observances.
Chapter 10 — Patriotic Customs

Sec.
170. National anthem; Star-Spangled Banner.
171. Conduct during playing.
172. Pledge of allegiance to flag; manner of delivery.
173. Display and use of flag by civilians; codification of rules and customs; definition.
174. Time and occasions for display.
    (a) Display on buildings and stationary flagstaffs in open; night display.
    (b) Manner of hoisting.
    (c) Inclement weather.
    (d) Particular days of display.
    (e) Display on or near administration building of public institutions.
    (f) Display in or near polling places.
    (g) Display in or near schoolhouses.
175. Position and manner of display.
176. Respect for flag.

177. Conduct during hoisting, lowering or passing of flag.
178. Modification of rules and customs by President.
179. Design for service flag; persons entitled to display flag.
180. Design for service lapel button; persons entitled to wear button.
181. Approval of designs by Secretary of Defense; license to manufacture and sell; penalties.
182. Rules and regulations.
182a to 184. Repealed.
185. Transferred.
186. National motto.
187. National floral emblem.
188. National march.
189. Flag of National League of Families POW/MIA.

§ 170. National anthem; Star-Spangled Banner

The composition consisting of the words and music known as The Star-Spangled Banner is designated the national anthem of the United States of America.
(Mar. 3, 1931, c. 436, 46 Stat. 1508.)

§ 171. Conduct during playing

During rendition of the national anthem when the flag is displayed, all present except those in uniform should stand at attention facing the flag with the right hand over the heart. Men not in uniform should remove their headdress with their right hand and hold it at the left shoulder, the hand being over the heart. Persons in uniform should render the military salute at the first note of the anthem and retain this position until the last note. When the flag is not displayed, those present should face toward the music and act in the same manner they would if the flag were displayed there.
(June 22, 1942, c. 435, § 6, 56 Stat. 380; Dec. 22, 1942, c. 806, § 6, 56 Stat. 1077; July 7, 1976, Pub.L. 94-344, § 1[18], 90 Stat. 812.)

§ 172. Pledge of allegiance to flag; manner of delivery

The Pledge of Allegiance to the Flag, "I pledge allegiance to the Flag of the United States of America, and to the Republic for which it stands, one Nation under God, indivisible, with liberty and justice for all.", should be rendered by standing at attention facing the flag with the right hand over the heart. When not in uniform men should remove their headdress with their right hand and hold it at the left shoulder, the hand being over the heart. Persons in uniform should remain silent, face the flag, and render the military salute.
(June 22, 1942, c. 435, § 7, 56 Stat. 380; Dec. 22, 1942, c. 806, § 7, 56 Stat. 1077; Dec. 28, 1945, c. 607, 59 Stat. 668; June 14, 1954, c. 297, 68 Stat. 249; July 7, 1976, Pub.L. 94-344, § 1[19], 90 Stat. 813.)

§ 173. Display and use of flag by civilians; codification of rules and customs; definition.

The following codification of existing rules and customs pertaining to the display and use of the flag of the United States of America is established for the use of such civilians or civilian groups or organizations as may not be required to conform with regulations promulgated by one or more executive departments of the Government of the United States. The flag of the United States for the purpose of this chapter shall be defined according to sections 1 and 2 of Title 4 and Executive Order 10834 issued pursuant thereto.

(June 22, 1942, c. 435, § 1, 56 Stat. 377; Dec. 22, 1942, c. 806, § 1, 56 Stat. 1074; July 7, 1976, Pub.L. 94-344, § 1[1], 90 Stat. 810.)

§174. Time and occasions for display.

(a) Displays on buildings and stationary flagstaffs in open; night display

It is the universal custom to display the flag only from sunrise to sunset on buildings and on stationary flagstaffs in the open. However, when a patriotic effect is desired, the flag may be displayed twenty-four hours a day if properly illuminated during the hours of darkness.

(b) Manner of hoisting

The flag should be hoisted briskly and lowered ceremoniously.

(c) Inclement weather

The flag should not be displayed on days when the weather is inclement, except when an all-weather flag is displayed.

(d) Particular days of display

The flag should be displayed on all days, especially on New Year's Day, January 1; Inauguration Day, January 20; Lincoln's Birthday, February 12; Washington's Birthday, third Monday in February; Easter Sunday (variable); Mother's Day, second Sunday in May; Armed Forces Day, third Saturday in May; Memorial Day (half-staff until noon), the last Monday in May; Flag Day, June 14; Independence Day, July 4; Labor Day, first Monday in September; Constitution Day, September 17; Columbus Day, second Monday in October; Navy Day, October 27; Veterans Day, November 11; Thanksgiving Day, fourth Thursday in November; Christmas Day, December 25; and such other days as may be proclaimed by the President of the United States; the birthdays of States (date of admission); and on State holidays.

(e) Display on or near administration building of public institutions

The flag should be displayed daily on or near the main administration building of every public institution.

(f) Display in or near polling places

The flag should be displayed in or near every polling place on election days.

(g) Display in or near schoolhouses

The flag should be displayed during school days in or near every school-house.

(June 22, 1942, c. 435, § 2, 56 Stat. 378; Dec. 22, 1942, c. 806, § 2, 56 Stat. 1074; July 7, 1976, Pub.L. 94-344, § 1[2]–[5], 90 Stat. 810.)

§ 175. Position and manner of display

The flag, when carried in a procession with another flag or flags, should be either on the marching right; that is, the flag's own right, or, if there is a line of other flags, in front of the center of that line.

(a) The flag should not be displayed on a float in a parade except from a staff, or as provided in subsection (i) of this section.

(b) The flag should not be draped over the hood, top, sides, or back of a vehicle or of a railroad train or boat. When the flag is displayed on a motor-car, the staff shall be fixed firmly to the chassis or clamped to the right fender.

(c) No other flag or pennant should be placed above or, if on the same level, to the right of the flag of the United States of America, except during church services conducted by naval chaplains at sea, when the church pennant may be flown above the flag during church services for the personnel of the Navy. No person shall display the flag of the United Nations or any other national or international flag equal, above, or in a position of superior prominence or honor to, or in place of, the flag of the United States at any place within the United States or any Territory or possession thereof: *Provided*, That nothing in this section shall make unlawful the continuance of the practice heretofore followed of displaying the flag of the United Nations in a position of superior prominence or honor, and other national flags in positions of equal prominence or honor, with that of the flag of the United States at the headquarters of the United Nations.

(d) The flag of the United States of America, when it is displayed with another flag against a wall from crossed staffs, should be on the right, the flag's own right, and its staff should be in front of the staff of the other flag.

(e) The flag of the United States of America should be at the center and at the highest point of the group when a number of flags of States or localities or pennants of societies are grouped and displayed from staffs.

(f) When flags of States, cities, or localities, or pennants of societies are flown on the same halyard with the flag of the United States, the latter should always be at the peak. When the flags are flown from adjacent staffs, the flag of the United States should be hoisted first and lowered last. No such flag or pennant may be placed above the flag of the United States or to the United States flag's right.

(g) When flags of two or more nations are displayed, they are to be flown from separate staffs of the same height. The flags should be of approximately equal size. International usage forbids the display of the flag of one nation above that of another nation in time of peace.

(h) When the flag of the United States is displayed from a staff projecting horizontally or at an angle from the window sill, balcony, or front of a building, the union of the flag should be placed at the peak of the staff unless the flag is at half-staff. When the flag is suspended over a sidewalk from a rope extending from a house to a pole at the edge of the sidewalk, the flag should be hoisted out, union first, from the building.

(i) When displayed either horizontally or vertically against a wall, the union should be uppermost and to the flag's own right, that is, to the observer's left. When displayed in a window, the flag should be displayed in the same way, with the union or blue field to the left of the observer in the street.

(j) When the flag is displayed over the middle of the street, it should be suspended vertically with the union to the north in an east and west street or to the east in a north and south street.

(k) When used on a speaker's platform, the flag, if displayed flat, should be displayed above and behind the speaker. When displayed from a staff in a church or public auditorium, the flag of the United States of America should hold the position of superior prominence, in advance of the audience, and in the position of honor at the clergyman's or speaker's right as he faces the audience. Any other flag so displayed should be placed on the left of the clergyman or speaker or to the right of the audience.

(l) The flag should form a distinctive feature of the ceremony of unveiling a statue or monument, but it should never be used as the covering for the statue or monument.

(m) The flag, when flown at half-staff, should be first hoisted to the peak for an instant and then lowered to the half-staff position. The flag should be again raised to the peak before it is lowered for the day. On Memorial Day the flag should be displayed at half-staff until noon only, then raised to the top of the staff. By order of the President, the flag shall be flown at half-staff upon the death of principal figures of the United States Government and the Governor of a State, territory, or possession, as a mark of respect to their memory. In the event of the death of other officials or foreign dignitaries, the flag is to be displayed at half-staff according to Presidential instructions or orders, or in accordance with recognized customs or practices not inconsistent with law. In the event of the death of a present or former official of the government of any State, territory, or possession of the United States, the Governor of that State, territory, or possession may proclaim that the National flag shall be flown at half-staff. The flag shall be flown at half-staff thirty days from the death of the President or a former President; ten days from the day of death of the Vice President, the Chief Justice or a retired Chief Justice of the United States, or the Speaker of the House of Representatives; from the day of death until interment of an Associate Justice of the Supreme Court, a Secretary of an executive or military department, a former Vice President, or the Governor of a State, territory or possession; and on the day of death and the following day for a Member of Congress. The flag shall be flown at half-staff on Peace Officers Memorial Day, unless that day is also Armed Forces Day. As used in this subsection —

(1) the term "half-staff" means the position of the flag when it is one-half the distance between the top and bottom of the staff;

(2) the term "executive or military department" means any agency listed under sections 101 and 102 of Title 5; and

(3) the term "Member of Congress" means a Senator, a Representative, a Delegate, or the Resident Commissioner from Puerto Rico.

(n) When the flag is used to cover a casket, it should be placed so that the union is at the head and over the left shoulder. The flag should not be lowered into the grave or allowed to touch the ground.

(o) When the flag is suspended across a corridor or lobby in a building with only one main entrance, it should be suspended vertically with the union of the flag to the observer's left upon entering. If the building has more than one main entrance, the flag should be suspended vertically near the center of the corridor or lobby with the union to the north, when entrances are to the east and west or to the east when entrances are to the north and south. If there are entrances in more than two directions, the union should be to the east.

(June 22, 1942, c. 435, § 3, 56 Stat. 378; Dec. 22, 1942, c. 806, § 3, 56 Stat. 1075; July 9, 1953, c. 183, 67 Stat. 142; July 7, 1976, Pub.L. 94–344, § 1[6]–[11], 90 Stat. 810, 811; Sept. 13, 1994, Pub.L. 103–322, Title XXXII, § 320922[b], 108 Stat. 2131.)

§ 176. Respect for flag

No disrespect should be shown to the flag of the United States of America; the flag should not be dipped to any person or thing. Regimental colors, State flags, and organization or institutional flags are to be dipped as a mark of honor.

(a) The flag should never be displayed with the union down, except as a signal of dire distress in instances of extreme danger to life or property.

(b) The flag should never touch anything beneath it, such as the ground, the floor, water, or merchandise.

(c) The flag should never be carried flat or horizontally, but always aloft and free.

(d) The flag should never be used as wearing apparel, bedding, or drapery. It should never be festooned, drawn back, nor up, in folds, but always allowed to fall free. Bunting of blue, white, and red, always arranged with the blue above, the white in the middle, and the red below, should be used for covering a speaker's desk, draping the front of the platform, and for decoration in general.

(e) The flag should never be fastened, displayed, used, or stored in such a manner as to permit it to be easily torn, soiled, or damaged in any way.

(f) The flag should never be used as a covering for a ceiling.

(g) The flag should never have placed upon it, nor on any part of it, nor attached to it any mark, insignia, letter, word, figure, design, picture, or drawing of any nature.

(h) The flag should never be used as a receptacle for receiving, holding, carrying, or delivering anything.

(i) The flag should never be used for advertising purposes in any manner whatsoever. It should not be embroidered on such articles as cushions or handkerchiefs or the like, printed or otherwise impressed on paper napkins or boxes or anything that is designed for temporary use and discard. Advertising signs should not be fastened to a staff or halyard from which the flag is flown.

(j) No part of the flag should ever be used as a costume or athletic uniform. However, a flag patch may be affixed to the uniform of military personnel, firemen, policemen, and members of patriotic organizations. The flag represents a living country and is itself considered a living thing. Therefore, the lapel flag pin being a replica, should be worn on the left lapel near the heart.

(k) The flag, when it is in such condition that it is no longer a fitting emblem for display, should be destroyed in a dignified way, preferably by burning.
(June 22, 1942, c. 435, § 4, 56 Stat. 379; Dec. 22, 1942, c. 806, § 4, 56 Stat. 1076; July 7, 1976, Pub.L. 94-344, § 1[12]–[16], 90 Stat. 812.)

§ 177. Conduct during hoisting, lowering or passing of flag

During the ceremony of hoisting or lowering the flag or when the flag is passing in a parade or in review, all persons present except those in uniform should face the flag and stand at attention with the right hand over the heart. Those present in uniform should render the military salute. When not in uniform, men should remove their headdress with their right hand and hold it at the left shoulder, the hand being over the heart. Aliens should stand at attention. The salute to the flag in a moving column should be rendered at the moment the flag passes.
(June 22, 1942, c. 435, § 5, 56 Stat. 380; Dec. 22, 1942, c. 806, § 5, 56 Stat. 1077; July 7, 1976, Pub.L. 94-344, § 1[17], 90 Stat. 812.)

§ 178. Modification of rules and customs by President

Any rule or custom pertaining to the display of the flag of the United States of America, set forth in sections 171 to 178 of this title, may be altered, modified, or repealed, or additional rules with respect thereto may be prescribed, by the Commander in Chief of the Armed Forces of the United States, whenever he deems it to be appropriate or desirable; and any such alteration or additional rule shall be set forth in a proclamation.

(June 22, 1942, c. 435, § 8, 56 Stat. 380; Dec. 22, 1942, c. 806, § 8, 56 Stat. 1077; July 7, 1976, Pub.L. 94-344, § 1[20], 90 Stat. 813.)

§ 179. Design for service flag; persons entitled to display flag

The Secretary of Defense is authorized and directed to approve a design for a service flag, which flag may be displayed in a window of the place of residence of persons who are members of the immediate family of a person serving in the armed forces of the United States during any period of war or hostilities in which the Armed Forces of the United States may be engaged.

(Oct. 17, 1942, c. 615, § 1, 56 Stat. 796; May 27, 1953, c. 70, 67 Stat. 35.)

§ 180. Design for service lapel button; persons entitled to wear button

The Secretary of Defense is also authorized and directed to approve a design for a service lapel button, which button may be worn by members of the immediate family of a person serving in the armed forces of the United States during any period of war or hostilities in which the Armed Forces of the United States may be engaged.

(Oct. 17, 1942, c. 615, § 2, 56 Stat. 796; May 27, 1953, c. 70, 67 Stat. 35.)

§ 181. Approval of designs by Secretary of Defense; license to manufacture and sell; penalties

Upon the approval by the Secretary of Defense of the design for such service flag and service lapel button, he shall cause notice thereof, together with a description of the approved flag and button, to be published in the Federal Register. Thereafter any person may apply to the Secretary of Defense for a license to manufacture and sell the approved service flag, or the approved service lapel button, or both. Any person, firm, or corporation who manufactures any such service flag or service lapel button without having first obtained such a license, or otherwise violates sections 179 to 182 of this title, shall, upon conviction thereof, be fined not more than $1,000.

(Oct. 17, 1942, c. 615, § 3, 56 Stat. 796; May 27, 1953, c. 70, 67 Stat. 35.)

§ 182. Rules and regulations

The Secretary of Defense is authorized to make such rules and regulations as may be necessary to carry out the provisions of sections 179 to 182 of this title.

(Oct. 17, 1942, c. 615, § 4, 56 Stat. 796; May 27, 1953, c. 70, 67 Stat. 35.)

§§ 182a to 182d. Repealed. Pub. L. 89-534, § 2, Aug. 11, 1966, 80 Stat. 345

§§ 183, 184. Repealed. Pub. L. 85-857, § 14(84), Sept. 2, 1958, 72 Stat. 1272

§ 186. National motto

The national motto of the United States is declared to be "In God we trust."

(July 30, 1956, c. 795, 70 Stat. 732.)

§ 187. National floral emblem

The flower commonly known as the rose is designated and adopted as the national floral emblem of the United States of America, and the President of the United States is authorized and requested to declare such fact by proclamation.

(Pub.L. 99-449, Oct. 7, 1986, 100 Stat. 1128.)

§ 188. National march

The composition by John Philip Sousa entitled "The Stars and Stripes Forever" is here designated as the national march of the United States of America.

(Pub.L. 100-186, Dec. 11, 1987, 101 Stat. 1286.)

§ 189. Flag of National League of Families POW/MIA

The National League of Families POW/MIA flag is hereby recognized officially and designated as the symbol of our Nation's concern and commitment to resolving as fully as possible the fates of Americans still prisoner, missing and unaccounted for in Southeast Asia, thus ending the uncertainty for their families and the Nation.

(Pub.L. 101-355, § 2, Aug. 10, 1990, 104 Stat. 416.)

Title 18, Crimes and Criminal Procedure, Part I — Crimes — Continued. Chapter 33 — Emblems, Insignia, and Names

§ 700. Desecration of the flag of the United States; penalties

(a)(1) Whoever knowingly mutilates, defaces, physically defiles, burns, maintains on the floor or ground, or tramples upon any flag of the United States shall be fined under this title or imprisoned for not more than one year, or both.

(2) This subsection does not prohibit any conduct consisting of the disposal of a flag when it has become worn or soiled.

(b) As used in this section, the term "flag of the United States" means any flag of the United States, or any part thereof, made of any substance, or any size, in a form that is commonly displayed.

(c) Nothing in this section shall be construed as indicating an intent on the part of Congress to deprive any State, territory, possession, or the Commonwealth of Puerto Rico of jurisdiction over any offense over which it would have jurisdiction in the absence of this section.

(Added Pub.L. 90-381, § 1, July 5, 1968, 82 Stat. 291.)

(d)(1) An appeal may be taken directly to the Supreme Court of the United States from any interlocutory or final judgment, decree, or order issued by a United States district court ruling upon the constitutionality of subsection (a).

(2) The Supreme Court shall, if it has not previously ruled on the question, accept jurisdiction over the appeal and advance on the docket and expedite to the greatest extent possible.

(As amended Pub.L. 101-131, §§ 2, 3, Oct. 28, 1989, 103 Stat. 777.)

Title 4, Flag and Seal of the United States. Chapter 1— The Flag

§ 3. Use of flag for advertising purposes; mutilation of flag

Any person who, within the District of Columbia, in any manner, for exhibition or display, shall place or cause to be placed any word, figure, mark, picture, design, drawing, or any advertisement of any nature upon any flag, standard, colors, or ensign of the United States of America, or shall expose or cause to be exposed to public view any such flag, standard, colors, or ensign upon which shall have been printed, painted, or otherwise placed, or to which shall be attached, appended, affixed, or annexed any word, figure, mark, picture, design, or drawing, or any advertisement of any nature; or who, within the District of Columbia, shall manufacture, sell, expose for sale, or to public view, or give away or have in possession for sale, or to be given away or for use for any purpose, any article or substance being an article of merchandise, or a receptacle for merchandise or article or thing for carrying or transporting merchandise, upon which shall have been printed, painted, attached, or otherwise placed a representation of any such flag, standard, colors, or ensign, to advertise, call attention to, decorate, mark, or distinguish the article or substance on which so placed shall be deemed guilty of a misdemeanor and shall be punished by a fine not exceeding $100 or by imprisonment for not more than thirty days, or both, in the discretion of the court. The words "flag, standard, colors, or ensign," as used herein, shall include any flag, standard, colors, ensign, or any picture or representation of either, or of any part or parts of either made of any substance or represented on any substance, or any size evidently purporting to be either of said flag, standard, colors, or ensign of the United States of America or a picture or a representation of either, upon which shall be shown the colors, the stars and the stripes, in any number of either thereof, or of any part or parts of either, by which the average person seeing the same without deliberation may believe the same to represent the flag, colors, standard, or ensign of the United States of America.

(July 30, 1946, c. 389, 61 Stat. 642; July 5, 1968, Pub.L. 90-381, § 3, 82 Stat. 291.)

Bibliography

There are two good booklets, available to the general public for a slight charge, that outline the flag code. One is titled "How to Respect and Display Our Flag." Prepared by the United States Marine Corps in 1955, it has been revised since. Copies are available from the Government Printing Office. The other is "The Star Spangled Banner," printed by the Smithsonian Institution in Washington, D.C. (Special publication #4529).

Either of these would make a fine and unusual gift for a child, especially one in a scouting program, or a thoughtful gift to all students in a school by a civic organization, or even a helpful gift to a person or business entrepreneur who makes a practice of flying the flag incorrectly.

If any reader becomes interested enough for further delving into the intriguing history behind the United States flag, there are other sources to probe. One of the very best overall is *The History of the United States Flag … From the Revolution to the Present* [1961, when it was published], *Including a Guide to Its Use and Display*, written by Milo Quaife, Melvin Weig, and Roy Appleman (Harper and Row). It is beautifully illustrated. This is an enlarged updating of *The Flag of the United States*, written by Mr. Quaife in 1942.

Readers wishing more detail in their learning might refer also to several older books: *The Stars and Stripes and Other American Flags* by Peleg D. Harrison (5th edition, Boston, 1914); *The Origin and Evolution of the United States Flag* by R.C. Ballard Thruston (Washington, 1926); and *The Flag of the United States* by Col. James A. Moss (Washington, 1941). These may have to be located in larger libraries, or perhaps arranged on loan from the Library of Congress through a local library.

Other sources consulted for this work are as follows.

"ABA Panel Supports Right to Burn Flag." *Lewiston (ID) Tribune*, 4 August 1989.
Angst, Walter. "Heraldic Plan for Redesign of the State Flags." *Smithsonian*, July 1973.
"Anthem Out at the Garden." *New York Times*, January 1973.
Army and Navy Journal, 27 February 1909.
Baer, John W. *The Pledge of Allegiance: A Centennial History, 1892–1992*. Annapolis, MD: self-published, 1992.

"The Banner Yet Waves." *Reader's Digest*, September 1989.

Barnard, Kathy, and Julie Bailey. "Area Retailers Are Caught in 'Desert Storm' of Patriotic Purchasing." *Lewiston (ID) Tribune*, 24 February 1991.

"Barr Admits Singing Was a Mistake." Associated Press, 28 July 1990.

"Barr Anthem Creates an Uproar." Associated Press, 7 July 1990.

"Battle Over Confederate Flag Continues." *Lewiston (ID) Morning Tribune*, 5 August 1994.

"Battle Streamers: Naval History on Parade." *All Hands*, March 1971.

"Battle Steamers of the United States Navy." Department of Navy, Naval History Division, 1972.

Bellamy, Francis, obituaries: *Boston Herald*, 30 August 1931; *Boston Evening Transcript*, 29 August 1931; *Boston Post*, 30 August 1931; *Boston Sunday Globe*, 30 August 1931.

Bennett, M.R., ed. *Old Glory: The Story of Our Flag*. Bellaire Bluffs, FL: Snibbe, 1972.

Billington, Joy. "Heraldry Is Everywhere." *Washington Star*, January 9, 1973.

"Blacks Try to Remove Rebel Flag." Associated Press, 3 February 1988.

Blevens, Fred. "Pledge Author Is Honored." *Tampa (FL) Tribune*, 22 November 1974.

"Bombs Bursting in Air." *Sports Illustrated*, 29 January 1973.

Bowlin, Brad. "Idaho Woman Is Expert on Creator of Flag." Associated Press, 5 July 1990.

Brooks, Stewart M. "The Origin of Memorial Day." *Yankee*, May 1968.

Brown, Marion Marsh. *Broad Stripes and Bright Stars*. Boy Scouts of America, 1955.

Buckley, Edith, and Lloyd J. Dockal. *Old Glory Around the World*. Milwaukee, WI: American Topical Assoc., 1970.

"Burn, Baby, Burn." *Lewiston (ID) Tribune*, 29 October 1989.

"Burning of UN Flag Results in Arrest." Associated Press, 19 March 1990.

"Change Our National Anthem, Congressman Says." *National Enquirer*, 3 September 1985.

"Children Lisp 'I Pledge Allegiance'—Who Wrote It?" *Tampa (FL) Tribune*, 11 March 1956.

Cooper, Grace. *Thirteen Star Flags*. Washington: Smithsonian Museum of History and Technology, 1973.

Corpin, Mary Anne. "First Ground Broken for Bellamy School." *Tampa (FL) Tribune*, 26 March 1974.

Corpin, Mary Anne. "New Bellamy School Honors 'Pledge' Author." *Tampa (FL) Tribune*, 11 November 1973.

Crouthers, David D. *Flags of America, History*. Maplewood, NJ: Hammond, 1962.

Dart, Bob. "Battle Brews as Court Strikes Flag Law." Cox News Service, 12 June 1990.

"Dedication Ceremony for Flag Pole Honoring Captain William Driver." Program. Nashville, TN: undated.

Desmond, Alice Curtis. *Your Flag and Mine*. New York: Macmillan.

"The Display and Use of the Flag of the United States." T10H Fact Sheet #6. United States Army, Institute of Heraldry, 14 July 1969.

District of Columbia Code, Annotated. Vol. 2. Charlottesville, VA: Michie, 1985.

"'Dont Tread on Me' ... Back on Jackstaffs." *All Hands*, January 1976.

DuBois, Arthur E. "New Stars for Our Flag." *American Weekly*, 6 May 1950.

Dunn, Jay Jay. "Bodies Politic: Uncle Sam." Letter to the Editor. *Troy (NY) Old Oregon*, 26 June 1986.

"The Early Navy and the Birth of the Nation." *All Hands*, January 1973.

Eggenberger, David. *Flags of the U.S.* New York: Crowell, 1964.

Eisenhower, Dwight D. "Proclamation #3269: Admission of the State of Alaska into the Union." 3 January 1959.

Eisenhower, Dwight D. "Proclamation #3309: Admission of the State of Hawaii into the Union." 21 August 1959.

Ellis, Linda. "The Stars and Stripes in a Huge Unfurling." *Washington Star*, 15 June 1980.

Epstein, Daniel Mark. "Star of Wonder." New York: Overlook Press, 1986.

Espo, David. "Some Legal Protection for Old Glory." Associated Press, 27 June 1995.

"Facts About the United States Flag." SIL-262. Washington: Smithsonian Institution, Div. of Military History, 1970.

Filby, P.W., and Edward G. Howard, comps. *Star Spangled Books*. Baltimore: Maryland Historical Society, 1972.

"First Court Test of Flag Burning Ban Underway." Associated Press, 1 November 1989.

"Flag Burning: States in No Rush to Consider Amendment." Associated Press, 17 June 1990.

"Flag Burning Issue." University of Maryland's *Argus Magazine*, February 1971.

"Flag Changes Proposed." Associated Press wirephoto and caption in *American Weekly*, 6 May 1950.

"Flag Day Shifts into High Gear Across the Country." *Forward*, June 1975.

The Flag of the United States of America. Boston: John Hancock Mutual Life Insurance Co., 1969.

"Flag Pledge Author Born 101 Years Ago." *Tampa (FL) Times*, 18 May 1956.

"Flag Sales Surge in Patriotic Boom." Associated Press, 22 August 1984.

"Flags at Sea." *All Hands*, March 1974.

"Flags on Hard Hats." *Lewiston (ID) Morning Tribune*, 28 March 1980.

Flags That Have Flown Over California. San Diego, CA: San Diego Gas & Electric Co., undated.

Fleming, Thomas. "One Flag from Many." *Reader's Digest*, September 1969.

"Flynt Arrested in Alaska." *Los Angeles Times*, 2 December 1983.

"Flynt Wears Flag as Diaper." Associated Press, 18 November 1983.

"Follow That Flag." *Washington Post*, 12 January 1972.

Fort McHenry brochure. Baltimore, MD: National Park Service, undated.

"Fort Stanwix." Washington: National Park Service, 1990.

"Francis Bellamy Is Vindicated in Washington." *Tampa (FL) Tribune*, 25 August 1957.

Francis Scott Key Foundation brochure. Washington, DC: undated.

"From Fancy Ideas to Family Heirlooms." *Country America*, July/August 1991.

Gagliaradi, Martha. "Flag and Peace Symbol Ringing Up the Sales." *Norfolk Virginian-Pilot*, 2 August 1970.

"George Washington Bridge Flag Data." Port Authority of New York brochure, July 1960.

"Georgia Governor Urges Removal of Confederate Emblem from Flag." *Lewiston (ID) Morning Tribune*, 29 May 1992.

Germond, Jack. *Whose Broad Stripes and Bright Stars*. New York: Warner Books, 1989

Getlein, Frank. "Flag on the Pants Seat." *Washington Star*, 3 April 1974.

"G.I. with Pants Flag Sentenced." *Norfolk Virginian-Pilot*, 24 September 1974.

"Girl Wins Right to Sit During Pledge." Associated Press, 18 August 1977.

"Girls Get $250 Fine, 30 Days for Wearing Flag on Jeans." *Norfolk Virginian-Pilot*, 4 August 1970.

Glatfelter, Charles H. *A Salutary Influence: Gettysburg College, 1832–1985*. Vols. 1 and 2. Gettysburg, PA: 1987.

The Glorious 50. Worcester, MA: State Mutual of America, 1973.

Gold, Vic. "For a New National Anthem." *Washington Star-News*, 18 April 1974.

The Guilford Flag. Raleigh: North Carolina Museum of History, 27 February 1992.

Haban, Rita D. *How Proudly They Wave*. Minneapolis: Lerner, 1989.

Hall, Bill. "A Lewiston Teacher Too Patriotic to Be Bland." *Lewiston (ID) Tribune*, 18 October 1991.

"Hanford Guard Suspended for Refusing to Fly Japanese Flag." Associated Press, 31 January 1992.

"Hard Hats Win Flag Decal Battle." *Lewiston (ID) Morning Tribune*, 28 March 1980.

Hedburg, Kathy. "U.S. Flag Has Visitor Seeing Red." *Lewiston (ID) Tribune*, 13 November 1985.

Hemmingway, Susan. "Tampa Woman Pledges Her Allegiance to Francis Bellamy." *Tampa (FL) Times*, 26 December 1978.

Hicks, F.C. *The Flag of the United States*. Washington: Privately printed, 1926.

"His Colors Tell His Stand." *Norfolk Virginian-Pilot*, 25 May 1970.

"Historic American Flags." Stamp sheet issued by Post Office Department, 4 July 1968.

"An Historic Flag to Fly Atop Capitol." *Washington Star-News*, 25 December 1973.

"History of the Rhode Island State Flag." Providence: Rhode Island Development Council, undated.

Holden, E.S. *Our Country's Flag and the Flags of Foreign Countries*. New York: Appleton, 1898.

Holt, Dean W. *American Military Cemeteries*. Jefferson, NC: McFarland, 1992.

Honors and Ceremonies: Watch Officer's Guide. Annapolis, MD: Naval Institute Press, 1987.

"House Votes to Ban Flag-Burning." *New York Times*, 13 September 1989.

"Hundreds Help Bathe Old Glory." *Lewiston (ID) Morning Tribune*, 16 March 1991.

"Idaho Woman Is Expert on Creator of the Flag." *Lewiston (ID) Monring Tribune*, 5 July 1990.

"Ike Okays New Type Flag Salute." United Press International, 15 June 1954.

James, Betty. "'75 Is the Year of the Flag." *Washington Star*, June 14, 1965.

Jansing, Tom. "A History of Flags." *All Hands*, March 1974.

"Justice to a Malden Man at Last: Play Pledge Credited to Upham." *Malden (MA) Evening News*. 6 and 7 February 1956.

Kaddy, Bedford O., Jr. "Where and Why the American Flag Flies Twenty-four Hours a Day." New York: privately printed, 1977.

Kelly, Patrick. "In Our Town." *Tampa (FL) Tribune*, 11 July 1965.

Leasem, Harold I., and George C. Mackenzie. "Fort McHenry." Washington, DC: National Park Service, United States Department of Interior, 1961.

Leavy, Jane. "Pomp and Comedy Mark Olympic Official Opening." *Washington Post*, 9 February 1984.

Letter from Allen R. Hoilman, Cataloger, Curation Branch, North Carolina Museum of History, Raleigh, NC, 27 February 1992.

Letters from Mayor Philip Bredesen and Librarian Virginia R. Lyle, Metropolitan Government of Nashville and Davidson County Public Library, Nashville, TN, 6 March 1992.

Letters from Rear Adm. J.L. Holloway, Jr., USN, Supt., and Michael J. Crawford, Head, Early History Branch, Naval Historical Center, U.S. Naval Academy, 1992.

"'Liberian' Flag Not Cause for Arrest." *Norfolk Virginian-Pilot*, 30 July 1970.

"Liberty's Five Flags." *Flag Plaza Standard*, Supp. to Vol. 20, #2. Pittsburgh: National Flag Foundation, 1988.

London, George. "Let's Have a National Anthem We Can SING." *Life*, 13 September 1968.

"Lousing Up the Used Flag Market." United Press International, 21 December 1954.

Luzader, John F. "The Stars and Stripes at Fort Stanwix: A Summary of the Evidence." *Fort Stanwix, Including Construction & Military History*. Washington: National Park Service, 1976.

"Make It Yourself." *Washington Star*, 26 October 1975.

Malone, Dumas, ed. *Dictionary of American Biography*. New York: Scribner, 1943.

Marshall, Diane P. "Shopping in the Great Philly Tradition." *Travel-Holiday*, December 1988.

Mastai, Boleslaw. *The Stars and Stripes*. New York: Knopf, 1973.

A Matter of Honor. Colorado Springs, CO: East Colorado Springs Rotary Club, pamphlet undated.

"The Medium Is Nail for Peace Message." *Los Angeles Daily News*, 26 January 1991.

Memorial to an American Patriot, the Life and Works of Bernard J. Cigrand, "The Father of National Flag Day." memorial pamphlet. 1946.

Mercier, Henry James. *Life in a Man-of-War, or Scenes in "Old Ironsides" During Her Cruise in the Pacific*. Boston: Houghton-Mifflin, 1927.

"A Metropolitan History: Old City Cemetery." Brochure. Nashville, TN: undated.

Military Courtesy, Honors, and Ceremonies: Naval Officer's Guide. Annapolis, MD: Naval Institute Press, 1983.

Miller, Margarette S. "The Origin and Authorship of the Pledge of Allegiance." *Portsmouth (VA) Star*, 20 September through 12 October 1942.

Mills, Paul C. *New Glory*. Part 1: Colonial and Revolutionary Era Flags. Santa Barbara (CA) Museum of Art, 1975.

Moss, James Alfred. *The Flag of the United States*. Washington, DC: 1930 and rev. 1941.

"National Flag Foundation Newsletter." Pittsburgh: National Flag Foundation, 12 October 1991.

"The National Memorial Cemetery of the Pacific." Washington, DC: Veteran's Administration pamphlet No. 40-1. November 1973.

"New National Anthem Favored." *Lewiston (ID) Morning Tribune*, 25 November 1989.

1992 Topical Stamp Publications. Johnstown, PA: American Topical Assoc., 1968.

Nishiwaki, Chris. "House Approves Flag-Burning memorial." *Lewiston (ID) Morning Tribune*, 26 January 1995.

"North American Vexillological Association." Brochure. Trenton, NJ: undated.

"O Say! Can You See?" *Sports Illustrated*, May 1968.

"O Say — It's Big, But Hard to See." Associated Press, 15 June 1991.

"Oklahoma Governor Balks at Flying Flag." Associated Press, 6 April 1988.

"Old Flag Valued at $5000." Associated Press, May 1973.

"Old Glory Has Its Ups and Downs." *Washington Star*, 21 April 1976.

"Old Glory Takes On a New Look in Bristol." *Worcester* (CT) *Pride*, July 1991.

"Optimists Honor McDonald's for Flying United States Flag." *Lexington Park* (MD) *Enterprise*, 1 July 1976.

Owen, F.A. *The Flag of the United States of America Manual*. San Francisco, CA: undated.

Panati, Charles. *Extraordinary Origins of Everyday Things*. New York: Harper & Row, 1987.

"Panel Oks $1 Fine for Beating of Flag Burners." *Lewiston (ID) Tribune*, 25 January 1990.

Papier, Deborah. "The Town That Remembers." *Mid-Atlantic Country*, May 1993.

Perrin, W.C. *British Flags, Their Early History, and Their Development at Sea*. Cambridge, England: Cambridge University Press, 1922.

"Philatelic News: Fifty State Flags." *Washington Star*, 11 January 1976.

"Places Where the United States Flag Is Flown Day and Night." GSA T10H Fact Sheet #8, 27 December 1972.

"Police Ban Confederate Battle Flags at Rededication of Alabama Capitol." *Lewiston (ID) Morning Tribune*, 12 December 1992.

"Policemen Loath to Lose Flag Patches." *Washington Star*, 3 January 1976.

Preble, G.H. *History of the Flag of the U.S.A.* 2nd rev. ed. Boston: A. Williams, 1880.

Proclamation 4064: Display of Flags at the Washington Monument. President of the United States of America. 6 July 1971.

"Protesters Burn Georgia Flag." *Lewiston (ID) Morning Tribune*, 20 July 1996.

Public Papers of the Presidents of the United States, Harry S Truman. 189: Statement by the President Announcing the Designation of General Douglas MacArthur to Lead the Allied Military Forces in Korea. Washington, DC: GPO, 1965.

"Puerto Rico's New Governor Says He'll Fight for Statehood." *Lewiston (ID) Tribune*, 3 January 1993.

Quaife, Milo M., Melvin J. Weig, and Roy E. Appleman. *The History of the United States Flag*. New York: Harper & Row, 1961.

"Quick! Call Betsy Ross!" United Press International, 29 June 1976.

Ralbavsky, Marty. "Waving the Flag: Pro Football and the Patriotic Game." *Washington Star-News*, 7 January 1973.

"Rally 'Round the Pennant." From Vol. 1, Chaplain Corps History. *All Hands*, 1924.

Reed, J.D. "Gallantly Screaming." *Sports Illustrated*, 3 January 1977.

Reed, Mary. "Remembrance Sunday." *Festival*, January 1989.

Ringo, S.H. "Uniform Addition" (picture and caption). *Norfolk Virginian-Pilot*, 9 July 1970.

"Ron Taylor to Sing for the Birds." *Lewiston (ID) Tribune*, 12 June 1991.

Rubin, James H. "First Amendment Permits Burning Flag." Associated Press, 22 June 1989.

"San Francisco Honors Slain Homosexual." United Press International, June 1977.

Schauffler, Robert Haven. *Our Flag in Verse and Prose*. New York: Dodd, Mead, 1936.

"Schroeder Accused of Disrespect." *Lewiston (ID) Morning Tribune*, 1 February 1988.

Schuller, Robert A. "Old Glory Speaks." Garden Grove, Calif.: Crystal Cathedral Ministries, 1986.

"The Seven Spikes of Lady Liberty's Crown." Letter to the Editor. *Pittsburgh Post-Gazette*, Reprinted in *Washington Star*, 29 August 1986.

Sherwood, John. "A Role, a Life." *Washington Star*, February 1976.

"Should We Change Our National Anthem?" *Parade*, 7 July 1988.

Shriners and Their Flags. Chicago: The Imperial Council of the Ancient Arabic Order Nobles of the Mystic Shrine, undated.

Smith, Whitney. "Brand New Look for States." *Smithsonian*, December 1973.

Smith, Whitney. *The Flag Book of the United States*. New York: Morrow, 1975.

"Southern Pride or Racism?" Associated Press, 25 July 1992.

"Stand-Up Joke." *Reader's Digest*, October 1975.

"Star in Starry Bikini Helps Five Find Freedom." *Norfolk Virginian-Pilot*, 16 October 1971.

"The Star Spangled Ban." *Washington Star*, 22 September 1981.

The Star Spangled Banner. Washington, DC: Smithsonian Institution, undated.

Steadman, Ethel. "Defacing of Old Glory Denied." *Norfolk Virginian-Pilot*, 5 July 1970.

"Students Oust President in Flag Flap." Associated Press, 7 November 1970.

Swan, Conrad. Letter on record of U.S. Coat of Arms and Arms of Registered Americans, York Herald of Arms, London, England, 15 February 1973.

"Tampans Rise in Defense of Bellamy Flag Pledge." *Tampa (FL) Tribune*, 15 April 1956.

"Teams Wear Flags to Show Support for Armed Forces." Associated Press, 18 October 1990.

"10,000 Bluejackets in Living Flag." *Great Lakes Naval Station Recruit*, December 1917, rep. *Navy Times*, January 14, 1970, and *Reminisce*, July/August 1973.

"This Is Our Flag—Be Proud of It." Flag poster by Government Printing Office. Washington, DC: July 1970.

"This Was a Funeral That Brought Joy." *Collegiate Baseball*, April 1985.

"Three Charged in Flag Defacing." *Lewiston (ID) Tribune*, 26 August 1989.

"Three Face Charges Over Flag Incident." Associated Press, 19 April 1984.

Thruston, Rogers C.B. *The Origin and Evolution of the U.S. Flag*. Washington: GPO, 1926.

Toner, Robin. "Flag Law Inflames Partisan Passions." *New York Times*, 28 July 1989.

"A Tradition of Independence." Providence: Rhode Island Development Council, 1972.

"Tradition of the Naval Reserve." *All Hands*, September 1973.

"A Trip Through the Home and Museum of Chief Justice Taney." Frederick, MD: undated.

Truly, Pat. "Stars and Stripes Forever? No, Not Exactly Forever." *Fort Worth (TX) Star-Telegram*, 4 July 1990.

"The Truth About Betsy Ross." *All Hands*, March 1974.

"The Turmoil of the Times." *Sports Illustrated*, May 1970.

"Two Acre Stars and Stripes Given to Reagan on Flag Day." *Los Angeles Times*, 15 June 1993.

"Two 'Dixies' Too Many at VMI?" *Washington Evening Star and Daily News*, 16 May 1973.

Umbreit, Kristi. "Catholic School Revises Pledge of Allegiance." Associated Press, 12 October 1990.

"Uncle Sam: Symbol of American Spirit Alive in Past and Present." *Grit*, 3 July 1994.

Uncle Sam Stamp. Issued by U.S. Postal Service, 3 June 1978.

United States Congress. Joint Committee on Printing. *Our Flag*. Washington, DC: GPO, 1979.

United States Marine Corps. *How to Respect and Display Our Flag*. March 1968.

U.S. Olympic Committee letter on Ralph Waldo Rose as first U.S. flag bearer to refuse to dip flag, in 1908. 14 February, 1992.

"U.S. Olympic Team Flag Bearers." In *The USA in the Olympic Movement*. Colorado Springs, CO: U.S. Olympic Committee, undated.

"'V-J Day' Holiday Said Racist," Associated Press, 14 August 1989.

Walker, Ben. "Baseball's Sound of Silence." Associated Press, 25 May 1986.

Waterloo Memorial Day Committee. *The History and Origin of Memorial Day in Waterloo, New York*. Geneva, NY: W.F. Humphrey, 1966.

Watson, Inez, ed. *South Carolina: State Symbols & Emblems*. Excerpted from *South Carolina Legislative Manual*, undated.

"Webster's Words." *Tampa (FL) Tribune*, 24 June 1956.

Wells, Robert L. "Marquis de Lafayette and a Flag That Never Come Down: 1834–1989." *Flag Plaza Standard*, Supp. to Vol. 21, #2. Pittsburgh: National Flag Foundation, 4 July 1989.

Welsh, Jonathan. "Oh Say Can You See ... Old Glory in Flames at a Boy Scout Bonfire?" *Wall Street Journal*, 6 July 1996.

"What's Your Problem?" *Newsday*, 29 March 1971.

White, Patricia. General Services Administration letter on government uses and costs of flags, 19 March 1992.

Williams, Elaine. "Lewiston Board Debates Flag Abuse." *Lewiston (ID) Tribune*, 15 October 1991.

Willis, George R. *The Story of Our Cruise in the U.S. Frigate* Colorado. Naval Historical Center report, 1873.

"With Order Rescinded, Deputy Will Wear Flag." Associated Press, 12 April 1991.

Witkin, Gordon. "Patriotism Is Back in Style." *U.S. News & World Report*, 9 July 1984.

"Woodrow Wilson Birthplace and Museum." Staunton, VA: undated.

"Woody Guthrie." *Esquire*, October 1980.

The World Almanac. New York: Newspaper Enterprise Association, 1973.

"Would Reagan Change in a Second Term?" *U.S. News & World Report*, 27 August 1984.

"Youth Sentenced to Year for Making Vest of Flag." Associated Press, 19 January 1970.

Index